Making Health Policy

Understanding Public Health

Series editors: Nick Black and Rosalind Raine, London School of Hygiene & Tropical Medicine

Throughout the world, recognition of the importance of public health to sustainable, safe and healthy societies is growing. The achievements of public health in nineteenth-century Europe were for much of the twentieth century overshadowed by advances in personal care, in particular in hospital care. Now, with the dawning of a new century, there is increasing understanding of the inevitable limits of individual health care and of the need to complement such services with effective public health strategies. Major improvements in people's health will come from controlling communicable diseases, eradicating environmental hazards, improving people's diets and enhancing the availability and quality of effective health care. To achieve this, every country needs a cadre of knowledgeable public health practitioners with social, political and organizational skills to lead and bring about changes at international, national and local levels.

This is one of a series of 20 books that provides a foundation for those wishing to join in and contribute to the twenty-first-century regeneration of public health, helping to put the concerns and perspectives of public health at the heart of policy-making and service provision. While each book stands alone, together they provide a comprehensive account of the three main aims of public health: protecting the public from environmental hazards, improving the health of the public and ensuring high quality health services are available to all. Some of the books focus on methods, others on key topics. They have been written by staff at the London School of Hygiene & Tropical Medicine with considerable experience of teaching public health to students from low, middle and high income countries. Much of the material has been developed and tested with postgraduate students both in face-to-face teaching and through distance learning.

The books are designed for self-directed learning. Each chapter has explicit learning objectives, key terms are highlighted and the text contains many activities to enable the reader to test their own understanding of the ideas and material covered. Written in a clear and accessible style, the series will be essential reading for students taking postgraduate courses in public health and will also be of interest to public health practitioners and policy-makers.

Titles in the series

Analytical models for decision making: Colin Sanderson and Reinhold Gruen
Controlling communicable disease: Norman Noah
Economic analysis for management and policy: Stephen Jan, Lilani Kumaranayake, Jenny Roberts, Kara Hanson and Kate Archibald
Economic evaluation: Julia Fox-Rushby and John Cairns (eds)
Environmental epidemiology: Paul Wilkinson (ed)
Environment, health and sustainable development: Megan Landon
Environmental health policy: Megan Landon and Tony Fletcher
Financial management in health services: Reinhold Gruen and Anne Howarth
Global change and health: Kelley Lee and Jeff Collin (eds)
Health care evaluation: Sarah Smith, Don Sinclair, Rosalind Raine and Barnaby Reeves
Health promotion practice: Maggie Davies, Wendy Macdowall and Chris Bonell (eds)
Health promotion theory: Maggie Davies and Wendy Macdowall (eds)
Introduction to epidemiology: Lucianne Bailey, Katerina Vardulaki, Julia Langham and Daniel Chandramohan
Introduction to health economics: David Wonderling, Reinhold Gruen and Nick Black
Issues in public health: Joceline Pomerleau and Martin McKee (eds)
Making health policy: Kent Buse, Nicholas Mays and Gill Walt
Managing health services: Nick Goodwin, Reinhold Gruen and Valerie Iles
Medical anthropology: Robert Pool and Wenzel Geissler
Principles of social research: Judith Green and John Browne (eds)
Understanding health services: Nick Black and Reinhold Gruen

Making Health Policy

Kent Buse, Nicholas Mays and Gill Walt

Open University Press

Open University Press
McGraw-Hill Education
McGraw-Hill House
Shoppenhangers Road
Maidenhead
Berkshire
England
SL6 2QL

email: enquiries@openup.co.uk
world wide web: www.openup.co.uk

and Two Penn Plaza, New York, NY 10121-2289, USA

First published 2005

Reprinted 2006 (Twice), 2007 , 2009
Second reprint 2009

A catalogue record of this book is available from the British Library

ISBN-10: 0 335 21839 3
ISBN-13: 978 0 335 21839 3

Library of Congress Cataloging-in-Publication Data
CIP data applied for

Typeset by RefineCatch Limited, Bungay, Suffolk
Printed in the UK by Ashford Colour Press Ltd, Gosport, Hampshire

Contents

Acknowledgements

Open University Press and the London School of Hygiene and Tropical Medicine have made every effort to obtain permission from copyright holders to reproduce material in this book and to acknowledge these sources correctly. Any omissions brought to our attention will be remedied in future editions.

We would like to express our grateful thanks to the following copyright holders for granting permission to reproduce material in this book.

p. 34 David Easton, *A Systems Analysis of Political Life*, 1965,Wiley, by permission of David Easton.

p. 181 A Glassman, MR Reich, Laserson, F Rojas 'Political analysis of health reform in the Dominican Republic', *Health and Policy Planning*, 1999, 14(1):115–126, by permission of Oxford University Press.

p. 129 Michael Howlett, 'Managing the "Hollow State": Procedural Policy Instruments and Modern Governance', *Canadian Public Administration*, 43, 4 (2000): 412–31, by permission of IPAC.

p. 69 Based on J Kingdon, *Agenda, alternatives and public policies*, 1984, Little Brown and Co.

p. 96 Simplified and adapted from Ministry of Health, *The health and independence report 2004: Director-General of Health's report on the state of public health*, by permission of Ministry of Health 2004.

p. 126 PA Sabatier, 'Top-down and bottom-up approaches to implementation research: a critical analysis and suggested synthesis', 1986, *Journal of Public Policy*, Cambridge University Press.

p. 41 Adapted from G Schmid, 'Economic and programmatic aspects of congenital syphilis control', *Bulletin of the World Health Organization*, 2004, by permission of World Health Organization.

p. 8 G Walt and L Gilson, 'Reforming the health sector in developing countries: the central role of policy analysis', *Health and Policy Planning*, 1994, 9:353–370, by permission of Oxford University Press.

p. 134 G Walt, 'Implementing health care reform: a framework for discussion' in RB Saltman, J Figueras and Sakellarides (editors), *Critical challenges for health care reform in Europe*, 1998, Open University Press. Reproduced with kind permission from Open University Press/McGraw-Hill Publishing Company.

Overview of the book

Introduction

This book provides a comprehensive introduction to the study of power and process in health policy. Much of what is currently available deals with the content of health policy – the 'what' of policy. This literature may use medicine, epidemiology, organizational theory or economics to provide evidence for, or evaluation of, health policy. Legions of doctors, epidemiologists, health economists and organizational theorists develop technically sound solutions to problems of public health importance. Yet, surprisingly little guidance is available to public health practitioners who wish to understand how issues make their way onto policy agendas (and how to frame these issues so that they are better received), how policy makers treat evidence (and how to form better relationships with decision makers), and why some policy initiatives are implemented while others languish. These political dimensions of the health policy process are rarely taught in schools of medicine or public health.

Why study health policy?

The book integrates power and process into the study of health policy. It views these two themes as integral to understanding policy. Who makes and implements policy decisions (those with power) and how decisions are made (process) largely determine the content of health policy and, thereby, ultimately people's health. To illustrate this point, take the case of developing HIV policy in a low income country. Were health economists primarily involved in advising the health minister, it is likely that prevention would be emphasized (as preventive interventions tend to be more cost-effective than curative ones). If, however, the minister also consulted representatives of people with HIV, as well as the pharmaceutical industry, it is likely that greater emphasis would be placed on treatment and care. In the unlikely event that powerful feminist organizations had the ear of the minister, they might lobby for interventions to empower women to protect themselves from unwanted and unprotected sex. The reconciliation of different views and the resulting policy depend on the power of various actors in the policy arena as well as the process of policy making (e.g. how widely groups are consulted and involved). Whether or not preventive, curative or structural HIV interventions are given priority will impact on the trajectory of the HIV epidemic.

All activity is subject to politics. For example, research into public health problems requires funding. In many universities, bench scientists and social scientists compete with each other for funds to support their research. Politics will determine the allocation of public funds to different research areas and academic disciplines and private firms will invest in those researchers and endeavours that are most likely to lead to the highest rates of return. Politics doesn't end with funding, as politics is likely to govern access to study populations and even publication. Unfavourable findings can be blocked or distorted by project sponsors and they can be disputed or ignored by decision makers or others who find them inconvenient. Politics is omnipresent. For this reason, understanding the politics of the policy process is arguably as important as understanding how medicine improves health. Stated differently, while other academic disciplines may provide necessary evidence to improve health, in the absence of a robust understanding of the policy process, technical solutions will likely be insufficient to change practice in the real world.

This book is for those who wish to understand the policy process so that they are better equipped to influence it in their working lives. It is intended as a guide for professionals who wish to improve their skills in navigating and managing the health policy process – irrespective of the health issue or setting.

Structure of the book

Conceptually, the book is organized according to an analytical framework for health policy developed by Walt and Gilson (1994). The framework attempts to simplify what are in practice highly complex relationships by describing them in relation to a 'policy triangle'. The framework draws attention to the 'context' within which policy is formulated and executed, the 'actors' involved in policy making, and the 'processes' associated with developing and implementing policy – and the interactions between them. The framework is useful as it can be applied in any country, to any policy, and at any policy level. A diverse range of theories and disciplinary approaches, particularly from political science, international relations, economics, sociology, and organizational theory are drawn upon throughout the book to support this simple analytical framework and provide further explanations of policy process and power.

Ten chapters cover different stages of the policy process. Chapter 1 provides an introduction to the importance and meaning of policy, an explanation of the policy analysis framework, and demonstrates how it can be used to understand policy change. Chapter 2 describes a number of theories which help explain the relationship between power and policy making, including those which deal with how power is exercised by different groups, how political systems and governments transform power into policies, how power is distributed, and how power affects decision making processes.

Chapter 3 introduces the state and the private for-profit sector. It traces the changing roles of these two important sectors in health policy and, thereby, provides a contextual backdrop to understanding the content and processes of contemporary health policy making. Agenda setting is the focus of the fourth chapter. Chapter 5 returns to actors by focusing on the different institutions of government and the influence they wield. Chapter 6 looks at actors outside government. Different types of interest groups in the health sector are compared in terms of their resources, tactics and success in the policy process.

Chapter 7 returns to the policy process by exploring policy implementation. It contrasts and reconciles 'top-down' and 'bottom-up' approaches to explaining implementation (or more often lack thereof). Chapter 8 shifts the focus to the global level and examines the role of various actors in the policy process and the implications for increasing global interdependence on domestic policy making. Chapter 9 looks at policy evaluation and explores the linkages between research and policy. The final chapter is devoted to doing policy analysis. It introduces a political approach to policy analysis, provides tips on gathering information for analysis, and guidance for presenting analysis. The aim of the chapter is to help you to develop better political strategies to bring about health reform in your professional life.

Each chapter has an overview, learning objectives, key terms, activities, feedback, and a brief summary and list of references. A number of the activities ask you to reflect on various aspects of a specific health policy which you select on the basis of having some familiarity with it. It would be helpful to begin to set aside documents related to your chosen policy for later use. These could be government documents, independent reports or articles from the popular press.

Acknowledgements

This book builds upon Gill Walt's book *Health Policy: An Introduction to Process and Power*, 2nd edition (1994). We thank Professor Calum Paton, Keele University, for reviewing a draft version and Deirdre Byrne (series manager) for help and support in preparing this book.

Reference

Walt G and Gilson L (1994). Reforming the health sector in developing countries: the central role of policy analysis. *Health Policy and Planning* 9: 353–70.

The health policy framework
Context, process and actors

Overview

In this chapter you are introduced to why health policy is important and how to define policy. You will then go on to consider a simple analytical framework that incorporates the notions of context, process and actors, to demonstrate how they can help explain how and why policies do or do not change over time.

Learning objectives

After working through this chapter, you will be better able to:

- **understand the framework of health policy used in this book**
- **define the key concepts used in this chapter:**
  - **policy**
  - **context**
  - **actors**
  - **process**
- **describe how health policies are made through the inter-relationship of context, process and actors**

Key terms

Actor Short-hand term used to denote individuals, organizations or even the state and their actions that affect policy.

Content Substance of a particular policy which details its constituent parts.

Context Systemic factors – political, economic, social or cultural, both national and international – which may have an effect on health policy.

Policy Broad statement of goals, objectives and means that create the framework for activity. Often take the form of explicit written documents, but may also be implicit or unwritten.

Policy elites Specific group of policy makers who hold high positions in an organization, and often privileged access to other top members of the same, and other, organizations.

Policy makers Those who make policies in organizations such as central or local government, multinational companies or local businesses, schools or hospitals.

Policy process The way in which policies are initiated, developed or formulated, negotiated, communicated, implemented and evaluated.

Why is health policy important?

In many countries, the health sector is an important part of the economy. Some see it as a sponge – absorbing large amounts of national resources to pay for the many health workers employed. Others see it as a driver of the economy, through innovation and investment in bio-medical technologies or production and sales of pharmaceuticals, or through ensuring a healthy population which is economically productive. Most citizens come into contact with the health sector as patients or clients, through using hospitals, clinics or pharmacies; or as health professionals – whether as nurses, doctors, medical auxiliaries, pharmacists or managers. Because the nature of decision making in health often involves matters of life and death, health is accorded a special position in comparison to other social issues.

Health is also affected by many decisions that have nothing to do with health care: poverty affects people's health, as do pollution, contaminated water or poor sanitation. Economic policies, such as taxes on cigarettes or alcohol may also influence people's behaviour. Current explanations for rising obesity among many populations, for example, include the promotion of high calorie, inexpensive fast food, the sale of soft drinks at schools, as well as dwindling opportunities to take exercise.

Understanding the relationship between health policy and health is therefore important so that it is possible to tackle some of the major health problems of our time – rising obesity, the HIV/AIDS epidemic, growing drug resistance – as well as to understand how economic and other policies impact on health. Health policy guides choices about which health technologies to develop and use, how to organize and finance health services, or what drugs will be freely available. To understand these relationships, it is necessary to better define what is meant by health policy.

What is health policy?

In this book you will often come across the terms policy, public policy and health policy.

Policy is often thought of as decisions taken by those with responsibility for a given policy area – it may be in health or the environment, in education or in trade. The people who make policies are referred to as policy makers. Policy may be made at many levels – in central or local government, in a multinational company or local business, in a school or hospital. They are also sometimes referred to as policy elites – a specific group of decision makers who have high positions in an organization, and often privileged access to other top members of the same, and other, organizations. For example, policy elites in government may include the members of the Prime Minister's Cabinet, all of whom would be able to contact and meet the top executives of a multinational company or of an international agency, such as the World Health Organisation (WHO).

Policies are made in the private and the public sector. In the private sector, multinational conglomerates may establish policies for all their companies around the world, but allow local companies to decide their own policies on conditions of service. For example, corporations such as Anglo-American and Heineken introduced anti-retroviral therapy for their HIV-positive employees in Africa in the early

2000s before many governments did so. However, private sector corporations have to ensure that their policies are made within the confines of public law, made by governments.

Public policy refers to government policy. For example, Thomas Dye (2001) says that public policy is whatever governments choose to do *or not to do*. He argues that failure to decide or act on a particular issue also constitutes policy. For example, successive US governments have chosen not to introduce universal health care, but to rely on the market plus programmes for the very poor and those over 65 years, to meet people's health care needs.

When looking for examples of public policy, you should look for statements or formal positions issued by a government, or a government department. These may be couched in terms that suggest the accomplishment of a particular purpose or goal (the introduction of needle exchange programmes to reduce harm among drug takers) or to resolve a problem (charges on cars to reduce traffic congestion in urban areas).

Policies may refer to a government's health or economic policy, where policy is used as a field of activity, or to a specific proposal – 'from next year, it will be university policy to ensure students are represented on all governing bodies'. Sometimes policy is called a programme: the government's school health programme may include a number of different policies: precluding children from starting school before they are fully immunized against the major vaccine-preventable childhood diseases, providing medical inspections, subsidized school meals and compulsory health education in the school curriculum. The programme is thus the embodiment of policy for school children. In this example, it is clear that policies may not arise from a single decision but could consist of bundles of decisions that lead to a broad course of action over time. And these decisions or actions may or may not be intended, defined or even recognized as policy.

As you can see, there are many ways of defining policy. Thomas Dye's simple definition of public policy being what governments do, or do not do, contrasts with the more formal assumptions that all policy is made to achieve a particular goal or purpose.

Health policy may cover public and private policies about health. In this book health policy is assumed to embrace courses of action (and inaction) that affect the set of institutions, organizations, services and funding arrangements of the health system. It includes policy made in the public sector (by government) as well as policies in the private sector. But because health is influenced by many determinants outside the health system, health policy analysts are also interested in the actions and intended actions of organizations external to the health system which have an impact on health (for example, the food, tobacco or pharmaceutical industries).

Just as there are various definitions of what policy is, so there are many ideas about the analysis of health policy, and its focus: an economist may say health policy is about the allocation of scarce resources for health; a planner sees it as ways to influence the determinants of health in order to improve public health; and for a doctor it is all about health services (Walt 1994). For Walt, health policy is synonymous with politics and deals explicitly with who influences policy making, how they exercise that influence, and under what conditions.

As you will see, this book takes this last view of health policy, and places it within a framework that incorporates politics. Politics cannot be divorced from health policy. If you are applying epidemiology, economics, biology or any other professional or technical knowledge to everyday life, politics will affect you. No one is unaffected by the influence of politics. For example, scientists may have to focus their research on the issues funders are interested in, rather than questions they want to explore; in prescribing drugs, health professionals may have to take into consideration potentially conflicting demands of hospital managers, government regulations and people's ability to pay. They may also be visited by drug company representatives who want to persuade them to prescribe their particular drugs, and who may use different sorts of incentives to encourage them to do so. Most activities are subject to the ebb and flow of politics.

Devising a framework for incorporating politics into health policy needs to go beyond the point at which many health policy analysts stop: the *content* of policy. Many of the books and papers written on health policy focus on a particular policy, describing what it purports to do, the strategy to achieve set goals, and whether or not it has achieved them. For example, during the 1990s attention was on the financing of health services, asking questions such as:

- Which would be a better policy – the introduction of user fees or a social insurance system?
- Which public health services should be contracted out to the private sector? Cleaning services in hospitals? Blood banks?
- Which policy instruments are needed to undertake major changes such as these? Legislation? Regulation? Incentives?

These are the 'what' questions of health policy. But they cannot be divorced from the 'who' and 'how' questions: who makes the decisions? Who implements them? Under what conditions will they be introduced and executed, or ignored? In other words, the content is not separate from the politics of policy making. For example, in Uganda, when the President saw evidence that utilization of health services had fallen dramatically after the introduction of charges for health services, he overturned the earlier policy of his Ministry of Health. To understand how he made that decision, you need to know something about the political context (an election coming up, and the desire to win votes); the power of the President to introduce change; and the role of evidence in influencing the decision, among other things.

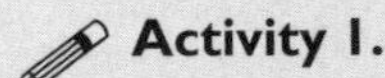

Activity 1.1

Without looking at the text, define:

- policy
- public policy
- health policy

Think of an example from your own country for each of those.

Feedback

- Policy is 'decisions taken by those with responsibility for a particular policy area'.
- Public policy refers to policies made by the state or the government, by those in the public sector.
- Health policy covers courses of action (and inaction) that affect the set of institutions, organizations, services and funding arrangements of the health care system (both public and private).

You may have found it tricky to define these words. This is because 'policy' is not a precise or self-evident term. For example, Anderson (1975) says policy is 'a purposive course of action followed by an actor or set of actors in dealing with a problem or matter of concern'. But this appears to make policy an 'intended' course of action, whereas many would argue that policies are sometimes the unintended result of many different decisions made over time. Policies may be expressed in a whole series of instruments: practices, statements, regulations and laws. They may be implicit or explicit, discretionary or statutory. Also, the word 'policy' does not always translate well: in English a distinction is often made between policy and politics, but in many European languages the word for policy is the same as the word for politics.

The health policy triangle

The framework used in this book acknowledges the importance of looking at the content of policy, the processes of policy making and how power is used in health policy. This means exploring the role of the state, nationally and internationally, and the groups making up national and global civil society, to understand how they interact and influence health policy. It also means understanding the processes through which such influence is played out (e.g. in formulating policy) and the context in which these different actors and processes interact. The framework, (Figure 1.1) focuses on content, context, process and actors. It is used in this book because it helps to explore systematically the somewhat neglected place

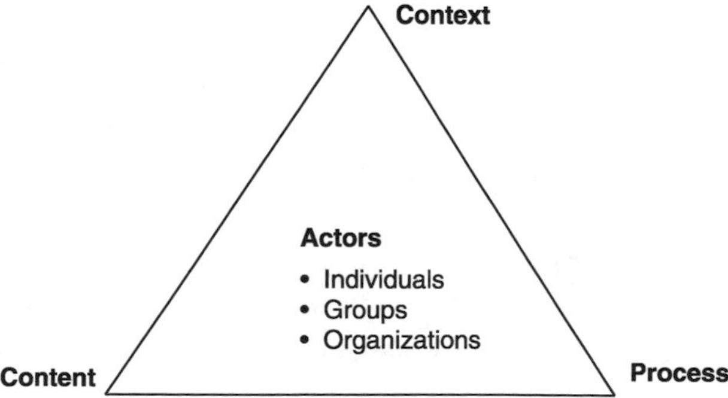

Figure 1.1 Policy analysis triangle
Source: Walt and Gilson (1994)

of politics in health policy and it can be applied to high, middle and low income countries.

The health policy triangle is a highly simplified approach to a complex set of inter-relationships, and may give the impression that the four factors can be considered separately. This is not so! In reality, actors are influenced (as individuals or members of groups or organizations) by the context within which they live and work; context is affected by many factors such as instability or ideology, by history and culture; and the process of policy making – how issues get on to policy agendas, and how they fare once there – is affected by actors, their position in power structures, their own values and expectations. And the content of policy reflects some or all of these dimensions. So, while the policy triangle is useful for helping to think systematically about all the different factors that might affect policy, it is like a map that shows the main roads but that has yet to have contours, rivers, forests, paths and dwellings added to it.

The actors who make policy

As you can see from Figure 1.1, actors are at the centre of the health policy framework. Actor may be used to denote individuals (a particular statesman – Nelson Mandela, the ex-President of South Africa, for example), organizations such as the World Bank or multinational companies such as Shell, or even the state or government. However, it is important to recognize that this is a simplification. Individuals cannot be separated from the organizations within which they work and any organization or group is made up of many different people, not all of whom speak with one voice and whose values and beliefs may differ.

In the chapters that follow you will look at many different actors and ways of differentiating between them in order to analyse who has influence in the policy process. For example, there are many ways of describing groups that are outside the realm of the state. In international relations it has been customary to talk about *non-state actors* (actors outside government). Political scientists talk about *interest or pressure groups*. In the development literature these groups are usually referred to as *civil society organizations* (organizations which fall between the state and the individual or household). What differentiates all these actors from government or state actors is that they do not seek formal political power for themselves, although they do want to influence those with formal political power.

Sometimes many different groups get together to demonstrate strong feelings about particular issues – these are called social movements or people's movements. For example, the activities of many different groups in the 1980s led to major political change in the socialist regimes of eastern Europe. Many social movements are struggles for independence, autonomy or against particular political regimes (e.g. the Zapatista movement in Chiapas province in Mexico is part of a movement all over Latin America to preserve the rights of indigenous people).

Actors may try to influence the policy process at the local, national, regional or international level. Often they become parts of networks, sometimes described as partners, to consult and decide on policy at all of these levels. At the local level, for example, community health workers may interact with environmental officers, teachers in local schools, even local businesses. At the other end of the spectrum, actors may be linked with others across state borders, for example, they may be members of inter-governmental networks (i.e. government officials in one department of government in one country, learning lessons about alternatives with government officials from another country); or they may be part of policy or discourse communities – networks of professionals who get together at scientific meetings or collaborate on research projects. Others may form issue networks – coming together to act on a particular issue. In Chapter 6 you will learn more about the differences between these groups and their role in the policy process.

To understand how much actors influence the policy process means understanding the concept of power, and how it is exercised. Actors may seek to influence policy, but the extent to which they will be able to do so will depend, among other things, on their perceived or actual power. Power may be characterized by a mixture of individual wealth, personality, level of or access to knowledge, or authority, but it is strongly tied up with the organization and structures (including networks) within which the individual actor works and lives. Sociologists and political scientists talk about the interplay between agency and structure, presenting the notion that the power of actors (agents) is intertwined with the structures (organizations) they belong to. You will look more closely at the notion of power in Chapter 2 but in this book it is assumed that power is the result of an interplay between agency and structure.

Activity 1.2

Make a list of the different actors who might be involved in health policy on HIV/AIDS in your own country. Put the actors into different groups.

Feedback

You might have grouped actors in different ways and in each country the list will differ and will change over time. The examples below may or may not apply to your country but they give an idea of the sorts of categories and sorts of actors you might have thought of. Where you do not know them, do not worry, there will be explanations and examples in later chapters:

- government (Ministry of Health, Ministry of Education, Ministry of Employment)
- international non-governmental organizations (Médecins Sans Frontières, Oxfam)
- national non-governmental organizations (People-Living-With-AIDS, faith-based organizations)
- pressure/interest groups (Treatment Action Campaign)
- international organizations (WHO, UNAIDS, the World Bank)
- bilateral agencies (DFID, USAID, SIDA)
- funding organizations (the Global Fund, PEPFAR)
- private sector companies (Anglo-American, Heineken, Merck)

Contextual factors that affect policy

Context refers to systemic factors – political, economic and social, both national and international – which may have an effect on health policy. There are many ways of categorizing such factors, but one useful way is provided by Leichter (1979):

- *Situational factors* are more or less transient, impermanent, or idiosyncratic conditions which can have an impact on policy (e.g. wars, droughts). These are sometimes called 'focusing events' (see Chapter 4). These may be a specific one-off occurrence, such as an earthquake which leads to changes in hospital building regulations, or much longer diffused public recognition of a new problem. For example, the advent of the HIV/AIDS epidemic (which took time to be acknowledged as an epidemic on a world scale) triggered new treatment and control policies on tuberculosis because of the inter-relationship of the two diseases – people who are HIV-positive are more susceptible to diseases, and latent tuberculosis may be triggered by HIV.
- *Structural factors* are the relatively unchanging elements of the society. They may include the *political system*, and extent to which it is open or closed and the opportunities for civil society to participate in policy discussions and decisions; structural factors may also include the *type of economy* and *the employment base*. For example, where wages for nurses are low, or there are too few jobs for those who have trained, countries may suffer migration of these professionals to other societies where there is a shortage. Other structural factors that will affect a society's health policy will include *demographic features* or *technological advance*. For example, countries with ageing populations have high hospital and drug costs for the elderly, as their needs increase with age. Technological change has increased the number of women giving birth by caesarian section in many countries. Among the reasons given are increasing professional reliance on high technology that has led to reluctance among some doctors and midwives to take any risks, and a fear of litigation. And of course, a country's *national wealth* will have a strong effect on which health services can be afforded.
- *Cultural factors* may also affect health policy. In societies where formal hierarchies are important, it may be difficult to question or challenge high officials or elder statesmen. The position of ethnic minorities or linguistic differences may lead to certain groups being poorly informed about their rights, or services that do not meet their particular needs. In some countries where women cannot easily access health services (because they have to be accompanied by their husbands) or where there is considerable stigma about the disease (for example, tuberculosis or HIV), some authorities have developed systems of home visits or 'door-step' delivery. Religious factors can also strongly affect policy, as was seen by the insistence of President George W. Bush in the early 2000s that sexual abstinence be promoted over the delivery of contraception or access to abortion services. This affected policy in the USA as well as many other countries, where NGO reproductive health services were heavily curtailed or their funds from the USA were cut if they failed to comply with President Bush's cultural mores.
- *International or exogenous factors* which are leading to greater inter-dependence between states, and influencing sovereignty and international cooperation in health (see Chapter 8). Although many health problems are dealt with by national governments, some need cooperation between national, regional or

multilateral organizations. For example, the eradication of polio has taken place in many parts of the world through national and regional action, sometimes with the assistance from international organizations such as WHO. However, even if one state manages to immunize all its children against polio, and to sustain coverage, the polio virus can be imported by people who have not been immunized crossing the border from a neighbouring country.

All these factors are complex, and unique in both time and setting. For example, in the nineteenth century, Britain sought to introduce public health policies about sexually transmitted diseases in the countries of the British Empire. Dominant colonial assumptions, regarding how the categories of race and gender operated in societies under colonial rule, produced policies that reflected the prejudices and assumptions of the ruling imperial power, rather than policies that were sensitive to local culture. Levine (2003) describes how in India, female sex workers were required to register with the police as prostitutes, a policy prompted by the British belief that prostitution carried neither shame nor stigma in India. Colonial policies on prostitution frequently focused on brothels, requiring them to be registered with the local authorities. The assumption that brothel owners were cruel, and denied their workers any freedom, led the colonial authorities to enforce registration which made brothel keepers responsible for ensuring all their workers submitted to a medical examination. In Britain, however, brothels were illegal and policies about female sex workers focused exclusively on those who 'walked the streets'.

An interesting example of how context affects policy is given by Shiffman and colleagues (2002). They compare reproductive rights in Serbia and Croatia, where, after the break-up of the Federal Republic of Yugoslavia, governments advocated measures to encourage women to have more children. The authors argue that these pro-natalist policies were due to perceptions by elites in both countries that national survival was at stake. Elite perceptions were due to several factors: one was a shift from a socialist philosophy committed to female emancipation to a more nationalist ideology that held no such pretensions. Another was the comparisons made by elites between low fertility rates among Serbs in Serbia and Croats in Croatia, and higher fertility rates in other ethnic groups in both countries.

To understand how health policies change, or do not, means being able to analyse the context in which they are made, and trying to assess how far any, or some, of these sorts of factors may influence policy outcomes.

Activity 1.3

Consider HIV/AIDS policy in your own country. Identify some contextual factors that might have influenced the way policy has (or has not) developed. Bear in mind the way context has been divided into four different factors.

Feedback

Obviously each setting is unique, but the sorts of contextual factors you may have identified are:

Situational

- a new prime minister/president coming to power and making AIDS policy a priority
- the death of a famous person acknowledged publicly to be due to AIDS

Structural

- the role of the media or NGOs in publicizing, or not, the AIDS epidemic – relating to the extent to which the political system is open or closed
- evidence of growing mortality from AIDS made public – perhaps among a particular group such as health workers

Cultural

The actions of religious groups – both negative and positive – with regard to those with HIV/AIDS or towards sexual behaviour

International

The role of international donors – the extra funds brought in by global initiatives such as the Global Fund to Fight AIDS, TB and Malaria

The processes of policy making

Process refers to the way in which policies are initiated, developed or formulated, negotiated, communicated, implemented and evaluated. The most common approach to understanding policy processes is to use what is called the 'stages heuristic' (Sabatier and Jenkins-Smith 1993). What this means is breaking down the policy process into a series of stages but acknowledging that this is a theoretical device, a model and does not necessarily represent exactly what happens in the real world. It is nevertheless, helpful to think of policy making occurring in these different stages:

- *Problem identification and issue recognition*: explores how issues get on to the policy agenda, why some issues do not even get discussed. In Chapter 4 you will go into this stage in more detail.
- *Policy formulation*: explores who is involved in formulating policy, how policies are arrived at, agreed upon, and how they are communicated The role of policy making in government is covered in Chapter 5 and that of interest groups in Chapter 6.
- *Policy implementation*: this is often the most neglected phase of policy making and is sometimes seen as quite divorced from the first two stages. However, this is arguably the most important phase of policy making because if policies are not implemented, or are diverted or changed at implementation, then

presumably something is going wrong – and the policy outcomes will not be those which were sought. These issues are discussed in Chapter 7.

- *Policy evaluation*: identifies what happens once a policy is put into effect – how it is monitored, whether it achieves its objectives and whether it has unintended consequences. This may be the stage at which policies are changed or terminated and new policies introduced. Chapter 9 covers this stage.

There are caveats to using this useful but simple framework. First, it looks as if the policy process is linear – in other words, it proceeds smoothly from one stage to another, from problem recognition to implementation and evaluation. However, it is seldom so clear or obvious a process. It may be at the stage of implementation that problem recognition occurs or policies may be formulated but never reach implementation. In other words, policy making is seldom a *rational* process – it is iterative and affected by interests – i.e. actors. Many people agree with Lindblom (1959) that the policy process is one which policy makers 'muddle through'. This is discussed in more detail in Chapter 2.

Nevertheless, the 'stages heuristic' has lasted for a long time and continues to be useful. It can be used for exploring not only national level policies but also international policies in order to try to understand how policies are transferred around the world.

Activity 1.4

The following extract on the rise and fall of policies on tuberculosis by Jessica Ogden and colleagues (2003) describes the different stages of the policy process, looking at context and actors as well as process.

As you read it, apply the health policy triangle:

1 Identify and write down who were the actors.
2 What processes can you identify?
3 What can you discern about the context?
4 What part did content play in determining policy?

Getting TB on the policy agenda and formulating the DOTS policy

1970s: the era of neglect and complacency

Throughout the 1970s TB control programmes were being implemented in many low and middle income countries, with only modest success. Only one international NGO, the International Union Against Tuberculosis and Lung Disease (IUATLD), explored ways of improving TB programmes, largely through the efforts of one of its public health physicians, Karel Styblo. From the early 1980s, Styblo and the IUATLD tried to develop a control strategy using a short-course regimen (six months) that would be feasible and effective in developing countries. At the time most TB programmes were using much longer drug regimens, and the public health community disagreed about best practice in treatment of TB.

Also, the international health policy context in the 1970s militated against support for the development of the IUATLD's vertical approach to TB control. This was the period when WHO, and in particular its then Director-General, Halfdan Mahler, espoused the goal of 'Health for All by the Year 2000'. This was to be achieved through concerted action to improve and integrate basic primary health care in poor countries. Health concerns therefore focused on integrating family planning and immunization in health services, rather than establishing vertical (specialized) disease control programmes.

The late 1980s: resurgence and experimentation

Interest in and concern over TB re-emerged from the mid-1980s as increasing numbers of cases, and alarming rises in multi-drug-resistant disease, were seen in industrialized countries, where most people had believed TB was a disease of the past. It was increasingly evident that TB and HIV/AIDS were linked, and many of the deaths from TB were linked to HIV.

Several international agencies initiated a process to get TB back on the international health policy agenda. The World Bank undertook a study of different health interventions as part of a health sector priorities review, and highlighted TB control as a highly cost-effective intervention. The *Ad Hoc* Commission on Health Research (made up of distinguished public health experts, with a secretariat at Harvard University) also identified TB as a neglected disease. Members of the Commission met Styblo, and were impressed with his approach. WHO expanded its TB Unit, and appointed Arata Kochi, an ex-UNICEF official, as its new head. One of his first appointments was an advocacy and communications expert.

The 1990s: advocacy opens up the window of opportunity

The WHO TB programme switched from a primarily technical focus to intensive advocacy in 1993. One of the first signs was a major media event in London in April 1993 declaring TB a 'Global Emergency'. The second was the branding of a new TB policy – DOTS – Directly Observed Therapy, Short-course. DOTS relied on five components: directly observed therapy (where health workers watched patients taking their drugs); sputum smear testing; dedicated patient recording systems; efficient drug supplies; and political commitment.

This branding process sent a tremor of shock waves through the academic and scientific communities. A rift developed between the political and operational experts who wanted to push the new strategy (which downplayed the importance of new vaccine and drug developments for TB) and the technical and scientific experts (including many in the academic community) who were concerned that the new WHO strategy not only oversimplified TB control measures, but would mean even less funding to research and development. Others objected to what was perceived initially as a very autocratic policy, with little room for discussion of alternative ways of controlling TB.

Feedback

1 You may have named the following as actors:

a) Karel Styblo, Halfdan Mahler, Arata Kochi (and the organizations within which they worked, which provided the base for their influence: IUATLD, WHO, UNICEF)

b) an un-named advocacy and communications expert
c) the World Bank; the *Ad Hoc* Committee on Health Research
d) networks: of public health community, TB specialists; technical and scientific experts interested in new drugs and vaccines research for TB.

2 Processes

The story is divided into decades that suggest a stage of neglect in the 1970s (with TB programmes being implemented in many countries but with no special attention to improving their impact); a stage when a problem was recognized in the 1980s as connections were made between the HIV/AIDS epidemic and increasing TB cases through research and experience. Then came the agenda-setting 1990s when concerted action put TB back on the international policy agenda.

3 Context

Some of the points you might make under context would be: complacency in the industrialized world up to the end of the 1980s, because TB was thought to be conquered. This was not true in low income countries, partly because of the relationship between TB and poverty. You might mention that WHO was promoting its 'Health for All' policy, which subscribed to integrated health care, and rejected special, vertical programmes, which was how TB programmes had been designed.

4 Content

You may have noted references to the technical content of TB policy such as short-course drug regime. You may also have noted what DOTS stood for and differences over what it should be.

Using the health policy triangle

You can use the health policy triangle to help analyse or understand a particular policy or you can apply it to plan a particular policy. The former can be referred to as analysis *of* policy, the latter as analysis *for* policy.

Analysis *of* policy is generally retrospective – it looks back to explore the determination of policy (how policies got on to the agenda, were initiated and formulated) and what the policy consisted of (content). It also includes evaluating and monitoring the policy – did it achieve its goals? Was it seen as successful?

Analysis *for* policy is usually prospective – it looks forward and tries to anticipate what will happen if a particular policy is introduced. It feeds into strategic thinking for the future and may lead to policy advocacy or lobbying. For example, before the UK government introduced legislation on compulsory use of car seatbelts to decrease mortality on the roads, it ran a national education campaign to persuade people of the evidence that seatbelts reduced deaths and it consulted the police and motor industry before introducing legislation that made it mandatory to have seatbelts in cars and for the police to enforce the law. In Chapter 10 you will learn some of the methods, such as stakeholder analysis, to help in prospective planning for policy.

An example of how analysis *of* a policy can help to identify action *for* policy is seen in a study undertaken by McKee et al. (1996) in which they compared policies across a number of high income countries to prevent sudden infant deaths – sometimes called 'cot deaths'. Research had highlighted that many of these deaths were avoidable by putting infants to sleep lying on their backs. The study showed that evidence has been available from the early 1980s but it was some years before it was acted on and some countries were quite slow to adopt measures to encourage parents to put their infants to sleep on their backs. The study suggests that statistical evidence seemed to have been of little importance as governments in many countries failed to recognize the steady rise in sudden infant deaths, even though the evidence was available to them. Instead focusing events such as television programmes which drew media attention, and the activities and feedback from NGOs were much more important. The lessons for policy depended to some extent on the political system: in federal forms of government, it seemed that authority was diffused, so strong central actions were difficult. This could be overcome by well-developed regional campaigning, and encouraging NGOs and the media to take an interest in the issue. In one country it seemed that a decentralized statistical service had led to delays in getting mortality data, so recognition of the problem took longer. The authors concluded that many countries needed to review their arrangements to respond to evidence of challenges to public health.

Summary

In this chapter you have been introduced to definitions of policy and health policy and a simple analytical framework of context, process and actors, to help you make sense of the politics which affect the policy making process. You have learned that the policy triangle can be used both retrospectively – to analyse past policy, and prospectively – to help plan how to change existing policy. Many of the concepts you have been introduced to will be expanded and illustrated in greater depth in the chapters that follow.

References

Anderson J (1975). *Public Policy Making*. London: Nelson

Dye T (2001). *Top Down Policymaking*. London: Chatham House Publishers

Leichter H (1979). *A Comparative Approach to Policy Analysis: Health Care Policy in Four Nations*. Cambridge: Cambridge University Press

Levine P (2003). *Prostitution, Race and Politics: Policing Venereal Disease in the British Empire*. New York: Routledge

Lindblom CE (1959). The science of muddling through. *Public Administrative Review* 19: 79–88

McKee M, Fulop N, Bouvier P, Hort A, Brand H, Rasmussen F, Kohler L, Varasovsky Z and Rosdahl N (1996). Preventing sudden infant deaths – the slow diffusion of an idea. *Health Policy* 37: 117–35.

Ogden J, Walt G and Lush L (2003). The politics of 'branding' in policy transfer: The case of DOTS for tuberculosis control. *Social Science and Medicine* 57(1): 163–72

Sabatier P and Jenkins-Smith H (1993). *Policy Change and Learning*. Boulder, CO: Westview Press

Shiffman J, Skarbalo M and Subotic J (2002). Reproductive rights and the state in Serbia and Croatia. *Social Science and Medicine* 54: 625–42

Walt G (1994). *Health Policy: An Introduction to Process and Power*. London: Zed Books
Walt G and Gilson L (1994). Reforming the health sector in developing countries: The central role of policy analysis. *Health Policy and Planning* 9: 353–70

2 Power and the policy process

Overview

In this chapter you will learn why understanding power is fundamental to policy analysis and be introduced to a number of theories which will help you understand the relationship between the two. These include explanations of power, its distribution in society and how governments make decisions. These theoretical insights help to explain why decision making is not simply a rational process but more likely is the result of power struggles between competing groups of actors.

Learning objectives

By working through this chapter, you will be able to:

- **differentiate between three dimensions of power and apply each to health policy making**
- **contrast theories which account for the distribution of power in society and understand their implications for who determines health policy**
- **define a political system, distinguish between various regime types, and understand their implications for participation in policy making**
- **contrast theories of decision making based on an appreciation of the role of power in the policy process**

Key terms

Authority Whereas power concerns the ability to influence others, authority concerns the right to do so.

Bounded rationality Policy makers intend to be rational but make decisions that are satisfactory as opposed to optimum, due to imperfect knowledge.

Elitism The theory that power is concentrated in a minority group in society.

Government The institutions and procedures for making and enforcing rules and other collective decisions. A narrower concept than the state which includes the judiciary, military and religious bodies.

Incrementalism Theory that decisions are not made through a rational process but by small adjustments to the status quo in the light of political realities.

Pluralism Theory that power is widely distributed in society.

Political system The processes through which governments transform 'inputs' from citizens into 'outputs' in the form of policies.

Power The ability to influence, and in particular to control, resources.

Rationalism Theory that decisions are made through a rational process by considering all the options and their consequences and then choosing the best among alternatives.

Sovereignty Entails rule or control that is supreme, comprehensive, unqualified and exclusive.

State A set of institutions that enjoy legal sovereignty over a fixed territorial area.

Introduction

You will be aware that power is exercised as a matter of course in many aspects of your everyday life. In the next chapter you will learn about the changing role of the state and that reforms of the late twentieth century aimed at 'rolling back the state' were resisted by various actors in many countries. Resistance is not surprising if you think of policy making as a struggle between groups with competing interests, some in favour of change and others opposed to it, depending on their interests or ideas. For example, health economists often wish to limit the professional autonomy of the medical profession so as to control spending patterns. Yet such reforms are often opposed by doctors – some of whom are concerned that this will usurp their professional authority and others because it may affect their income. Policy making is, therefore, often characterized by conflicts that arise when change is proposed or pursued which threatens the status quo. The outcome of any conflict depends on the balance of power between the individuals and groups involved and the processes or rules established to resolve those conflicts. Therefore, understanding policy making requires an understanding of the nature of power, how it is distributed and the manner through which it is exercised.

This chapter outlines several theories which help to understand the relationship between power and health policy making. While different theories hold true in different circumstances, it is also the case that it is up to you to decide which is the more persuasive since all are somewhat dependent on different views of the world. First, the meaning of power is explained. Then, a number of theories on the distribution of power are presented – particularly contrasting pluralism and forms of elitism. We then turn to how policy making takes place in political systems to explain how the pluralists and elitist theorists may both be right, depending on the policy content and context. In light of the role that power plays in policy making, finally you will learn the extent to which decision making is a rational process or one in which reason is sacrificed to power.

This chapter deepens your understanding of the *process* dimension of the policy triangle and provides the basis for more in-depth analysis of agenda setting and policy formulation, implementation and evaluation. The chapter also identifies specific *actors* in broad terms, particularly the state, organized interest groups, and individual decision makers, who have power and exercise it through the policy process.

What is power?

Power is generally understood to mean the ability to achieve a desired outcome – to 'do' something. In policy making, the concept of power is typically thought of in a relational sense as in having 'power over' others. Power is said to be exercised when A has B do something that B would not have otherwise done. A can achieve this end over B in a number of ways, which have been characterized as the three 'faces' or 'dimensions' of power: power as decision making; power as non-decision making; and power as thought control.

Power as decision making

'Power as decision making' focuses on acts of individuals and groups which influence policy decisions. Robert Dahl's classic study, *Who Governs?*, looked at who made important decisions on contested issues in New Haven, Connecticut, USA (Dahl 1961). He drew conclusions about who had power by examining known preferences of interest groups and comparing these with policy outcomes. He found that the resources which conferred power on citizens and interest groups varied and that these resources were distributed unequally: while some individuals were rich in some political resources, they were likely to be poor in others. Different individuals and groups were therefore found to be able to exert influence on different policy issues. These findings led Dahl to conclude that different groups in society, including weak groups, could 'penetrate' the political system and exercise power over decision makers in accordance with their preferences. While only a few people had direct influence over key decisions, defined as successfully initiating or vetoing policy proposals, most had indirect influence by the power of the vote.

What is meant by political resources? From a long list of potential assets, Dahl singled out social standing, access to cash, credit and wealth, legal trappings associated with holding official office, jobs, and control over information as particularly important in this policy arena. The range of resources at the disposal of actors in health policy is equally diverse – and will be a function of the particular policy content and context.

Power as non-decision making

Dahl's critics argued that his analysis, which focused on observable and contested policy issues, was blind to some important dimensions of power because it overlooked the possibility that dominant groups exert influence by limiting the policy agenda to acceptable concerns. Bachrach and Baratz (1962) argued that 'power is also exercised when A devotes his energies to creating or reinforcing social and political values and institutional practices that limit the scope of the political process to public consideration of only those issues which are comparatively innocuous to A'. Consequently, power as agenda-setting highlights the way in which powerful groups control the agenda to keep threatening issues below the policy radar screen. Expressed differently, power as 'non-decision making' involves 'the practice of limiting the scope of actual decision making to safe issues by manipulating the dominant community values, myths and political institutions and procedures' (Bachrach and Baratz 1963). In this dimension of power, some issues remain latent and fail to enter the policy arena.

Activity 2.1

Consider how one person (A) may exercise power over another (B), that is how someone gets another person to do what they would otherwise not have done.

Feedback

You may have identified three possible ways:

- intimidation and coercion (the stick)
- productive exchanges involving mutual gain (the carrot)
- the creation of obligations, loyalty and commitment (the hug)

Some have suggested that it is useful to differentiate between hard and soft power where hard power corresponds to the carrot and the stick and soft to the hug. Soft power involves 'getting others to want what you want' (Nye 2002). Soft power relies on co-opting others by shaping their preferences and is associated with resources such as attractive and enviable culture, values, ideas, and institutions.

Activity 2.2

What differentiates authority from coercion and persuasion? Why might this distinction be important in relation to one person getting another to support a policy that s/he wouldn't have otherwise done?

Max Weber (1948) identified three sources of authority. First, *traditional authority* exists where one obeys on the basis of custom and the established way of doing things (for example, a king or sultan has traditional authority). People conform as part of everyday life on the basis of socialization. For example, poor pregnant women in rural Guatemala do not question whether the practices and advice of their midwife are evidence-based, but surrender to her authority because of trust that society places in midwives based on their experience and the expectation that they know best.

Second, *charismatic authority* is based on intense commitment to a leader and their ideology or other personal appeals. Those exercising authority on the basis of charisma, such as religious leaders, statesmen (e.g. Nelson Mandela) and health gurus do so on the basis of being perceived as having authority.

Feedback

Authority is defined as the right to rule or govern. It exists when subordinates accept the dictates of their rulers without question. When authority exists, personal judgement is surrendered to an authority on the basis of trust and/or acceptance.

Weber's third category is *rational–legal authority*. It is based on rules and procedures. In this case, authority is vested in the office as opposed to the attributes of the particular office holder. As a result, the office holder, irrespective of his/her training or expertise, is *in* authority. Many countries with a history of British colonial rule designate the Secretary as the most senior bureaucrat in the Ministry of Health. The Health Secretary is rarely a doctor but instead is a professional administrator. While many doctors implement the dictates of the Secretary, they do so on the basis of his/her rational-legal authority rather than on the basis of traditional or charismatic authority. Indeed, given the role that knowledge and expertise play in the health policy process, it may be useful to add to Weber's classification (traditional, charismatic, rational-legal) a category entitled *technical authority*. Patients respect the advice of their doctors (for the most part) on the basis of the technical knowledge that doctors are thought to possess.

This raises the question of what induces people to surrender their personal judgement to authorities and that is where the concept of legitimacy is useful. Authority is considered legitimate if personal judgement is based on trust and acceptance. This is different from being coerced to yield judgement on the basis of threat (e.g. by the police). Legitimate authority occupies that space in the middle of the spectrum between coercion (stick) and persuasion (carrot).

To return to the question of A getting B to support a policy that s/he might not otherwise have: approaches which are based on either too much coercion or persuasion may result in policies which enjoy little popular legitimacy, may not be readily accepted, and may be difficult and costly to secure compliance for implementation.

An example of power as non-decision making can be identified in the health sector. In 1999, an independent committee of experts reviewed tobacco industry documents to assess the influence of the industry on the World Health Organisation. Its report revealed that the industry used a variety of tactics, including staging events to divert attention from the public health issues raised by tobacco use and secretly paying 'independent' experts and journalists to keep the focus of the Organisation on communicable, as opposed to non-communicable, diseases (Zeltner et al. 2000).

Power as thought control

Steven Lukes (1974) conceptualizes 'power as thought control'. In other words, power is a function of the ability to influence others by shaping their preferences. In this dimension, 'A exercises power over B when A affects B in a manner contrary to B's interests'. For example, poor people voted for President Bush in 2004 in spite of his domestic policies which were not in their interests.

Lukes argues that A gains B's compliance through subtle means. This could include the ability to shape meanings and perceptions of reality which might be done through the control of information, the mass media and or through controlling the processes of socialization. McDonald's, the fast food company, spends billions of dollars on advertising annually. Its symbolic Golden Arches are reported to be more widely recognized than the Christian cross. In China, children have been indoctrinated to accept that the company's mascot, Ronald McDonald, is 'kind, funny, gentle and understands children's hearts' thereby subtly conditioning this emerging market of young consumers to think positively about McDonald's and its products. McDonald's targets decision makers as well as consumers. Prior to a parliamentary debate on obesity in the UK, the company sponsored 20 parliamentarians to attend the European Football Championships in Portugal in 2004.

Activity 2.3

Why might McDonald's send parliamentarians to watch football?

Feedback

Without access to internal company documents, one can only speculate on the aims of such largesse. One plausible explanation is that McDonald's hoped to instil in these legislators an association between McDonald's and the company's actions to support increased physical activity as a route to reducing obesity; an association which might displace other associations that the policy makers might have between, for example, the company's products and any relationship that may exist between their consumption and obesity.

Lukes finds this dimension of power the 'supreme' and 'most insidious' form as it dissuades people from having objections by 'shaping their perceptions, cognitions and preferences in such a way that they accept their role in the existing order of things, either because they can see or imagine no alternative to it, or because they see it as natural and unchangeable, or because they value it as divinely ordained and beneficial'.

The largely unregulated market for complementary treatments and tonics may be growing as a result of this form of power. Such treatments are popular and widely used in many countries. In Australia, more than half the population regard vitamins, minerals, tonics or herbal medicine as helpful for treating depression. Surveys in the USA suggest that over 50 per cent of respondents who reported anxiety attacks or severe depression had used complementary therapies in the previous 12 months (Kessler et al. 2001). Yet a systematic review of the evidence of the effectiveness of a number of the most popular complementary therapies to treat depression concluded that there is no evidence to suggest that they are effective (Jorm et al. 2002). Meanwhile, adverse reactions to such treatments have doubled in the past three years (WHO 2004). Arguably, the interests of consumers, or at least poor consumers, would be better served if they were to allocate their limited health care expenditure to items proven to be efficacious. Yet marketing has apparently manipulated these consumers' interests to reflect those of industry.

Activity 2.4

The following describes a classic study of air pollution in the USA. As you read it consider:

1 Which dimension of power is described?
2 Does the study indicate that power as thought control may also have been in play?

The un-politics of air pollution

In the 1960s, Matthew Crenson sought to explain why air pollution remained a 'non-issue' in many American cities. In particular, he attempted to identify relationships between the neglect of air pollution and characteristics of political leaders and institutions.

Crenson's approach, examining why things do not happen, contrasted with that of Robert Dahl's which looked at why they do (1961). Crenson adopted this strategy to test whether or not the study of political inactivity (or non-decision making) would shed new light on ways of thinking about power. He also wondered if this different approach would support the claims made by Dahl that the policy making process was open to many groups in society.

Crenson began by demonstrating that action or inaction on pollution in US cities could not be attributed to differences in actual pollution level or to differences in social attributes of the populations in different cities. The study involved two neighbouring cities in Indiana which were both equally polluted and had similar demographic profiles. One of the cities, East Chicago, had taken action to deal with air pollution in 1949, while the other, Gary, did nothing until 1962. Crenson argues that the difference arose because Gary was a single-employer town dominated by U.S. Steel, with a strong political party organization, while Chicago was home to a number of steel companies and had no strong party organization when it passed air pollution legislation. In Gary, anticipated negative reactions from the company were thought to have prevented activists and city leaders from placing the issue on the agenda. Crenson also interviewed political leaders from 51 American cities. These suggested that 'the air pollution issue tends not to flourish in cities where industry enjoys a reputation for power'.

Crenson's major findings were that, first, power may consist of the ability to prevent some items from becoming issues. Second, that power does not need to be exercised for it to be effective: the mere reputation for power can restrict the scope of decision making. Third, those affected by political power, 'the victims', may remain invisible, because the power or reputation of the powerful may deter the less powerful from entering the policy making arena. He concluded that 'non-issues are not politically random oversights but instances of politically enforced neglect'.

Feedback

1 Crenson's study describes and provides an empirical basis for power as non-decision making.

2 Given that people would probably prefer not to be poisoned by air pollution, the case suggests that people will not necessarily act on their preferences and interests. This is presumably due to some form of manipulation or indoctrination, policy making by thought control.

Activity 2.5

From what you have learned so far, provide three simple answers on how a relationship between A and B reveals that A is exercising power over B.

Feedback

A can get B to do what B may not have otherwise done. A can keep issues that are of interest to B off the policy agenda. A can manipulate B in a way that B fails to understand his/her true interests.

So far, you have learned that power is the ability to achieve a desired result irrespective of the means. It concerns the ability to get someone to do what they would not have otherwise done. Dahl, who examined decision making, concluded that power is widely distributed in society but was criticized as having failed to identify the true winners and losers – particularly the losers who do not enter the policy arena. Lukes takes the position that power can be exercised in a more subtle manner through keeping issues off the agenda or through psychological manipulation. Common to all these perspectives is the notion that the policy process involves the exercise of power by competing actors to control scarce resources. The manner in which these struggles are resolved depends in large part on who has power in society, a topic which you will now consider.

Who has power?

If power concerns the ability to influence others, it raises the question 'who has the power to impose and resist policies?'. The three 'dimensions' of power suggest different views as to who wields power and how widely it is shared in policy processes. There is no correct answer to this question as the distribution of influence will depend on the specific policy content and context. For example, in a country where tobacco constitutes a considerable proportion of the gross domestic product and is valuable source of government revenue, is the tobacco industry or the Ministry of Health and public health and consumer interest groups likely to have more influence over a tobacco control policy? Yet, in the same country, industry may have less influence over policy to screen for cancer than, for example, the Ministry of Health, the medical profession, and patient groups.

Despite the differences that policy content and context exert over the distribution of power in a given policy process, attempts have been made to arrive at general theories. These theories turn on the nature of society and the state. While some theories locate power in society as opposed to the state, all are concerned with the role of the state and the interests which the state is thought to represent in the policy process. The focus is on the state because of the dominant role that it usually plays in the policy process. Theorists differ, however, in two important respects. First, in their assessment of whether the state is independent of society or a reflection of the distribution of power in society (state- and society-oriented respectively). Second, in their view of the state serving a common good or the interests of a privileged group. You will now learn about how the theories differ and consider the implication of these differences for health policy.

Pluralism

Pluralism represents the dominant school of thought as far as theories of the distribution of power in liberal democracies are concerned. In its classical form, pluralism takes the view that power is dispersed throughout society. No individual group holds absolute power and the state arbitrates among competing interests in the development of policy.

The key features of pluralism are:

- open electoral competition among a number of political parties
- ability of individuals to organize themselves into pressure groups and political parties
- ability of pressure groups to air their views freely
- openness of the state to lobbying for all pressure groups
- state as a neutral referee adjudicating between competing demands
- although society has elite groups, no elite group dominates at all times

For pluralists, health policy emerges as the result of conflict and bargaining among large numbers of groups organized to protect the specific interests of their members. The state selects from initiatives and proposals put forward by interest groups according to what is best for society.

Pluralism has been subject to considerable scepticism for its portrayal of the state as a neutral umpire in the distribution of power. The major challenge on the first count comes from public choice theorists and on the second from elite theorists.

Public choice

Public choice theorists agree with the pluralists that society is made up of competing groups pursuing self-interested goals but they dispute the claim of the state's neutrality. Public choice theorists assert that the state is itself an interest group which wields power over the policy process in pursuit of the interests of those who run it: elected public officials and civil servants. To remain in power, elected officials consciously seek to reward groups with public expenditure, goods, services and favourable regulation in the expectation that these groups will keep them in power. Similarly, public servants use their offices and proximity to political decision makers to derive 'rents' by providing special access to public resources and regulatory favouritism to specific groups. As a result, public servants hope to expand their bureaucratic empires as this will lead to bigger salaries and more opportunities for promotion, power, patronage and prestige. The state is, therefore, said to have an inbuilt dynamic which leads to the further growth and power of government.

Public choice theorists argue that the self-interested behaviour of state officials will lead to a policy that is captured by narrow interest groups. As a result, policies are likely to be distorted in economically negative ways and are not in the public's interest. Adherents of this school would argue that health policies which involve rolling back the state will be resisted by bureaucrats, not because of the technical merits or demerits of the policy, but because bureaucrats favour policies which further entrench their positions and extend their spheres of influence. In Bangladesh, for example, Ministry of Health and Family Welfare officials resisted proposals to contract out public sector facilities to non-governmental organizations for management and service delivery as well as a related proposal to establish an autonomous organization to manage the contracting process. Public choice adherents would explain this resistance on the basis of fear of staff redundancies, diminished opportunities for rent-seeking and patronage, and concerns about the diminution of statutory responsibilities.

Critics suggest that public choice overstates the power of the bureaucracy in the policy process and is largely fuelled by the ideological opposition to escalating public spending and big government.

Elitism

Elitist theorists contend that policy is dominated by a privileged minority. They argue that public policy reflects the values and interests of this elite or aristocracy – not 'the people' as is claimed by the pluralists. Modern elitists question the extent to which modern political systems live up to the democratic ideals suggested by the liberal pluralists. For example, in the democratic USA, scholars have shown how an elite shapes key decisions. President G.W. Bush and his father, the former President, have considerable financial interests in the defence and energy sectors while Vice-President Dick Cheney was chief executive of a major oil firm before assuming his post. In contrast, groups representing small business, labour and consumer interests are only able to exert influence at the margins of the policy process.

As far as health policy is concerned, does elitist theory overstate the capacities of the elite to wield power? Certainly, most health policy is considered to be of relatively marginal importance and, consequently, it may be that elitist theories are less useful in accounting for power in health policy. Such marginal issues are sometimes referred to as 'low politics'. Nonetheless, you will see many examples in this book which suggest that an elite wields considerable influence in this relatively mundane level of policy making.

Others who examine elites closely distinguish between a 'political elite' made up of those who actually exercise power at any given time and which include:

> members of the government and high administration, military leaders, and, in some cases, politically influential families . . . and leaders of powerful economic enterprises, and a political class which includes the political elite as well as leaders of opposition political parties, trade union leaders, businesspeople and other members of the social elite. (Bottomore 1966)

It can be inferred that for elite theorists, power may be based on a variety of resources: wealth, family connections, technical expertise, or office. Yet what is also important is that for any one member of the elite, power is unlikely to depend on one source.

According to elite theorists:

- Society is comprised of the few with power and the many without. Only the few who have power make public policy.
- Those who govern are unlike those who do not. In particular, the elite come from the higher socio-economic strata.
- Non-elites may be inducted into the governing circles if they accept the basic consensus of the existing elite.
- Public policy reflects the values of the elite. This may not always imply a conflict

with the values of the masses. Indeed, as Lukes (1974) argued, the elite can manipulate the values of the masses to reflect their own.

- Interest groups exist but they are not all equally powerful and do not have equal access to the policy making process.
- The values of the elite are conservative and consequently any policy change is likely to be incremental.

It would appear that elitist theory is relevant to many countries in Latin America, Africa and Asia, where politicians, senior bureaucrats, business people, professionals and the military make up tight policy circles that become a dominant or ruling class. In some places, the elite may be so few in number that they can be recognized by their family name.

The notion that not all interest groups are equally influential holds similar intuitive appeal. There is an increasing concentration of ownership in certain industries, for example, tobacco, alcohol, and pharmaceuticals. These powerful groups will have more leverage over policy than will public health groups. The following highlights the results of a study by Landers and Sehgal (2004) on the resources spent by some of these groups lobbying at the national level in the US.

Healthcare lobbying in the United States

The term 'lobby' as a noun relates to the areas in parliaments where citizens can make demands on legislators and where policy makers meet. The term is also used as a verb, meaning to make direct representation to a policy maker. Lobby and interest groups are similar in that they both attempt to influence policy makers. Lobbyists are hired by various organizations to represent the interests of their clients on a commercial basis.

In 2000, health care lobbyists spent US$237 million, more than any other industry, to influence US Senators and representatives, the Executive and other federal agencies at the national level. Of this amount, drug and medical supply companies accounted for over a third ($96 million); physicians and other health professionals ($46 million), hospitals and nursing homes ($40 million); health insurance and managed care companies ($31 million); disease advocacy and public health organizations ($12 million).

The greater the amount of funding, the more likely it is that interest groups are able to put across their perspectives to legislators. Doctors commenting on the study expressed concern that 'health policy is at risk of being unduly influenced by special interest groups that can bring the most financial resources to the table' (Kushel and Bindman 2004).

During the three-year period of the study, the number of organizations employing lobbyists increased by 50 per cent, suggesting that lobbying is an increasing popular tool to curry influence in the American political system.

Activity 2.6

At this point it is useful to consider how it was possible for scholars to arrive at such different conclusions as to the distribution of power in the United States. Dahl (1961), you will recall, argued that many groups can influence the policy process while others have asserted a ruling class or elite could be identified, consisting of the captains of business, political executive and the military establishment.

Feedback

The answer lies in what the scholars have observed and studied. Dahl focused on actual conflicts among groups over municipal politics. Elitist theorists studied 'reputations for power'. Elitists assert that those with a reputation for power were effective at keeping controversial issues off the policy agenda, which are, therefore, beyond the purview of the conflicts studied by Dahl.

There are a number of other important elitist frameworks which locate power in specific groups in society. Marxism argues that power is vested in a ruling capitalist class and that this class controls the state. Professionalism draws attention to the power of specific professional groups and the way they wield influence over the policy process. You will learn more about the special position of the medical profession in health policy in Chapter 6. Feminism focuses on the systematic, pervasive and institutionalized power which men wield over women in the domestic/private and public spheres. In its extreme form, women remain in the private domain (as mothers and wives) while public affairs, such as the state, are run by and for men. In patriarchal societies, men define the problems and their solutions, decide which issues are policy-worthy and which are not, and, in line with Lukes's conceptualization of power as thought control (1974), have socialized many women to accept their status within this schema. Between 1990 and 2000, the proportion of seats held by women in national parliaments increased, from 13 to 14 per cent. There were distinct regional variations, while women's participation improved in Nordic countries and approached 40 per cent, the proportion in Western Asia slipped from 5 to 4 per cent (UN 2002).

Activity 2.7

As you read the following piece about sex-selective abortions, consider whether or not the claim that health policy in India is captured by men is valid.

Gendered policy implementation

In India, antenatal ultrasound technology which was ostensibly introduced to identify congenital complications, has transformed the cultural preference for male progeny into a process through which those who can afford a scan, which is an increasingly large proportion, may pre-select males by identifying females during pregnancy and selectively terminating female foetuses. This has resulted in an intensification of the 'masculinization' of the sex ratio in the country. The 2001 census revealed a national child (0–6 years of age) sex ratio of 933 females to 1,000 males (whereas one would expect a roughly equal number of girls and boys surviving in a gender-equal society). Some states have higher differentials than others. For example, Punjab reports a ratio of 793 per 1,000 boys in that age group.

In response to the problem, the federal government passed the Pre-natal Diagnostic Techniques Act in 1994. Little was done to implement the Act until 2001 when an NGO filed a public interest claim with the Supreme Court. The Court directed certain states to take action (seizing machines in clinics without licences) but one prominent demographer contends that the law is 'totally ineffective'. Apparently, no action has been taken against unlicensed users in places such as Delhi, but the problem remains that licensed providers continue to use the machines in defiance of the law. The issue has become all the more urgent with new technologies for sex-selection marketed to Indians by US firms and available over the Internet. Consequently, there have been calls for amendments to the legislation. It has, however, been argued that there are limits to what the law and the courts can do in face of deep-rooted prejudices against girl children.

Feedback

While it is clear that sex discrimination is pervasive in India, some might point to the existence of the 1994 law as proof that women can successfully penetrate the policy process. Feminists would argue, however, that the law was too little, too late, and too poorly implemented. Explaining such failure would require more information on how the problem was framed and who put it on the policy agenda (likely to have been women) and who was responsible for implementation, mainly men!

Activity 2.8

The following is an account of work by Kelley Lee and Hillary Goodman (2002) on the distribution of power in international health in relation to health care financing policy.

As you read it, make notes of why Lee and Goodman describe the actors as part of a global policy network and what might account for its success. Also consider why you might argue that the existence of this network is insufficient proof of a policy elite in health sector reform.

International health financing reform: dominated by an elite?

In an attempt to demonstrate the impact of globalization on the processes of health policy making, Lee and Goodman (2002) undertook an empirical analysis of health care financing reform during the 1980s and 1990s. While it was apparent that a plethora of non-state actors were increasingly involved in the provision and financing of health services, it was less clear whether or not this huge diversity was similarly reflected in debating and formulating health policy. Lee and Goodman were sceptical of the claims that globalization had increased the range and heterogeneity of voices in the policy process so they set out to establish who had been responsible for the ideas and content of health care financing policy.

The study began by tracing the significant changes in the content of health care financing policy during the period, marked by a transition from strong reluctance to a broader acceptance of private finance for a range of health care services. The key individuals and institutions involved in the discourse on financing policy were identified through a systematic search of the literature. This resulted in a list of individuals who had published frequently in key journals, been frequently cited, and/or contributed to seminal policy documents on the topic. The institutional base, source of funding, and nationality of these key actors were noted. These individuals were interviewed to elicit their views on the most influential documents, individuals, institutions and meetings in the policy area and their curriculum vitae were procured. Finally, the researchers studied records of attendance and presentations at meetings reported by informants to have been seminal in the evolution of the policies.

Network maps were developed linking the institutions and individuals. The authors discovered that a small (approximately 25) and tightly knit group of policy makers, technical advisers and academics had dominated the process and content of health financing reform. This group, which was connected by multiple linkages in a complex network, was based in a small number of institutions led by the World Bank and USAID. Network members were observed as following a common career progression. Revolving doors circulated members among key institutions, thereby enabling them to occupy various roles as researchers, research and pilot project funders policy advisers, and decision makers.

Lee and Goodman conclude that a global elite had dominated policy discussion through their control of resources, but more importantly through their 'control of the terms of debate through expert knowledge, support of research, and occupation of key nodes' in the network. What concerned the authors was not that a small group of leaders shaped the policy debates, but rather that the leadership was not representative of the interests at stake: 'the global policy network has been narrowly based in a small number of institutions, led by the World Bank and USAID [but including Abt Associates, a private consultancy firm and Harvard University], in the nationality and disciplinary background of the key individuals involved'. Lee and Goodman were also concerned that policy did not result from a 'rational convergence of health needs and solutions'. Instead, the elite is described as having exercised its influence on national agendas through both coercive (conditionalities on aid in the context of extreme resource scarcity) and consensual (collaborative research, training and through co-option of policy elites) approaches.

The authors argue that this case contradicts pluralist claims that globalization is opening up decision making for a wider range of individuals and groups.

Feedback

The group which governs the health care financing agenda can be portrayed as an elite in that it is small in number, and members have similar educational, disciplinary and national backgrounds. Over a 20-year period, this policy elite is demonstrated to have successfully established an international health care financing agenda and formulated policies that were adopted in numerous countries. It was able to do this in part because of its gateway to development assistance but more importantly, through its control of technical expertise, expert knowledge and positions and occupation of key nodal points in the network. The existence of this network is not proof that an elite dominates all health reform policy. If it were found that other policy issues in the broader international policy context were influenced by individuals and institutions which were based in other countries, and staffed by decision makers with different credentials and backgrounds, you might conclude that a form of pluralism exists.

A variety of theories on the distribution of power in society and the character of the state in policy making have been presented. The differences between them are not trivial in that they carry important implications for who has power and what explains policy change. Some of the discrepancies can be accounted for by different methodological approaches. Taking into consideration critiques, methodological constraints and new empirical evidence, these and other theorists have modified and updated their approaches. Most pluralists now acknowledge that the policy making playing field is not even. They note the privileged position of organized business and the role that the media and socialization play in most political systems.

Despite the fact that there is some overlap among the theories and convergence on some points as well, it still remains that there is reasonable empirical evidence for many of the competing theoretical claims. Hence, it is useful to return to the point made at the outset. To some extent, the actual distribution of power will depend on the policy context and content. Issues of great national importance are likely to be made by a power elite whereas more mundane issues are likely to be more highly debated and influenced by a range of interest groups. What is ultimately useful about the models is that they provide different ways of trying to understand given policy issues.

Power and political systems

David Easton's (1965) systems model of policy making provides one approach to simplifying the complexities of political decision making and understanding its key universal components. A system is a complex whole which is constituted by a number of inter-related and inter-dependent parts. The system's parts may change as they interact with one another and the wider environment. While these changes and processes of interaction result in a constant transformation within the system, overall they must remain broadly in balance or equilibrium if the system is to survive.

The political system is concerned with deciding which goods, services, freedoms, rights and privileges to grant (and to deny) and to whom they will be granted (or denied). The wider environment affects the political system in that it provides opportunities, resources, obstacles and constraints to political decision making. For example, there may be a shortage of nurses. This might provoke action (policy decision) from the political system to deal with the shortage. Among policy alternatives, the political system may increase the number of nursing places in higher educational facilities, provide monetary incentives such as loans to encourage students to enter the nursing speciality, recruit nurses from other countries, increase the skills of para-medical staff to take on some nursing functions, or do nothing.

Activity 2.9

Identify some of the obstacles and constraints to each of the policy responses proposed above to deal with the shortage of nurses. For example, an increase in the number of nursing places in higher education will require additional funds, will not necessarily attract additional students, and will take a number of years to resolve the problem.

Feedback

1 Providing monetary incentives to nursing students will require additional funds, might be perceived as unfair by other students and disciplines, may be difficult to administer, and may not attract additional students.

2 Recruiting foreign nurses will require additional funds, may require changes to existing foreign worker regulations, and may be resisted by domestic nursing unions, xenophobic groups or patients.

3 Increasing the skills of another cadre of staff to assume nursing functions may result in demand from them to be remunerated as nurses, may require additional funds, and may be resisted by nursing unions.

The key processes which the systems model highlights are 'inputs' and 'outputs' and the linkages between them (Figure 2.1). Inputs take the form of demands and support from the populace (the energy which drives the system). Demands on the system are made by individuals and groups. In the health sector, these may include higher expenditure on health care, free or more affordable care, more convenient services, the right to abortion (or the 'right to life'), and so on. These preferences are transformed into demands when they are communicated by citizens to decision makers directly or indirectly through interest groups, lobbyists and political parties. Support comprises action taken by the public to underpin (or oppose) the political system by paying taxes, voting and complying with the law (or not paying taxes, defacing the ballot, using illicit services – for abortion, for example).

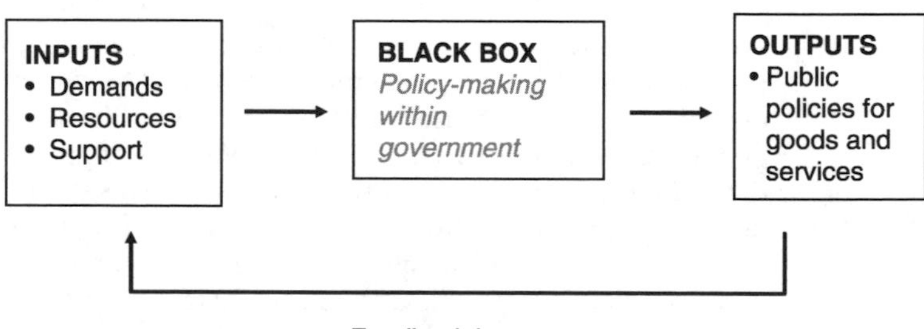

Figure 2.1 Easton's political systems model
Source: Adapted from Easton (1965)

Inputs are fed into policy making to produce outputs; the decisions and policies of government including legislation, imposition of taxation, and resource allocation. Easton provided relatively few details on how the conversion process takes place and therefore government decision making is considered a 'black box'. Some outputs are obvious and visible, such as a decision by government to train more nurses. Some outputs may be less obvious and even largely invisible. As Bachrach and Baratz (1963) remind us, some decisions may be subtle or non-decisions which perpetuate the existing allocation of values or keep issues off the policy agenda. For example, while some citizens may demand more nursing staff, the government may take no action. Inside the black box a resource allocation decision has been taken without any visible policy making.

The outputs of the policy process are distinguished from their impact. Policy impact relates to the effects of policy decisions on individuals and groups in society. Ultimately, for example, citizens will be interested in the impact of any policy to address the nursing shortage on the number of nurses in the health care system and the effect that this has on the quality of care.

The logic of the systems approach dictates that policy outputs and impacts generate 'feedback' which influences future demands and support on the system – creating a loop. The feedback is characterized as continuous or iterative to capture the evolving interdependency within the components of the system. To carry on with the nursing example, if the policy which is adopted fails to achieve its aims or results in unanticipated consequences (poorer quality nursing, for example), affected groups will likely alter their preferences, demands and support in relation to other policy alternatives. These inputs will in turn affect the constraints and opportunities presented to decision makers working within the black box and condition their subsequent approach to the problem.

Easton's model explains why political systems are responsive to public pressure. The model also breaks down the policy making process into discrete stages which will be analysed in further detail later in this book. Moreover, its very general nature means that it can be applied to most political systems. Yet, as with any model, its simplification of reality also has some drawbacks, some of which should be apparent to you, given the discussion of power.

Activity 2.10

Consider whether or not Easton's political system model deals adequately with: (1) the distribution of power in society; (2) the neutrality of the state; and (3) the possibility that the state may be self-interested. Write a few sentences to critique the model on each of these issues.

Feedback

1 The model fails to grapple with the issue of the balance of power in society and how this balance might affect the allocation of values through the political system. For example, an elite may value a separate and superior health service subsidized by the state and may be able to articulate its demands and support for this preference in a way that is not possible for the masses to articulate their demands for a service which is accessible to all social classes.

2 Easton's model appears to suggest that the state is neutral in its allocation of values among competing demands. The model assumes that the state develops policy by balancing demands as opposed to taking account of the relative power of those making different demands on the system and providing it with different types of support. In the real world, those groups which can make campaign finance contributions or spend the largest sums on lobbyists are more likely to have their demands preferentially treated by decision makers than those groups that lack finances to amplify their demands or back up their support.

3 The model does not appear to provide scope for the state acting in its own interest (as argued by public choice theorists). Decision makers, and especially decision implementers, often tailor policy outputs to suit their own interests rather than bending to the demands and support from the wider environment.

As a result of the latter two concerns, it is argued that the model fails to explain why governments may employ repression and coercion, as many have at some time, to curb demands. A further criticism is, the model does not account for policy that arises from decision making within private organizations, for example, voluntary industry codes such as on child labour or private regulation pertaining to technical matters. Furthermore, as already alluded to, the model places too little emphasis on what happens inside the black box. Are decisions made in a rational way by policy makers or in an incremental manner depending on the exercise of power by interest groups? These questions will be discussed later in this chapter.

Despite these shortcomings, the concept of the political system provides an important key to understanding the discrete stages of the decision making cycle. Yet before turning to these stages, you need to understand about inputs, in an effort to clarify the relationship between them and the policy making process – particularly citizens' ability to influence the policy process. This relationship hinges around the nature of participation in the political system.

Classifying political systems: participation, benefits and openness

Broadly speaking, citizens can participate either directly or indirectly in the policy process. Direct participation describes attempts to influence policy through face-to-face or other forms of personal contact with policy makers. For example, constituents may meet with their parliamentary representative to discuss options for reducing the length of the local hospital waiting list. Indirect participation refers to actions by individuals to influence the selection of government representatives. This normally takes place by joining political parties, campaigning for particular parties or individuals and voting in elections.

The extent to which people can participate in the political system either directly or indirectly is partially a function of the culture and nature of the political system – clearly not all political systems are alike. There have been attempts to classify political systems based on the extent to which they allow for participation in the political system and on the basis of the kinds of outputs they produce. Based on an analysis of Greek city–states, Aristotle developed a taxonomy of six political systems on the basis of who rules and who benefits (Table 2.1). Aristotle's categories

Table 2.1 Aristotle's forms of government

		Who rules?		
		One person	*The few*	*The many*
Who benefits?	Rulers	Tyranny	Oligarchy	Democracy
	All	Monarchy	Aristocracy	Polity

Source: Adapted from Heywood (2002)

remain widely understood today. In his view, democracy, oligarchy and tyranny were all debased forms of government as the governors served their own interests.

More recent attempts at classifying political systems have added a further dimension: how open is the system to deliberation of alternatives (how liberal or authoritarian)? On the basis of these criteria, five groups of political systems have been distinguished:

- *liberal democratic regimes*. This category is marked by governments that operate with relatively stable political institutions with considerable opportunities for participation through a diverse number of mechanisms and groups: elections, political parties, interest groups, and 'free media'. It includes the countries of North America, Western Europe as well as countries such as India and Israel. They tend neither to be highly inegalitarian (with the exception of the USA) nor highly egalitarian. Health policy varies considerably from market-oriented in the USA to the responsibility of the welfare state in Western Europe.
- *egalitarian-authoritarian*. Characterized by a closed ruling elite, authoritarian bureaucracies and state-managed popular participation (i.e. participation-regimented and less a democratic opportunity than an exercise in social control). Close links often exist between single political parties and the state and its bureaucracies. During the 1970s, the Soviet Union, China, Vietnam, Angola, Mozambique and Cuba might have been included. These states were intendedly egalitarian – although the scope and nature of equality were often contested. These countries had well-developed social security systems and health care was financed and delivered almost exclusively by the state (private practice was banned in some cases) and treated as a fundamental human right. Few egalitarian-authoritarian political systems now exist.
- *traditional-inegalitarian*. These systems feature rule by traditional monarchs which provide few opportunities for participation. Saudi Arabia provides an example of this increasingly rare system. Health policy relies heavily on the private sector with the elite using facilities in advanced countries as the need arises.
- *populist*. These are based upon single or dominant political parties, highly nationalist and leadership tends to be personalized. Participation is highly regimented through mass movements controlled by the state or political party. Elites may have some influence on the government either through kinship with the leader or membership of the political party – as long as they support the nationalist and populist causes. Many newly independent states of Africa and South America began with populist political systems. While the colonial health services had only been available to the ruling elite, populists attempted to provide health for all as a basic right.
- *authoritarian-inegalitarian*. These political systems have often occurred in reaction to populist and liberal democratic regimes. They are often associated with military governments and involve varying degrees of repression. In the mid-1980s, over half the governments in Sub-Saharan Africa were military – and many were marked by autocratic personal rule. Health policy reflected the interests of a narrow elite: a state-funded service for the military while others had to rely heavily on the private sector.

In light of the profound political upheaval at the end of the 1980s, the above classification of political systems has been shown to be somewhat dated and no clear substitutes have emerged. Francis Fukuyama, an American political scientist, published a paper in 1989 provocatively entitled 'The end of history?' He claimed that the collapse of communism and the wave of democratization of the late 1980s signalled the recognition of liberal democracy as the superior and 'final form of human government'. Although it is true that some form of democracy is the most common form of political system, Fukuyama's analysis is western-centric, based on values such as individualism, rights and choice; moreover, it fails to account for the persistence and rise of new forms of political systems which tend to be more complex and diverse. Heywood (2002) tentatively puts forward a classification reflecting the current political world:

- *Western polyarchies*. Equates with liberal democracies as outlined above. The nomenclature was changed for two reasons, one of which was the recognition that in many of these countries the practice fell short of the ideal of democracy.
- *new democracies*. A wave of democratization began in 1974 with the overthrow of authoritarian governments in Greece, Portugal and Spain. These countries were joined by many former Soviet Republics in 1989–91. All these countries have introduced multiparty elections and radical market-oriented reforms. From a political point of view, the distinction between these and the established Western polyarchies is the incomplete consolidation of democracy and the co-existence of certain forms of authoritarianism which limit participation. Massive social sector reforms have undermined social safety nets, mass redundancy of medical personnel and a shift to private finance.
- *East Asian regimes*. While the countries of the western rim of the Pacific Ocean are largely polyarchic, they differ from the Western ones on the basis of cultural differences which have been shaped by Confucian ideas and values as opposed to liberal individual ones. Consequently, East Asian regimes are characterized by 'strong' governments, powerful ruling parties, respect for leadership, emphasis on community and social cohesion. Low tax rates and low public spending result in limited public provision of health care.
- *Islamic regimes*. Found in countries in North Africa, the Middle East and parts of Asia. The goal of Islamic systems is to develop a theocracy in which political institutions and processes reflect higher religious principles and beliefs. Fundamental Islamic regimes are associated with Iran, Afghanistan under the Taliban, and Saudi Arabia. Malaysia provides an example of a pluralist Islamic state. These states form a heterogeneous group, and consequently generalizing on their nature is difficult. In terms of health policy one might expect religion to have a marked effect on reproductive and sexual health services.

It is apparent that there are significant differences between the above groups of political systems. One of the most important features is the extent to which they encourage or stifle participation. This in turn has major implications for how health policy is made and whose interest's health policies serve.

Activity 2.11

Match the health policy with one of these political systems: East Asian; liberal-democratic; Islamic; military.

1 policy which bars unmarried women from access to publicly provided contraceptive services
2 policy of exemption of military personnel for paying for publicly provided health care services
3 diverse and competitive public and private provision; public sector may play a large role in financing and delivery
4 diverse and competitive public and private provision; limited public finance; limited participation in policy making

Feedback

1 Islamic

2 military

3 liberal-democratic (Western polyarchy)

4 East Asian

Making decisions inside the black box

Now consider three contrasting views on decision making with the aim of understanding their implications for health policy making. There has been an ongoing debate between theorists who portray decision making as a 'rational' process, others who refer to 'incremental' models which describe a process by which decision makers 'muddle through' in response to political influence to which they are subjected, and attempts by others to reconcile these two views. The case of congenital syphilis is employed to illustrate the different approaches to understanding decision making but any health issue could have been used. At the end, the links are made between this debate over decision making and the analysis of power and the role of the state contained earlier in this chapter.

Activity 2.12

While reading about the four models (rationalism; bounded rationalism; incrementalism; mixed scanning), make a note of whether they aim to be descriptive of the way that decisions are actually made, prescriptive of the way decisions ought to be made (that is, normative), or possibly both. In addition, write down two or three problems inherent in each model.

Rational models of decision making: too idealistic?

It is often assumed that policies and decisions are made in a rational way. The rational model of decision making is associated with Simon's (1957) work on how organizations should make decisions. Simon argued that rational choice involves selecting from among alternatives that option which is most conducive to the achievement of the organizational goal(s) or objective(s). To achieve the desired outcome, decision makers must work through a number of steps in a logical sequence. First, decision makers need to identify a problem which needs to be solved and isolate that problem from others. For example, in Sub-Saharan Africa, syphilis infection rates among pregnant women are over 10% in some areas. To isolate the problem, they may have to decide whether or not it is a true increase or an artefact of improved detection capacity and whether their over-riding concern is with the infection of children or with the burden of syphilis in the population more generally.

Second, the goals, values and objectives of decision makers need to be clarified and ranked. For example, would policy makers prefer to reduce the incidence of congenital syphilis by screening all pregnant women (a strategy which might be equitable) or only screen those perceived to be at high risk (a strategy which might be more cost-effective)?

Third, decision makers list all alternative strategies for achieving their goal. Depending on the country, such strategies might include:

- increase the coverage of ante-natal care, increase the number of women seeking care early in their pregnancy, and train health care providers to deliver effective screening and management of syphilis
- advocate presumptive syphilis treatment for all pregnant women
- target presumptive treatment for groups at high risk; or
- control genital ulcer disease in the population through, for example, condom promotion

Figure 2.2 illustrates the relative effect of these options.

The fourth step would involve rational decision makers undertaking a comprehensive analysis of all the consequences of each of the alternatives. In relation to congenital syphilis, decision makers would need to calculate the reduction in the incidence of syphilis as well as the costs associated with each of the alternatives (some of which have been listed above). Attempting to quantify the extent to which the intervention meets the objective and the related costs can be quite complex. Fifth, each alternative and its set of consequences would need to be compared with the other options. Finally, the policy makers would choose that strategy which maximizes their values and preferences as far as goal attainment is concerned. By working through this logical and comprehensive process, a rational decision is taken in that the means are selected which most effectively achieve the policy aim.

It is extremely unlikely that decision makers involved in establishing a policy undertake the process and steps described above to arrive at their policy decision. The failure to adhere to such a rational process can be explained by the difficulties that many analysts of decision making find in the approach which essentially

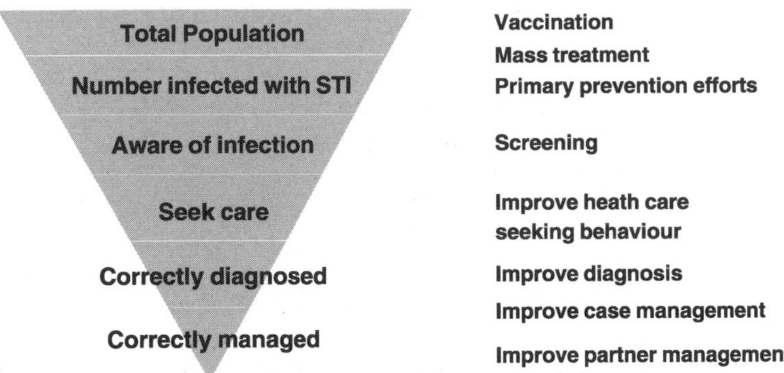

Figure 2.2 Inverted public health pyramid for prevention and care of people infected with syphilis

Source: Adapted from Schmid (2004)

prescribes how policy *ought* to be made rather than *describing* how it is *actually* made in the real world.

One challenge to the rational model lies in the area of problem definition. The precise nature of the problem is not always clear-cut. For example, in relation to congenital syphilis, is the problem one of trying to bring down the overall rate of syphilis in the general population (which includes, of course, pregnant women), or is it one of trying to improve screening and treatment facilities for pregnant women?

The rational model has also been criticized in relation to specifying values and objectives. Whose values and aims are to be adopted? No organization is homogeneous and different parts of an organization may pursue different, if not competing, objectives based on differing values. For example, Zafrullah Chowdhury's (1995) analysis of the formulation of an Essential Drugs Policy in Bangladesh drew attention to the conflicting responses of the World Bank to the policy. The Bank's Industry and Energy Unit in Dhaka conveyed its objections to the policy while its Population and Health Unit provided whole-hearted support to the government.

A third conclusion lies in the assumption that all possible strategies can be considered. Many contending policy alternatives may be foreclosed by prior investments, commitments and political realities. For example, a congenital syphilis policy aiming to increase ante-natal services in rural areas by relocating doctors to serve in rural facilities would likely face considerable resistance from the professional medical association.

A fourth, rather obvious, shortcoming relates to its impracticality. In the real world, the problem of gathering information on all alternatives will face budget and time constraints. Allocating sufficient time and money to collect all the relevant data on all possible options to make every decision would not be justified or sanctioned in most organizations.

Others provide a different kind of critique of the model which contests the very idea of understanding the world in a 'rational' manner. They challenge the idea that the human world is simply natural and given and argue that it is an artefact that is constructed through social processes. In this view, decision makers have a subjective understanding of problems and their solutions – in effect, they create the meaning of the problem and fix it in a manner which corresponds to their values. As Edelman (1988) has argued, policy makers may 'construct' problems so as to justify solutions and in so doing a policy may be a success as a political device even if it fails to address or ameliorate a reality in the sense that 'the operation was a success, but the patient died'.

Simon answered some of these problems by arguing that the rational model provides an idealized approach; describing the way that policy ought to be made rather than how it is actually done in practice. Later he proposed 'bounded rationality' as a model of the practice of policy making in the real world. Acknowledging the complexities of rational choice and the costs and incompleteness of information facing decision makers, Simon argues that they simplify decision making in two ways. First, they find ways to deal with recurrent problems so as not to have to assess each in a comprehensive manner. As a result, many strategies are not subject to exacting scrutiny. Second, decision makers do not aim to achieve optimal solutions to problems but rather to find solutions or choose strategies that meet satisfactory standards in what is termed 'satisficing' (March and Simon 1958). Consequently, Simon argues that decision makers are deliberately rational, but are subject to real-world constraints which limit their ability to make perfectly rational choices. In terms of congenital syphilis policy, decision makers adhering to the bounded rationality model behave as rationally as possible within the constraints of time, information and ability to recognize the consequences of every possible solution.

Incremental models of decision making: more realistic; but too conservative?

Charles Lindblom (1959) proposed an alternative account of decision making which he entitled 'muddling through'. According to Lindblom, decision makers 'muddle' in the sense that they take incremental steps from the initial situation by comparing only a small number of possible alternatives which are not terribly different from the status quo. Lindblom argues that decision makers will test the political waters in deciding whether or not to pursue a given course of action. The test of a good policy is not whether it maximizes or even satisfices the values of the decision makers (as was the case with the rationalist model) but whether it secures the agreement of the various interests at stake. If opposition is too strong, an option closer to the status quo will be tested. Subsequent attempts at policy change will again seek to compare options which may challenge the status quo, but only in a marginal way. For Lindblom, the decision making process is marked by mutual adjustment by the affected stakeholders.

Lindblom argued that muddling through provides a better recipe for taking policy decisions in that damaging policy mistakes can be avoided by taking incremental steps whose effects can be assessed prior to taking the subsequent one. Moreover, it is argued that it provides a more democratic and practical approach to finding more 'sensible politics' than the hierarchical, centrally coordinated approaches promoted by the rationalists.

To return to the example of congenital syphilis policy, incremental decision making would eschew bold policy initiatives which attempted to eliminate the condition. Instead, decision makers might proceed initially by piggy-backing ante-natal syphilis screening onto routine HIV testing in ante-natal settings. If this intervention were broadly accepted by HIV/AIDS activists, health workers, and women attending ante-natal clinics, decision makers might then take another incremental step by pursuing a policy of allocating some additional resources to increase the number of pregnant women attending ante-natal clinics. If, however, HIV/AIDS activists baulk at attempts to highjack 'their' services, or health workers will not accept the additional workload, decision makers would likely explore other incremental steps, such as expanding dedicated syphilis screening programmes.

While the incremental model presents a more realistic account of decision making than does the rational one, it too has been the subject of intense criticism. One critique of the model revolves around its inability to explain how fundamental and radical decisions are taken. If decision making involves small exploratory steps from the existing policy, how can one account for policies that involve fundamental reforms of an entire health care system? In addition to this limitation to its descriptive capacity, are concerns about its prescriptive or normative position on policy making. In effect, incrementalism advocates a conservative approach to decision making. Policy makers are discouraged from pursuing strategies which result in goal maximization if these are found to run up against vested interests. In that change is most likely to be resisted precisely where it is most needed, incrementalist approaches are unlikely to foster innovation or significant progress and are likely to be unfair as they favour those with more power. Incrementalism, in theory and practice, fails to address the unequal distribution of power among interest groups or to tackle the possibilities that bias excludes certain items from policy consideration.

Lindblom rejected this criticism and argued that a succession of minor steps could amount to fundamental change (Lindblom and Woodhouse 1993). For example, advocates of a particular policy could over time whittle away at political opposition towards a longer-term goal. Others have been more sceptical, arguing that in practice the approach does not deal with what will guide the incremental steps. These 'may be circular – leading to where they started, or dispersed – leading in many directions at once but leading nowhere' (Etzioni 1967). As a result, a middle way has been proposed which could guide the incremental steps.

Mixed-scanning approach to decision making: the middle way

Attempts have been made to combine the idealism of the rational-comprehensive approach with the realism of the incremental models while overcoming the unrealistic requirements of rationalism and the conservative slant of incrementalism. In particular, Amitai Etzioni proposed a 'mixed-scanning' model to decision making which was based on weather forecasting techniques (1967) in which broad scans of an entire region are coupled with images of selected areas of turbulence. In the context of decision making, mixed scanning would involve a wide sweep of the general problem as a whole and more detailed analysis of a select component of the problem. Etzioni drew a distinction between fundamental and minor decisions. In his view, with respect to major decisions, policy makers undertake a broad analysis of the area without the detailed analysis of the policy options as suggested by the rationalists. More detailed reviews are conducted of options in relation to less important steps which might lead up to or follow from a fundamental decision. Mixed scanning is thought to overcome the unrealistic expectations of rationalism by limiting the details required for major decisions, while the broad view helps overcome the conservative slant of incrementalism by considering the longer-run alternatives. Etzioni claimed that mixed scanning was not only a desirable way of making decisions but also provided a good description of decision making in practice.

Applying the mixed-scanning model to congenital syphilis policy making might describe the following practice which obtains in some countries. On the one hand, Ministries of Health undertake exercises aimed at estimating and quantifying the overall burden of disease associated with major disease categories on a periodic basis which provide the basis for attempts to prioritize specific disease programmes and establish broad targets for resource allocation across competing expenditure categories. On the other hand, disease-specific programme managers undertake more detailed analysis of the options available in relation to funding specific interventions. However, in practice, in many resource-constrained countries, decision making proceeds in a much less structured way, either through unplanned drift or in response to political pressures or opportunities or funds provided by global initiatives.

Feedback

Compare your answers with those in Table 2.2. Most people like to think that they are rational and prize the use of rationality in decision making. Simon's rational model of decision making proposes that a series of logical steps is undertaken so that the best option can be identified and selected. Rational models serve mainly prescriptive purposes as there are many constraints to practising rationality in the real world. Bounded rationalism acknowledges that decision makers intend to be rational but, given information uncertainties and the costs of knowledge, reach a decision that 'satisfices'. Incremental models explicitly take power into account and provide a largely descriptive account of how policy makers muddle through in response to complex political pressures. While critics claim that incrementalism is biased in favour of the status quo, Lindblom has argued that a series of small steps can cumulatively result in major changes and that small steps may serve to guard against major policy disasters. Mixed scanning has been proposed as a middle ground. Many analysts suggest that mixed scanning provides a relatively accurate account of decision making in the real world – even if the distinction between major and minor decisions remains conceptually murky.

Table 2.2 Decision making theories compared

Theory/model	*Major proponent*	*Descriptive vs. Prescriptive*	*Criticisms*
Rationalism	Simon	Prescriptive	problem definition problematic who sets goals many options foreclosed impractical/impossible to collect data
Bounded rationalism	Simon	Prescriptive and descriptive	problem definition problematic who sets goals many options foreclosed
Incrementalism	Lindblom	Mainly descriptive Claims for prescription	doesn't explain major policy change/reform inbuilt conservative bias
Mixed scanning	Etzioni	Prescriptive and descriptive	distinction between fundamental and routine decisions not clear

Summary

This chapter has introduced theoretical frameworks to enable you to apply the concept of power in relation to policy making. Power was defined and the three ways that it is exercised were illustrated. The debate on how power is distributed in society with pluralists and elitists occupying two extreme positions was introduced. In practice, the distribution of power will depend on the policy issue, its significance and the political system in which the policy is being made. A generalized account of how decision making takes place in any political system was also introduced. Although there has been a long debate concerning the manner in which policy decisions are made, between rationalists on the one hand and incrementalists on the other, the role that power plays in decision making is incontrovertible. The rational view has often been described as prescriptive (how policies ought to be made) and the incremental view as descriptive (of how policy is actually made). Health policy making is likely to be characterized by mixed scanning and muddling through. Understanding the interests of various actors and the manner in which they wield power is therefore intrinsic to an understanding of the policy process and essential for any attempt to influence that process.

References

Bachrach P and Baratz MS (1962). The two faces of power. In Castles FG, Murray DJ and Potter DC (eds) *Decision, Organisations and Society*. Harmondsworth: Penguin

Bachrach P and Baratz MS (1963). Decisions and nondecisions: an analytical framework. *American Political Science Review* 57: 641–51

Bottomore TB (1966). *Classes in Modern Society*. New York: Pantheon Books

Chowdhury Z (1995). *Essential Drugs for the Poor*. London: Zed

Crenson M (1971). *The Unpolitics of Air Pollution*. Baltimore, MD: The Johns Hopkins University Press

Dahl RA (1961). *Who Governs? Democracy and Power in an American City*. New Haven, CT: Yale University Press

Easton D (1965). *A Systems Analysis of Political Life*. New York: Wiley

Edelman M (1988). *Constructing the Political Spectacle*. Chicago: Chicago University Press

Etzioni A (1967). Mixed scanning: a 'third approach' to decision making. *Public Administrative Review* 27: 385–92

Fukuyama F (1989). The end of history? *National Interest*. Summer, 3–18

Heywood A (2002). *Politics*. 2nd edn. Houndsmill: Palgrave Macmillan

Jorm AF, Christensen H, Griffiths KM and Rodgers B (2002). Effectiveness of complementary and self-help treatments for depression. *Medical Journal of Australia* 176(10 Suppl): S84–95

Kessler RC, Soukup J, Davis RB, Foster DF, Wilkey SA, Van Rompay MI and Eisenberg DM (2001). The use of complementary and alternative therapies to treat anxiety and depression in the United States. *American Journal of Psychiatry* 158(2): 289–94

Kushel M and Bindman AB (2004). Health care lobbying. Time to make patients the special interest. *American Journal of Medicine* 116(7): 496–97

Landers SH and Sehgal AR (2004). Health care lobbying in the United States. *American Journal of Medicine* 116(7): 474–7

Lee K and Goodman H (2002). Global policy networks: The propagation of health care financing reform since the 1980s. In Lee K, Buse K and Fustukian S (eds) *Health Policy in a Globalising World*. Cambridge: Cambridge University Press, pp. 97–119

Lindblom CE (1959). The science of muddling through. *Public Administrative Review* 19: 79–88

Lindblom CE and Woodhouse EJ (1993). *The Policy-Making Process*. 3rd edn. Englewood Cliffs, NJ: Prentice-Hall

Lukes S (1974). *Power: A Radical Approach*. London: Macmillan

March JG and Simon HA (1958). *Organizations*. New York: John Wiley and Sons

Nye J (2002) *The Paradox of American Power: Why the World's Only Superpower Cannot Go it Alone*. Oxford: Oxford University Press

Schmid G (2004). Economic and programmatic aspects of congenital syphilis control. *Bulletin of the World Health Organization* 82(6): 402–9

Simon HA (1957). *Administrative Behaviour*. 2nd edn. New York: Macmillan

UN (2002). *Implementation of the UN Millennium Declaration. Report of the Secretary General*. Fifty-seventh session. Item 44 of the provisional agenda. A/57/270. New York: UN General Assembly

Weber M (1948). *From Max Weber: Essays in Sociology*. London: Routledge and Kegan Paul

WHO (2004). *Guidelines on Developing Consumer Information on Proper Use of Complementary and Alternative Medicine*. Geneva: WHO

Zeltner T, Kessler DA, Martiny A and Randera F (2000). *Tobacco Company Strategies to Undermine Tobacco Control Activities at the World Health Organization*. Geneva: WHO

3 The state and the private sector in health policy

Overview

This chapter introduces you to two of the most important actors in health policy – the state and the private for-profit sector – although in some situations other actors can play influential roles. The chapter traces the changing roles of these two sectors in health policy and thereby provides the context to understanding the content and processes of contemporary health policy making.

Learning objectives

After working through this chapter, you will be better able to:

- **understand why the state is at the centre of health policy analysis**
- **describe and account for the changing role of the state in the past few decades, and what this has implied for the state's role in health**
- **identify a range of private sector organizations with an interest in health policy**
- **explain how the private sector increasingly influences health policy**

Key terms

Company Generic term for a business which may be run as a sole proprietorship, partnership or corporation.

Corporation An association of stockholders which is regarded as a 'person' under most national laws. Ownership is marked by ease of transferability and the limited liability of stockholders.

Decentralization The transfer of authority and responsibilities from central government to local levels, which are thereby strengthened.

Industry Groups of firms closely related and in competition due to use of similar technology of production or high level of substitutability of products.

Multinational corporation Firm which controls operations in more than one country, even if it does not own them but controls through a franchise.

New public management An approach to government involving the application of private sector management techniques.

Private sector That part of the economy which is not under direct government control.

Privatization Sale of publicly owned property to the private sector.

Regulation Government intervention enforcing rules and standards.

Transnational corporation Firm which owns branch companies in more than one country.

Introduction

This chapter concerns the changing role of the state in health policy. The state is typically a central focus of policy analysis, this is in part the result of its omnipresence and, in part, because it does more than any other body to decide what policies should be adopted and implemented. Policy decisions of governments extend deeply into people's lives from the relatively trivial to the life-changing. Depending on where you live, the state may, for example:

- regulate the number of children you have (China)
- decide whether or not divorcees are allowed a second child (allowed in Shanghai but not in the rest of China)
- prohibit private medical practice (Cuba)
- determine the age at which sex-change therapy is allowed (presently 13 years in Australia)
- determine whether or not emergency contraception is available over-the-counter (not available in the USA but available in the UK)

The state may also:

- subject persons of different race, ethnicity, or religion to different laws
- imprison suspected terrorists indefinitely without charge (France) or suspend protections of Geneva Conventions for enemy combatants (USA).

For much of the twentieth century the state has played a dominant role in the economies of most countries: airlines were owned and operated by the state as were other utilities such as railways, water, electricity, and telephones. Many governments presided over command and control economies in the context of rigid five-year development plans. In many newly independent countries, the government also became the major employer. For example, in Tanzania the government's workforce grew from 27 per cent of those formally employed in 1962 to over 66 per cent in 1974 (Perkins and Roemer 1991). By the 1980s things began to change; states were rolled back and the private sector was encouraged to enter fields that were once the preserve of the state – including health care. This shift has had implications both for the content of health policy as well as the actors participating in the health policy process.

In this chapter, you will chart the changes to the roles of the state and market. The activities of different branches of government in the policy process are explored in greater detail in Chapter 4. The chapter begins by exploring state involvement in health and presents arguments which justify its prominent role. You will then learn why disillusion with the state has grown over the past two decades and why this has given impetus to a world-wide movement of health sector reform. The emergence of the private for-profit sector in health services is highlighted and three ways that it increasingly affects health policy are illustrated.

The role of the state in health systems

By the early 1980s, the state had assumed a leading place in health care finance and in service delivery in most countries. In addition, it played the central role in allocating resources among competing health priorities and in regulating a range of activities which impinge upon health. To take just one example, think of the role that states might play with respect to the regulation of health care service delivery. Mills and Ranson (2005) have identified the following regulatory mechanisms which have been applied in low and middle income countries.

To regulate the quantity and distribution of services, the state has:

- licensed providers (in all countries) and facilities (increasingly common for hospitals)
- placed controls on the number and size of medical schools (common), controlled the number of doctors practising in certain areas, and limited the introduction of high technology (being considered in Thailand and Malaysia)
- provided incentives to practise in rural areas (many countries for doctors)

To regulate prices of services, governments have:

- negotiated salary scales (Zimbabwe, Argentina)
- set charges (South Africa)
- negotiated reimbursement rates (many social insurance schemes)

To regulate quality of health services, governments have:

- licensed practitioners
- registered facilities
- controlled the nature of services provided
- required providers to establish complaints procedures
- required provision of information for monitoring quality
- controlled training curricula
- set requirements for continuing education
- introduced accreditation of facilities

In addition to the finance, provision and regulation of health services, most states have assumed a range of public health functions, for example, they:

- ensure safe water and food purity
- establish quarantine and border control measures to stop the spread of infectious diseases
- regulate roads and workplaces to reduce the threat of injuries
- legislate, aimed at curbing environmental and noise pollution
- set standards for food labelling, the level of lead in petrol, and tar and nicotine in cigarettes
- regulate and license industries as well as force them to adopt different technologies on public health grounds
- add chlorine to drinking water

You could likely add to the above list which is meant to illustrate the state's deep and wide involvement in health at the beginning of the twenty-first century. This raises the question of how such growth has been justified.

Activity 3.1

The following reviews the rationale for the involvement of the state in health. While reading through the section, makes notes as to the main reasons for the state involvement in the health systems.

Economists have focused on market failure as the principal reason for a pronounced role for the state in health care finance and provision. Efficient markets depend on a number of conditions. These are often not met because of specific characteristics of health and health services. First, the optimal amount of health services will not always be produced or consumed because the externalities (costs and benefits) are not taken into consideration by consumers or producers. For example, childhood immunization rates in the UK are decreasing because parents' decisions relate to the perceived costs and benefits of protecting their children as opposed to the benefits of protection of others by reducing the pool of susceptible children. Second, the market will fail to provide many so-called 'public goods' because of the lack of incentives to do so. Public goods are those that are 'non-rival' in consumption (consumption by one person does not affect consumption of the same good by others) and 'non-excludable' (it is not possible to prevent a consumer from benefiting – by making them pay), for example, control of mosquito breeding or producing knowledge through research. Third, monopoly power may lead to overcharging. Monopolies could be established by the medical profession, the drug industry or a hospital in a given catchment area. However, some economists argue that the lack of efficient health care markets provide relatively weak justification for state delivery of health services (except in relation to public and preventive health services) as these could be dealt with through regulation.

Another argument in favour of a strong state role hinges around information asymmetry between consumer and providers. Consumers are at a disadvantage and private providers are in an unusually strong position to take advantage of this imbalance through profit seeking and over-treatment. Another characteristic of the market is that the need for health care is uncertain and often costly. This provides an argument in favour of insurance. However, experience suggests that private insurance markets do not work well in health. Both of these reasons provide compelling support for state involvement.

Yet it is rather unlikely that these economic arguments can account for the prominent role of the state in health. If any theoretical or philosophical principle were invoked, it would likely be related to equity and the concern that some individuals will be too poor to afford health care and require the support and protection of the state. This touches on the wider debate on the ethical underpinnings of a health care system. There are those who argue that health services should be treated similarly to other goods and services for which access depends on ability and willingness to pay. Others argue that access to health care is a right of all citizens, irrespective of their income or wealth.

In practice, the role of the state in health service finance and provision has varied significantly between countries, depending on whether or not private markets have developed for insurers and for providers and whether or not the state has taken responsibility for providing for the whole population (e.g. India and Zambia) or catered more for the poor (e.g. Mexico and Thailand). Nonetheless, what was uniform across all countries was an expansion of the role of the state in health during the twentieth century, with the state assuming the central and primary responsibility for health services and thereby taking the centre stage for health policy making.

Feedback

The main justifications for state involvement are:

- market failure
- information asymmetry between consumer and provider
- need for care uncertain and often costly
- to achieve social equity of access to care

The critique of the state

Considerable disaffection with the expanded role of the state took place during the 1980s and led to a reassessment of its appropriate role in the health sector. This happened in the context of a global economic recession, mounting government indebtedness, and spiralling public expenditure. Conservative governments came to power in the USA and the UK which questioned what they saw as bloated and inefficient public sectors presiding over important areas of the economy. Reforms were introduced which involved liberalizing trade, selling off publicly owned industries, deregulating utilities and private industry, and curbing public expenditure. Tapping into widespread dissatisfaction with state administrations generally, which were often viewed as distant, undemocratic, unresponsive, unaccountable and even corrupt, the idea of rolling back the state spread to other high income countries and later to middle and low income countries as well. International financial institutions, such as the World Bank and the International Monetary Fund, pressured governments to reduce their deficits, and control public expenditure by implementing what were termed 'structural adjustment programmes'. In return for targeted loans and grants, governments promised to reform their economies principally by privatization and by reducing the involvement and responsibility of the state, particularly in service provision.

The decade was marked by a global turn in favour of the market, with a concomitant scepticism about the merits of pursuing social solidarity through government action. The collapse of the Soviet Union further discredited the notion of centrally planned, state-controlled economies. Anti-state, pro-market philosophy was promoted around the world by international agencies and private foundations. They, often rightly, claimed that the public sector too often provided patronage instead of service, employment rather than goods and services, and used office to secure political support. As proof, they pointed to poorly performing, costly and overstaffed bureaucracies, providing inadequate service in disintegrating facilities.

These trends were reflected in the health sector and led to a movement for health sector reform (Roberts et al. 2004). The state was widely regarded as having failed to provide services for everyone, despite rising levels of expenditure. Political pressures had resulted in public finance of health services which were not cost-effective while more cost-effective services were not widely provided. The political demands of the economic elite and the self-interest of urban-based bureaucrats resulted in a disproportionate allocation of resources to urban tertiary facilities at the expense of basic services for the bulk of the population. Poor management decreased their efficiency and resulted in problems such as lack of continuous drug supplies. In many low income countries, inadequate finance meant poor equipment, poorly paid staff, leading to poor quality care. Public providers were often absent from their posts (sometimes attending illegal private practice), poorly motivated, seen as unresponsive, and charging patients illicit fees for services that governments proclaimed were freely available to all. Those people who required publicly financed services most often failed to access them while those who were politically connected were able to capture this state subsidy. Many, including the poor in the poorest countries, were in practice relying heavily on the private sector – often facing catastrophic payments to do so.

Reinvention of government and health sector reform

Given the widespread problems experienced in the sector, it is not surprising that the idea of reform was seized upon so readily. Yet the means for reform were greatly influenced by the prevailing ideology of the appropriate role for the state and the delivery of public health services. The state was to be slimmed down, health provision was to be made more efficient by introducing competition and decentralizing decision making, and the private sector was to be afforded a much larger role (Harding 2003).

Prevailing neo-liberal economic thinking was brought to bear to understand the root causes of the malaise in the health sector and greatly influenced prescriptions on the appropriate role for the state. Two theories stand out: public choice and property rights. *Public choice*, discussed in Chapter 2, deals with the nature of decision making in government. It argues that politicians and bureaucrats behave like other participants in the political system in that they pursue their own interests. Consequently, politicians can be expected to promote policies which will maximize their chances of re-election while bureaucrats can be expected to attempt to maximize their budgets because budget size affects bureaucrats' rewards either in terms of salary, status or opportunities to engage in corruption. As a result of these perverse incentives, the public sector is deemed to be wasteful and not concerned with efficiency or equity. *Property rights* theorists explained poor public sector performance through the absence of property rights. They argue that in the private sector, owners of property rights, whether owners of firms or shareholders, have strong incentives to maximize efficiency of resource use as the returns to investment depend upon efficiency. In contrast, such pressure does not arise in the public sector; staff may perform poorly at no cost to themselves, resulting in a poorly performing systems overall. They have few reasons to do well because they cannot benefit personally from goal performance, unlike in a business. Both theories draw attention to the incentives which motivate state officials and how these influence the policies that they pursue.

These beliefs gave rise to proposals to curb the state – to radically contain public expenditure – but also to introduce 'new public management' in those areas of the health sector which were not privatized. It was new in the sense that it sought to expose public services to market pressures by establishing internal markets within the public sector. Internal markets were established by forcing public providers (e.g., general practitioner groups) to compete for contracts from public purchasers, contracting out service provision by competitive tendering (for hospital catering and cleaning services, for example) and devolving significant decision making to organizations, particularly hospitals, and to lower levels of government. These reforms involved the creation of purchasing agencies and the introduction of contractual relationships within the public sector.

In addition to reforms within public administration, new mechanisms to finance health care were put on the policy agenda (such as out-of-pocket fees for service use), restrictions on private providers were lifted, diversity of ownership in the health sector was promoted, and efforts were made to improve the accountability of providers to consumers, patients and communities.

Decentralization, another popular reform, aimed to transfer the balance of power within the state. In one form, functions held by the Ministry of Health (MOH) were transferred to newly established executive agencies which assumed management responsibility at the national level (for example, in Ghana and Zambia). The MOH could then focus its efforts on policy and oversight. In other cases, authority was transferred to district or local levels. Decentralization can also involve providing autonomy to hospitals by giving them control over their budgets. Decentralization distributes power from the MOH to other organizations.

Although the state has been slimmed down in many countries in the course of such reforms, it is almost universally agreed that the state ought to (and often does) retain a variety of functions. On the one hand, governments need to 'steward' the sector. Stewardship involves safeguarding population health by developing policy, setting and enforcing standards, rationing and setting priorities for resource allocation, establishing a regulatory framework, and monitoring the behaviour of providers. On the other hand, governments need to 'enable' – whether that is enabling the private sector or ensuring the fair financing of service provision through tax or mandatory insurance in high income countries and targeting public expenditure towards the poor in low income countries.

The World Bank was highly influential in promoting these reforms in low income countries, both through policy advice and through conditions attached to lending programmes. While these reforms have been nothing short of revolutionary in their intent, they have had mixed results on the ground. Although most governments have embraced reform, at least rhetorically, few have managed successfully to implement them. Implementation has also sometimes resulted in unanticipated consequences. While user fees for public services were introduced primarily to raise resources, they have not been very successful in this regard but have often had a negative impact on the use of essential services. Arrangements to protect the poor from charges have been difficult to administer. In China, reforms have resulted in fewer people being covered by health insurance. While 71 per cent of the population had some form of health insurance in 1981 (including 48 per cent of the rural population), by 1993 the level had fallen to 21 per cent, with 7 per cent coverage of the rural population (WHO 1999).

Activity 3.2

Make a list of health reforms which have been discussed or introduced during the past decade in your country. See if you can find reference to each of the reforms listed above, and if possible others, using Table 3.1. Depending on your general knowledge of health sector reform in your country, you may need to do some research. If you live in a low or middle income country, one approach to gathering the information would be to consult the World Bank's website where you can search for analytic or project lending reports (staff appraisal reports) for your country. If you live in a high income country, you can consult the European Observatory on Health Systems and Policies (www.euro.who.int/observatory) which covers a number of countries outside of Europe as well.

Table 3.1 Health reform checklist

Health reform	*Yes*	*No*
Liberalizing laws on the private providers		
Introducing user fees and strategies to exempt poor		
Introducing community-based insurance		
Introducing social health insurance		
Creation of purchasing agencies		
Introduction of contractual relationships and management agreements		
Decentralization of health service		
Decentralization of hospital management		
Encouraging competition and diversity of ownership		

Feedback

It is not likely that you ticked 'yes' to all reforms, as the content of reforms differed across countries. Nevertheless, it is likely that you identified a number of them, as virtually no health system has remained untouched by these sorts of reform.

The reform movement highlights the power of ideas and ideology in policy change. Yet reforms have provoked significant resistance. Some opposition has been based on philosophical and ideological grounds. Many have questioned the lack of evidence upon which reforms were based as well as the imposition of 'blueprints' without due consideration of national and local context (Lee et al. 2002). Yet reforms were more often resisted on the basis of the costs that they imposed on the incomes and interests of those actors who had benefited from the prevailing system. Consequently, successive rounds of reforms have rolled out unevenly across countries, with considerable evidence of limited progress and poor results, leaving the agenda largely unfinished in many countries (Roberts et al. 2004). Part of the failure of reform programmes rested on the disproportionate emphasis placed on the technical content of reform at the expense of the politics of the reform process.

Yet reforms continue to be announced. In 2004, for example, Russian President Vladimir Putin's government drafted a bill aimed at reforming its 'bloated' health bureaucracy by sacking approximately half (300,000) of its doctors and health workers in the next few years (Osborn 2004).

The for-profit sector and health policy

The assault on the state in the 1980s and 1990s provided an opportunity for the private for-profit sector in health. While the private sector was already active in many countries in terms of health service delivery, it was usually overlooked in relation to health policy and regulation. This is surprising because it is difficult to identify health policies in which the private sector does not have an interest or play some role. But what exactly is the for-profit sector and how is it involved in health policy? The following provides a brief overview of the types of private sector actors in health and differentiates the three main ways that the private sector is involved in health policy.

What is the private sector?

The private for-profit (or commercial) sector is characterized by its market orientation. It encompasses organizations that seek to make profits for their owners. Profit, or a return on investment, is the central defining feature of the commercial sector. Many firms pursue additional objectives related, for example, to social, environmental or employee concerns but these are, of necessity, secondary and supportive of the primary objective which concerns profit. In the absence of profit, and a return to shareholders, firms cease to exist.

For-profit organizations vary considerably. The sector consists of firms which may be large or small, domestic or multinational. In the health sector there are single doctor's surgeries and large group practices, pharmacies, generic drug manufacturers and major pharmaceutical companies, medical equipment suppliers, and private hospitals and nursing homes.

When thinking about the role of the commercial sector in health policy, it is often useful to broaden the scope of analysis and include organizations that are registered as not-for-profit in their legal status. These may have charitable status but are established to support the interests of a commercial firm or industry. These may include business associations or trade federations. For example, both PhRMA (American Pharmaceutical Manufacturers Association) and BIO, the biotechnology industry organization, are engaged in the health policy process.

A wide range of industry-funded think tanks, 'scientific' organizations, advocacy groups (such as patient groups) and even public relations firms working for industry are actors engaged in the health policy arena. For example, the tobacco company Philip Morris established the Institute of Regulatory Policy as a vehicle to lobby the US federal government and delay the publication of a report by the Environmental Protection Agency on environmental tobacco smoke (Muggli et al. 2004). The International Life Sciences Institute (ILSI) was established in 1978. The Institute's first President envisioned it as a mini-World Health Organisation. It describes itself as a 'Global Partnership for a Safer, Healthier World' which employs strategic alliances to bring scientific solutions to important public health issues, particularly in areas such as diet, tobacco and alcohol. While it is at pains to present itself as a scientific body, its first President served simultaneously as a Vice-President of the Coca-Cola Company and it is predominantly funded by the food industry. It has gone to great lengths to conceal the commercial sponsorship of its research and publications and present itself as scholarly and independent (James 2002).

Industry also organizes and supports patient groups to influence health policy decisions of governments. For example, 'Action for Access' was set up by Biogen in 1999 to get the UK National Health Service to provide interferon beta for multiple sclerosis patients (Boseley 1999). In some health policy debates, public relations firms play important roles. Firms are employed to put across industry views, through the media or other means, as disinterested third parties. In 2002, the five leading health care public relations firms in the USA earned over US$300 million for planning pre-launch media coverage of new drugs, cultivating prescribers, publishing medical journals and supporting patient groups with the aim of influencing health care policy and practice (Burton and Rowell 2003).

Looser groups supported by industry can also be influential in the health policy process. ARISE, Associates for Research into the Science of Enjoyment, promotes the pleasures of smoking, alcohol, caffeine and chocolate. With support from companies such as British American Tobacco, Coca-Cola, Philip Morris, RJR, Rothmans, Miller Beer and Kraft, it publishes articles that promote and advocate consumer freedom in relation to those substances and deride the necessity of public regulation. One publication called *Bureaucracy against Life: The Politicisation of Personal Choice* attacks the European Community for restriction of individual choice in connection to 'the alleged dangers associated with alcohol, tobacco, caffeine and an increasing range of foods' as paternalistic.

Activity 3.3

Look at the business section of a major national or international newspaper. Find examples of each of the types of commercial organizations listed above with a linkage to a health issue (either due to the goods or services they manufacture, promote, distribute, sell or regulate). Provide one or two examples of each category of commercial entity, the health issue in which they have an interest, what they manufacture, distribute, sell, or promote, and the relationship of these goods or services to health (either positive or negative). Also, see if you can find any references to less formal commercial organizations – this may be more difficult. You may need to collect newspapers for a few days to get an example of each type of organization.

The types of organization to consider are:

- Small firm
- MNC or TNC
- Business association
- Professional association
- Think tank
- Patients' group
- Commercial scientific network
- Public relations firm
- Loose network

Feedback

It should be evident that a wide range of organizations and groups associated with the private sector are interested and involved in health policy in your country. It may also be evident from the news clippings that these organizations vary tremendously in relation to their size (by staff, sales or market capitalization – value on the stock exchange), organizational form, and interest in particular health policies.

What makes the private sector a powerful actor in health policy?

Power is the ability to achieve a desired result. Resources often confer power and, on that basis, the power of some industries and firms may be obvious to you. Of the top 100 'economies' in the world 49 are countries, but 51 are firms when measured by market capitalization. Figure 3.1 compares the market capital of ten of the largest companies in the world, ten leading pharmaceutical firms, with the gross national income of those low income countries for which there was data in 2003 – note how the firms dwarf the size of the collective economies of the poorest countries. The revenue of the top 50 pharmaceutical firms amounted to US$466 billion in 2003 which had increased from US$296 billion just two years earlier (Sellers 2004). Contrast the magnitude of corporate sales with the annual budget of WHO: it is a paltry US$1 billion and has remained stagnant for over a decade.

Firms provide governments with tax revenues, some are major employers in the economy, and governments gain influence in international affairs on the coat tails of their large corporations and are therefore interested in their success. In many sectors, firms have specialist knowledge which governments rely on in making policy and regulations. For these reasons, small and large businesses are often important actors in policy debates.

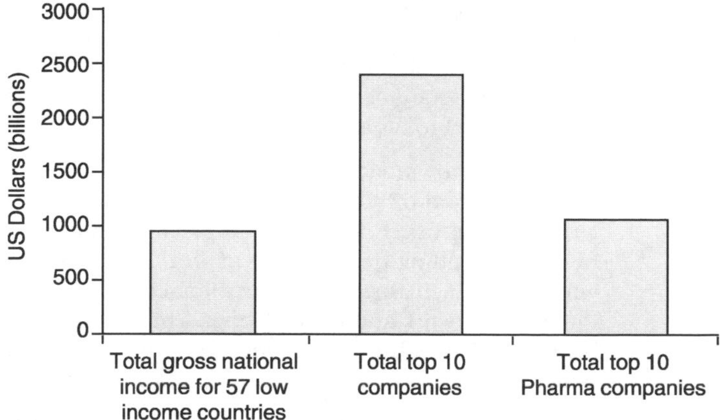

Figure 3.1 Market capitalization of largest companies compared with gross national incomes of 57 low income countries, 2003

Sources: World Bank (2005) and Bureau Van Dijk (2005)

How is the private sector involved in health policy?

In Chapter 1 a distinction between public and private policy was made. You learned that the private sector develops policy related to health – whether it is a firm setting down rules for its staff (e.g., on sick leave) or an industry federation establishing policies for its members (e.g., in relation to environmental pollution). This is one way that the private sector is involved in health policy, through self-regulation. You will now explore private health policy making in further detail as well as two additional mechanisms through which the private sector is involved in health policy. One of these is likely to be obvious to you after having completed Table 3.1, namely, the private sector's involvement in public policy making. In addition, a new form of engagement, referred to as 'co-regulation', provides a middle ground between self-regulation and public policy.

Self-regulation

Self-regulation concerns efforts by private companies to establish their own rules and policies for operating within a specific domain. For example, rules governing how to design, categorize, produce and handle particular goods and services are routinely adopted by groups of companies and industries.

One can distinguish between two types of self-regulation. First are those efforts which attempt to regulate what might be termed private 'market' standards and, second, the regulation of 'social standards'. In the case of market standards, aspects of products, process and business practice are subject to self-regulation for the purpose of facilitating commerce. Common standards support business by reducing transaction costs, ensuring compatibility, and creating fair competition for all firms in the market. There are thousands of examples of self-regulation from codes of conduct on advertising (which, for example, might restrict advertising of unhealthy products to children) to standards governing voltages within medical equipment to standards on electronic medical claims.

Self-regulation through social standards is generally undertaken in response to concerns raised by consumers, shareholders, or due to the threat of impending public regulation which may be more onerous. Initiatives include corporate social responsibility, voluntary codes and reporting initiatives, and some corporate philanthropic programmes. These initiatives sometimes govern social issues that are already subject to (often ineffective) statutory regulation.

Company and industry-wide codes of conduct represent one increasingly prominent form of self-regulation through social standards. Currently voluntary codes cover a variety of corporate practices that are important determinants of health. Depending on your line of work, you may be aware of voluntary codes which cover such aspects as occupational health and safety, wages and hours, minimum age of work and forced labour. The promise and perils of codes are set out below to allow you to judge whether or not they are good substitutes for public policy.

It is relatively easy to understand why firms and industries adopt voluntary codes governing social issues. First, by doing so, firms are often able to generate public relations material and improve their corporate image. Second, early adoption of a code can differentiate a firm from a competitor and thereby increase its market share. Third, adoption of codes in response to consumer or shareholder demand permits firms to demonstrate that they listen and can boost sales and investment. Depending on the issue, codes can be used to stave off consumer boycotts and also public regulation. As you can see, there is a market logic to codes.

Codes can also be good for society. The introduction of a standard by one firm or a group of firms can compel other firms to adopt similar standards so as to prevent the loss of market share. By pulling up the laggards, leading firms can ratchet up standards across an industry. Second, in some contexts compliance with voluntary codes may be more effective than compliance with statutory regulation. The theory is that companies adopt codes so as to gain market share and comply with them so as not to lose the confidence of their consumers/shareholders. Codes are also promoted as curbing government expenditure on public regulation.

At first glance codes appear to represent a win-win situation but closer inspection reveals some weaknesses in this form of private policy making. One analyst concludes that 'corporate codes of conduct are treated with disdain and largely dismissed by knowledgeable and influential opinion leaders among various stakeholder groups, as well as by outside analysts and the public-at-large' (Sethi 1999).

Activity 3.4

Based on your general knowledge of codes, take the following test to see if you can deduce why Sethi made such pessimistic remarks:

1 Do codes typically:

a) enunciate general principles; or
b) provide specific standards (i.e., quantifiable and measurable indicators)?

2 Do codes typically:

a) focus on concerns of consumers in high income countries (e.g., child labour, or pesticide residue on organic fruit); or
b) concerns of local employees (e.g., right to collective bargaining, pesticide exposure)?

3 Is code compliance likely to be:

a) linked to internal reward structures in the company (are there incentives to ensure that the code is implemented?; or
b) divorced from reward structure, operating procedures, or corporate culture?

4 Do companies typically make public:

a) the process by which they seek to comply with the code and the findings related to the code; or
b) only those aspects of the findings which are favourable?

5 Is reporting of code implementation typically:

a) subject to external scrutiny; or
b) handled internally by the company?

Feedback

While there are undoubtedly exceptions to the rule, Sethi (1999) concludes that codes typically comprise lofty statements of intent, are largely responsive to consumer pressure and therefore highlight issues in consumer-sensitive industries (e.g. clothing) while ignoring many others, and that companies tend to lack the means to communicate compliance with the code in reliable and believable ways. The correct answers are all 'b'.

A review of voluntary codes of pharmaceutical marketing concluded that they lacked transparency and public accountability because consumers were not involved in monitoring and enforcement, they omitted major areas of concern, and lacked timely and effective sanctions (Lexchin and Kawachi 1996). Similarly, a former Executive Director of WHO argues that self-regulation in the case of tobacco manufacturing and smoke-free policies 'failed miserably' (Yach 2004).

Another problematic aspect of voluntary codes relates to their reliance on company 'commitment' to stakeholders. Undertaking to voluntarily uphold a particular principle is qualitatively distinct from being held accountable under law to ensuring specific rights, for example, of those affected by company operations. As a consequence, patchwork self-regulation results in 'enclave' social policy which governs select issues and groups of workers at a specific point in their working lives (e.g. only those workers in a specific plant and only while they hold their jobs). Some fear that these self-regulatory efforts will erode societal commitment to universal rights and entitlements.

In summary, an increasing number of self-regulatory mechanisms are being adopted by the business community in areas which affect health. Private actors are involved in policy formulation, adoption and implementation, often without reference to state actors. While private policy may promote health, it may also have negative impacts. Consequently, the need for public regulation remains – and unsurprisingly, the private sector has a stake in public policy – a topic now addressed.

The private sector and public policy

In the following chapters you will learn more about how the government makes and implements public policy – here examples are provided to illustrate the involvement of the private sector in the process. The private sector is often affected by public policy and, as a result, may attempt to influence the content of such policy. The private sector wields influence in a number of ways. Firms will often provide finance to political parties and to political campaigns in the hope that once those parties and politicians are in office they will be more responsive to demands that firms may make in the policy process.

Private organizations will also lobby for or against particular policies. Influence can also be wielded through corporate participation in government committees and working groups. Moreover, corporate executives also compete for public office, and, if successful, may take positions in line with business interests.

Co-regulation

Co-regulation presents a 'third way' between statutory regulation and self-regulation. It may be viewed as public sector involvement in business self-regulation. The idea is that public and private sectors will negotiate on an agreed set of policy or regulatory objectives. Subsequently, the private sector will take responsibility for implementation of the provisions. Monitoring compliance may remain a public responsibility or may be contracted out to a third party – sometimes an interested non-governmental watchdog. Co-regulatory initiatives often involve public, private and civil society actors working in partnership.

Co-regulation is relatively new, with limited experience at the national and regional levels. For example, in the UK, the Advertising Standards Authority has a range of sanctions against misleading advertisements which is backed up by statutory regulations of the Office of Fair Trading which can secure a High Court injunction to prevent a company publishing the same or similar advertisements. In other words, the statutory backing gives the self-regulatory code teeth. The European Union is also experimenting with co-regulation particularly with respect to the Internet, journalism and e-commerce.

Summary

In this chapter you have learned why the state is considered the most important actor in policy making. While it is important to understand the role of the state in policy making, an analysis focused entirely on the state is no longer sufficient. This is because the role of the state has changed and the private sector now features more prominently in health policy making – either independently or in association with the state.

References

Boseley S (1999). Drug firm asks public to insist NHS buy its product. *The Guardian*. 29 September

Bureau Van Dijk. Osiris database, Dow Jones Global Index, latest company information. Accessed at: http://osiris.bvdep.com, 2 March 2005.

Burton B and Rowell A (2003). Unhealthy spin. *British Medical Journal* 326: 1205–7

Financial Times (2000). *Human Development Report 2000*. FT500, 4 May

Harding A (2003). Introduction to private participation in health services. In Harding A and Preker AS (eds) *Private Participation in Health Services*. Washington, DC: The World Bank, pp. 7–74

James JE (2002). Third-party threats to research integrity in public–private partnerships. *Addiction* 97:1251–5

Lee K, Buse K and Fustukian S (eds) (2002). *Health Policy in a Globalising World*. Cambridge: Cambridge University Press

Lexchin J and Kawachi I (1996) Voluntary codes of pharmaceutical marketing: controlling promotion or licensing deception? In Davis P (ed.) *Contested Ground: Public Purpose and Private Interest in the Regulation of Prescription Drugs*. New York: Oxford University Press, pp. 221–35

Mills AJ and Ranson MK (2005). The design of health systems. In Merson MH, Black RE and

Mills AJ (eds) *International Public Health: Disease, Programs, Systems and Policies*. Sudbury, MA: Jones and Bartlett

Muggli ME, Hurt RD and Repace J (2004). The tobacco industry's political efforts to derail the EPA report on ETS. *American Journal of Preventive Medicine*. 26(2): 167–77

Osborn A (2004). Half of Russia's doctors face sack in healthcare reforms. *British Medical Journal* 382(7448): 1092

Perkins D and Roemer M (1991). *The Reform of Economic Systems in Developing Countries*. Cambridge, MA: Harvard University Press

Roberts MJ, Hsiao W, Berman P and Reich MR (2004). *Getting Health Reform Right: A Guide to Improving Performance and Equity*. Oxford: Oxford University Press

Sellers RJ (2004). PharmExec 50. *Pharmaceutical Executive*. May: 61–70

Sethi PS (1999). Codes of conduct for multinational corporations: an idea whose time has come. *Business and Society Review* 104(3): 225–41

WHO (1999). *The World Health Report 1999: Making a Difference*. Geneva: WHO

World Bank (2005). *World Development Report 2005: A Better Investment Climate for Everyone*. Washington, DC: World Bank. Available at http://siteresources.worldbank.org/INTWDR2005/Resources/wdr2005_selected_indicators.pdf, accessed 15 March 2005

Yach D (2004). Politics and health. *Development* 47(2): 5–10

4 Agenda setting

Overview

This chapter looks at how issues are identified as a matter of concern for policy. Why do some issues gain attention to the extent that action of some sort is likely to be taken? According to the simple 'stages model' of the policy process introduced in Chapter 1, problem identification is the first step in the process of changing and implementing policy. However, it can be surprisingly difficult to explain how and why some issues become prominent in the eyes of policy makers and others recede from view. In terms of the health policy triangle, set out in Chapter 1, the explanation most often relates to changes in the policy context which enable those among the policy actors concerned to change policy to persuade others that action should be taken. The focus in this chapter will be on government policy making and why governments choose to act on some issues but not on others. The chapter also looks at the range of interest groups that contribute to agenda-setting, paying particular attention to the role of the mass media since they often play an important part in issue recognition.

Learning objectives

After working through this chapter, you will be better able to:

- **define what is meant by the *policy agenda***
- **understand different explanations as to how issues get onto the policy agenda and how certain issues get priority for policy development over others**
- **compare the respective roles of a range of interest groups in setting the policy agenda**

Key terms

Agenda setting Process by which certain issues come onto the policy agenda from the much larger number of issues potentially worthy of attention by policy makers.

Feasibility A characteristic of issues for which there is a practical solution.

Legitimacy A characteristic of issues that policy makers see as appropriate for government to act on.

Policy agenda List of issues to which an organization is giving serious attention at any one time with a view to taking some sort of action.

Policy stream The set of possible policy solutions or alternatives developed by experts, politicians, bureaucrats and interest groups, together with the activities of those interested in these options (e.g. debates between researchers).

Policy windows Points in time when the opportunity arises for an issue to come onto the policy agenda and be taken seriously with a view to action.

Politics stream Political events such as shifts in the national mood or public opinion, elections and changes in government, social uprisings, demonstrations and campaigns by interest groups.

Problem stream Indicators of the scale and significance of an issue which give it visibility.

Support A characteristic of issues that the public and other key political interests want to see responded to.

What is the policy agenda?

The word 'agenda' can be used in a number of different ways, for example, to describe the sequence of business to be conducted at a committee meeting. At other times, people are accused of having a 'hidden agenda', meaning that they have ulterior motives for their actions. In relation to policy making, the term agenda means:

> the list of subjects or problems to which government officials and people outside of government closely associated with those officials, are paying some serious attention at any given time . . . Out of the set of all conceivable subjects or problems to which officials could be paying attention, they do in fact seriously attend to some rather than others. (Kingdon 1984)

Activity 4.1

List some of the health-related subjects or problems that you are aware of that the government has recently paid serious attention to in your country. If you cannot remember any, have a look at the newspapers for the past few months to see which health issues and policies have been mentioned.

Feedback

Out of the potentially wide range of health and related issues that the government could be attending to, there is usually a shorter list of 'hot' topics actively under discussion. For example, the government could be concerned about the health of recent migrants to the country, the recruitment and retention of nurses in hospitals, the immunization rate in remote rural areas, recent upward trends in sexually transmitted disease and which drugs primary care nurses should be able to prescribe.

Activity 4.2

Why do you think these particular subjects or problems received high priority? List the reasons that occur to you.

Feedback

You may have given reasons such as the number of people affected by the health issue; the health impact, say of a disease, or a rapid increase in incidence; pressure from an influential group or from the public; criticism from opposition politicians or an international agency; the publication of a research report highlighting the issue or showing it in a new way; the arrival of a new Minister of Health or a change of government; and so on. These and other factors will be considered in a more structured way in the rest of the chapter.

Obviously the list of problems under active consideration varies from one section of the government to another. The president or prime minister will be considering major items such as the state of the economy or relations with other countries. The Minister and Ministry of Health will have a more specialized agenda which may include a few 'high politics' issues, such as whether a system of national health insurance should be established, as well as a larger number of 'low politics' issues such as whether a particular drug should be approved for use and, if so, whether it is worth being reimbursed as part of the publicly financed health care system.

Why do issues get onto the policy agenda?

Sometimes it is obvious why policy makers take particular issues seriously and then act upon their understanding of them. For instance, if a country is invaded, the government will rapidly recognize this as a problem requiring a government response. It will then act to mobilize the armed forces to attempt to repel the invader. But this sort of appreciation and reaction to a crisis is not typical of most policy making. Most policy making is, as Grindle and Thomas (1991) put it, 'politics-as-usual changes': a response to routine, day-to-day problems that need solutions. Given that there are always more such problems being publicly discussed than government time, energy and resources to deal with them, where does the impetus for change or response to a particular problem come from when there is no crisis (obviously what is perceived to be a 'crisis' will vary from place to place and over time)? Several explanations have been put forward as to how and why some issues are taken seriously by government officials when there is no apparent crisis.

Agenda setting in politics-as-usual circumstances

Early explanations of what constituted a public problem, as against something that individuals and families would have to deal with themselves, assumed that problems existed purely in objective terms and were simply waiting to be recognized by government acting in a rational manner, for example, because the problems threatened the well-being of the population. According to this explanation, governments would actively scan the horizon and the most 'important' issues would become the subject of policy attention (e.g. in health terms, government would focus on the diseases responsible for the greatest share of death and disability). A more sophisticated variant of this approach was to argue that what made its way onto the policy agenda was more a function of long-term changes in socio-economic conditions that produced a set of problems to which governments had to respond eventually even if there had been no systematic assessment of potential policy problems. From this perspective, countries with ageing populations will have to respond eventually to the implications for retirement pensions, health services, long-term care, transport, and so on.

Later political scientists and sociologists argued that recognizing something as a problem for government is very much more of a social process, involving defining what is 'normal' in a society and what is an unacceptable deviation from that position (Berger and Luckman 1975). This perspective draws attention to the ideology and assumptions within which governments operate and how they shape what is defined as an issue for government attention as well as how it is regarded. The manner and form in which problems are understood are important influences on how they will eventually be tackled by policy makers (Cobb and Elder 1983). So, for example, if the problem of people with mental illness is framed by the media in terms of the risk they pose to themselves, this will have quite different consequences for the policy agenda than if the problem is articulated as one of protecting the public from the threat of violence from people with mental illness. In neither scenario are the prevalence and incidence of mental illness central to the question of whether the issue will be taken seriously.

This perspective also recognizes that not everyone will necessarily agree on how a phenomenon should be framed (i.e. what sort of a problem is this?) and whether it should be a matter for government action. Important policy actors can clash and compete in attempting to persuade government not only to put an issue on the agenda but also in the way they wish to see it presented and dealt with.

There are a number of theoretical models of agenda setting. Two of the most prominent and widely used are described below.

The Hall model: legitimacy, feasibility and support

This approach proposes that only when an issue and likely response are high in terms of their *legitimacy, feasibility* and *support* do they get onto a government agenda. Hall and her colleagues provided a simple, quick-to-apply model for analysing which issues might be taken up by governments (Hall et al. 1975).

Legitimacy

Legitimacy is a characteristic of issues with which governments believe they should be concerned and in which they have a right or even obligation to intervene. At the high end, most citizens in most societies in the past and the present would expect the government to keep law and order and to defend the country from attack. These would be widely accepted as highly legitimate state activities.

Activity 4.3

Which health-related government policies and programmes are generally regarded as highly legitimate?

Feedback

Probably the most widely accepted role for government in relation to health is to act to reduce the risk of an infectious disease being established and spreading through the population. Another is regulating pollution. Even in these areas, there is usually some debate about the precise nature and limits of government action.

However, there are many other areas where legitimacy is contentious. Legitimacy varies greatly from country to country and changes over time. Things that were not seen as the domain of government regulation in the past (e.g. control of smoking in work-places) are now increasingly accepted as legitimate and vice versa (e.g. relaxation of laws prohibiting homosexual activity in many countries). Typically, in times of perceived external threats, the public and politicians are more willing to curb individual liberties because they believe that such actions will protect the community from worse harm.

Feasibility

Feasibility refers to the potential for implementing the policy. It is defined by prevailing technical and theoretical knowledge, resources, availability of skilled staff, administrative capability and existence of the necessary infrastructure of government. There may be technological, financial or workforce limitations that suggest that a particular policy may be impossible to implement, regardless of how legitimate it is seen to be.

Activity 4.4

Which policies would you like to introduce into the health system in your country but which are likely to face major feasibility problems?

Feedback

You may have made all sorts of suggestions. One common one is in achieving geographical equity of provision of health service despite the reluctance of health care professionals to work in 'less desirable' areas such as remote, rural locations. Another common feasibility problem relates to health care financing in low income countries. Their governments may wish to introduce more public finance into their health care systems but frequently lack robust tax systems to raise the revenue because so many people work in the informal sector of the economy.

Support

Finally, *support* refers to the elusive but important issue of public support for government, at least in relation to the issue in question. Clearly, more authoritarian and non-elected regimes are less dependent on popular support than democratic governments, but even dictatorships have to ensure that there is some support among key groups, such as the armed forces, for their policies. If support is lacking, or discontent with the government as a whole is high, it may be very difficult for a government to put an issue on the agenda and do anything about it (see Easton's model of the political system in Chapter 3).

Thus the logic of the Hall model is that governments will estimate whether an issue falls at the high or low end of the three continua of legitimacy, feasibility and support. If an issue has high legitimacy (government is seen as having the right to intervene), high feasibility (there are sufficient resources, personnel, infrastructure) and high support (the most important interest groups are supportive – or at least not obstructive), then the odds of the issue reaching the policy agenda and faring well subsequently are greatly increased.

Of course, this does not rule out more tactical reasons for putting an issue onto the policy agenda. Sometimes, governments will publicly state their position on a particular issue to demonstrate that they care, or to appease donors who demand a response as a condition of aid, or to confound the political opposition, even when they do not expect to be able to translate their concern into a policy that could be implemented because it has low feasibility and/or support.

The Kingdon model: policy windows and three streams of policy process

John Kingdon's (1984) approach focuses on the role of policy entrepreneurs inside and outside government who take advantage of agenda-setting opportunities – known as *policy windows* – to move items onto the government's formal agenda. The model suggests that the characteristics of issues combine with the features of political institutions and circumstances, together with the development of policy solutions, in a process that can lead to the opening and closing of windows of opportunity to shift an issue onto the agenda. He conceives of policy emerging through three separate 'streams' or processes – the *problem stream*, the *politics stream* and the *policy stream*. Policies are only taken seriously by governments when the three streams run together (Figure 4.1). Kingdon's 'windows' are the metaphorical launch 'windows' in a space mission. Blast-off can only occur when all the conditions are favourable.

Three streams of policy process

The *problem stream* refers to the perceptions of problems as public matters requiring government action and is influenced by previous efforts of government to respond to them. Officials learn about problems or socio-economic conditions through indicators, feedback from existing programmes, pressure groups, or sudden, focusing events such as crises. Indicators may include routine health statistics, for example, showing an increase in childhood obesity or a return of TB to a

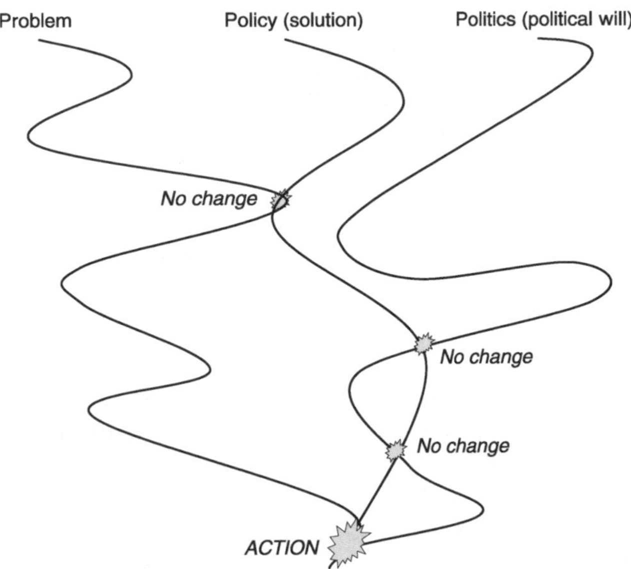

Figure 4.1 Kingdon's three stream model of agenda setting
Source: Adapted from Kingdon (1984)

population previously free of the disease. However, such facts rarely if ever 'speak for themselves' and lead directly to action (see Chapter 9 for more on the links between research and policy).

The *policy stream* consists of the ongoing analyses of problems and their proposed solutions together with the debates surrounding these problems and possible responses. In this stream of ideas a range of possibilities is explored and, at times, may be progressively narrowed down or promoted. For an idea or solution to get to the surface, it must be technically feasible, consistent with dominant social values, be capable of handling future feasibility constraints (such as on finance and personnel), be publicly acceptable and must resonate with politicians.

The *politics stream* operates quite separately of the other two streams and is comprised of events such as swings of national mood, changes of government and campaigns by interest groups.

Kingdon identifies visible and hidden participants affecting the coming together of the streams. The visible participants are organized interests that highlight a specific problem, put forward a particular point of view, advocate a solution and use the mass media to gain attention. Visible participants may be inside or outside government. For example, a new president or prime minister may be a powerful agenda setter because he/she has only recently been elected and is given the benefit of the doubt by the electorate. The hidden participants are more likely to be the specialists in the field – the researchers, academics and consultants who work predominantly in the policy stream – developing and proposing options for solving problems which may get onto the agenda. Hidden participants may play a part in getting issues onto the agenda, particularly if they work with the mass media. Increasingly, universities, which are competing with one another for research funds, encourage their staff to promote their research findings in the mass media. This may mean that some academics shift from hidden to more visible roles in the agenda-setting process.

Policy windows

According to Kingdon's model, the three streams work along different, largely independent channels until at particular times, which become *policy windows*, they flow together, or intersect. This is when new issues get onto the agenda and policy is highly likely to change. As a result, policies do not get onto the agenda according to some logical series of stages. The three streams flow simultaneously, each with a life of its own, until they meet, at which point an issue is likely to be taken seriously by policy makers. The meeting of the streams cannot easily be engineered or predicted.

Activity 4.5

Suggest possible reasons why the three streams might meet, leading to a problem moving onto the policy agenda. Locate each possible reason in one of Kingdon's three 'streams'.

Feedback

The main reasons why the three streams might converge and open a policy window include:

- the activities of key players in the *political stream* who work to link particular policy 'solutions' to particular problems and at the same time create the political opportunity for action. These people are known as *policy entrepreneurs* since this is the political version of the activity of bringing buyers, sellers and commodities together on which commerce thrives
- media attention to a problem and to possible solutions (*policy stream* influencing the *politics stream*)
- a crisis such as a serious failure in the quality or safety of a service or other unpredictable event (*problem stream*)
- the dissemination of a major piece of research (*policy stream* which may affect the *policy stream*)
- changes of government after elections or other regular, formal landmarks in the political process (e.g., budgets) (*politics stream*)

Thus, in reality, participants in the policy process rarely proceed from identification of a problem to seeking solutions. Alternative courses of action are generated in the policy stream and may be promoted by experts or advocates over long periods before the opportunity arises (the policy window opens) to get the issue they relate to and the solutions onto the agenda.

The two models you have just read about are useful because they can be applied to a wide range of health policies, including those you know about in your own country. They should be able to help explain why a particular issue is on the policy agenda, or why it has not reached the policy agenda.

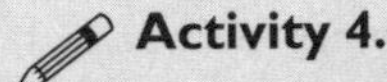

Activity 4.6

Read the following account, based on Reich (1994), which describes the introduction of an essential drugs policy in Bangladesh. Apply the two models to this case study to explain the events that took place.

Getting the issue of essential drugs onto the policy agenda in Bangladesh

Lieutenant-General and Army Chief of Staff HM Ershad seized power in a military coup in Bangladesh in 1982. Within four weeks of the coup he had established an expert committee of eight to confront widely discussed problems in the production, distribution and consumption of pharmaceuticals. Less than three months later the Bangladesh (Control) Ordinance of 1982 was issued as a Declaration by Ershad, based on a set of 16 guidelines that would regulate the pharmaceutical sector. The main aim of the Ordinance was to halve the 'wastage of foreign exchange through the production and/or importation of unnecessary drugs or drugs of marginal value'. The drugs policy was to be applied to both private and public sectors and created a restricted national formulary of 150 essential drugs plus 100 supplementary drugs for specialized use which could be produced at relatively low cost. Over 1,600 products deemed 'useless, ineffective or harmful' were banned.

The formulation of the drugs policy was initiated by a group of concerned physicians and others with close links to the new president, without external consultation and discussion. The Bangladesh Medical Association was represented by one member of its pharmaceuticals sub-committee, but its General-Secretary was not officially involved because of his known connections to a transnational pharmaceutical corporation. The pharmaceutical industry was not represented at all on the expert committee. It was argued that its presence would distort and delay policy change. Once the policy was on the agenda and had been promulgated, the industry, both domestic and transnational, launched an advertising campaign against the drugs list.

Among the physicians on the committee was a well-known doctor, Zafrullah Chowdhury, who had established the Gonoshasthaya Kendra (GK) health care project soon after independence in 1971. Among other activities, GK manufactured essential generic drugs in Bangladesh. Production had begun in 1981 and by 1986 GK Pharmaceuticals Ltd was producing over 20 products. Later Dr Chowdhury was accused of promoting the interests of GK Pharmaceuticals through the committee.

Feedback

Applying the Hall model

The policy of essential drugs had *legitimacy* because Ershad's government was new and new policies were both expected and allowed. Further, there was a strong case for limiting the number of drugs imported both because many were deemed ineffective or harmful and because they wasted scarce foreign currency which a poor country like Bangladesh could ill afford.

It was *feasible* to introduce radical change because it could be done by passing an Ordinance from the President: it did not require a long parliamentary process. Its passage was made more feasible by keeping opposition to a minimum by acting very quickly. In addition, there were virtually no financial implications for the government, if anything, this would reduce public drug expenditure.

Support was more difficult: there was considerable resistance from health professionals, from multinational pharmaceutical firms, and initially from national drug companies. But, as the people and national industries gained support (through lower prices and greater local production), so support for the policy grew. In addition, as a dictator, Ershad was able to ignore initial opposition since he did not need parliamentary support for his policy to be enacted.

Applying the Kingdon model

The problem of ineffective and expensive drugs had been floating in the *problem stream* for some time before Ershad took power, but without any action being taken. However, in 1982, a new president took over, eager to win popular support by showing his willingness to act on recognized problems that affected many people (change in the *politics stream*). The most obvious losers included foreign pharmaceutical companies that were unlikely to be widely supported within Bangladesh. A small group of Bangladeshi health professionals, chaired by a celebrated doctor with an interest in health projects and the local pharmaceutical industry, had been highly concerned about the pharmaceutical issue for some time before Ershad took power. Some of its members were hidden participants in the *policy stream*, collecting information and monitoring the situation, and others were visible participants, advocating change explicitly. They recognized an opportunity to get an essential drugs policy on the agenda when the government changed and had close links to the new president. The technical feasibility, public acceptability and congruence with existing values were all judged to be favourable, and so the three streams came together, putting essential drugs on the policy agenda.

Agenda setting and policy change under crisis

You have seen that a perceived crisis is one reason why policy windows open. Policy making in times of crisis is different from ordinary, business-as-usual policy making. For example, it is easier to get radical policies seriously considered in times of crisis than other times. A crisis exists when important policy makers perceive that one exists, that it is a real and threatening set of circumstances, and that failure to act could lead to even more disastrous consequences. Events that do not have all these characteristics are not likely to be considered a crisis. However, where the gravity of the situation is confirmed by pressure from outside government, such as a dramatic fall in the price of a key export crop, and the government has access to corroborating information from its own experts, then the chances are that the government will see the problem as a crisis, and pay it serious attention. This may or may not, in turn, lead to an actual change of policy.

Many examples of new policies moving onto the agenda occur in times of economic crisis. Radical reforms in macro economic, trade, labour market and social welfare policy in New Zealand after 1984 were prompted by a conviction on the part of the incoming Labour government, its principal advisers in the Treasury and influential segments of the business community that the country was on the brink of economic collapse. This justified a radical change in the issues on the policy agenda and subsequent policies favouring the free market in many areas of national life. The reforms included major changes to the operation of the health care system. The public part of the system was split into purchasers (regional health authorities, responsible for procuring services for their populations) and providers (autonomous public hospitals and private and voluntary sector providers) who competed for the business of the purchasers in a publicly financed market (see Chapter 2 for more on this kind of thinking). It is unlikely that the cascade of changes to the economy and the public services, including health care, would have occurred in the way they did over a relatively short period without the impetus of a strong sense of economic crisis coupled with a change of government.

Crises can be acute or more chronic. The New Zealand case had elements of both the acute and chronic since some participants had identified major problems with the country's economic policies a decade before 1984.

Since crises are defined by the intersection of 'objective' conditions and perceptions of the gravity of those conditions, there is always scope for interest groups and governments to heighten the sense of crisis in order to pave the way for changes they particularly want to introduce. One interpretation of the change strategy for the British National Health Service of the Blair government, between 1997 and 2005, was that it comprised identifying problems and solutions, but also engendering a strong sense that the NHS was in grave crisis – that without reform it could not continue in its present form and would have to be abolished and replaced by something quite different. Thus, the Blair government identified the quality of cancer services and long waiting times as major problems threatening the very existence of a tax-financed, universal system. The government also used scandals of poor clinical quality at particular hospitals as a rationale for general changes to the regulation and oversight of clinicians.

Non-decision making

While both crisis and politics-as-usual models are useful in helping to explain how issues come onto the policy agenda and are acted upon, or why eventually they are not (because they may lack legitimacy, feasibility or support or because the three policy streams do not come together in favourable circumstances to provide a 'window of opportunity'), observable action provides an incomplete guide to the way all policies are decided. In other words, you need to think about the possibility of *non-policy making,* or *non-decision making* when thinking about what gets onto the public policy agenda (see Chapter 2 for a fuller discussion of this). Those with enough power are not only capable of stopping items reaching the agenda, they are also able to shape people's wishes so that only issues deemed acceptable are discussed, never mind acted on.

Activity 4.7

Until the 1970s, stopping smoking was widely seen as almost entirely an individual matter (except for deterring children from smoking). As a result, there was not even discussion about the possibility of limiting where smoking could take place in the health interests both of smokers and non-smokers.

Do you think the lack of discussion of smoking bans in the 1970s is an example of non-decision making through force, prevailing values or avoidance of conflict on the part of Western governments?

Feedback

The main reason for non-decision making related to the prevailing values of the time, which, in turn, were supported by tobacco industry advocates. In addition, governments were reluctant to face conflict with the tobacco industry and court public unpopularity. This anticipation of conflict kept the issue off the agenda for many years.

Another example of non-decision making relates to the fact that the often radical 'market' reforms of many health care systems in the 1990s rarely if ever challenged the monopoly control exercised by the medical profession over who can and cannot initiate treatment and prescribe drugs for patients. While many previous assumptions as to how health care systems should be organized and directed were overturned (e.g., privatization of public hospitals and competition between providers), the fundamental interests of the dominant occupational group prevented any concerted debate about opening medical work to other professions.

Who sets the agenda?

In the rest of this chapter you will explore how the main actors in the policy process, particularly the government and the media, put issues on the policy agenda. Since you will be moving on to consider government policy making in the next chapter, and the business community, the medical profession and other interest groups in Chapter 6, more time will be spent here on the role of the media than any of the other actors in agenda setting. Furthermore, in most circumstances, the media's primary role in policy making is likely to be in helping to set the policy agenda rather than in other aspects of the process.

Governments as agenda-setters

Governments, particularly of large, wealthy countries, can be very influential in setting the international policy agenda. For example, the Bush administration in the USA actively promoted its 'ABC' ('abstinence, be faithful and condom use') strategy for HIV/AIDS prevention and control within the international public health community and high prevalence countries, particularly in Sub-Saharan Africa, in the face of criticism from many experts and activists. It was able to do so because of the large sums of money it was making available for HIV/AIDS prevention and the conditions it applied to the use of these funds.

Within their own countries, governments are plainly crucial agenda-setters since they control the legislative process and often initiate policy change (see the next chapter for more on this process). It became fashionable in the 1990s for political parties to set the agenda for their term of office in advance by publishing relatively detailed election manifestos and promising to implement the changes set out in the manifesto if elected as a way of establishing the trust of the electorate. This is one of the more obvious ways in which governments can attempt to set the agenda. However, being in the manifesto only increases the likelihood of an issue getting onto the agenda and being acted on, it is not a guarantee. For example, political activists writing the manifesto may not give enough weight to the feasibility of what they have proposed.

Other than in their pre-election party manifestos, how far do governments pursue an active programme of issue search – looking for items that need to go on the policy agenda? Hogwood and Gunn (1984) argue that governments *should* do so because they need to anticipate problems before they occur in order to minimize any adverse consequences or to avert a potential crisis. Perhaps the most obvious reasons for issue search lie in the external environment such as demography, technology, and so on. In almost all countries, the growing numbers and proportion of older people in the population have to be taken into account in setting health policy in areas such as paying for services, long-term care of frail people and the management of chronic diseases. New solutions become available to old problems such as linking patients' records kept by different institutions. New problems begin to assume clear contours such as the potential effect of climate change on agrarian economies and the nature of public health risks. As well as serving the elected government of the day, one of the functions of a responsible civil service is to provide reports identifying and drawing future policy issues to the attention of ministers, particularly those which are largely inescapable, such as the effects of global warming. However, there is no guarantee that the government of the day will want to respond to what it may perceive to be a long-term issue that its successors and not they themselves can deal with.

The mass media as agenda-setter

How far and in which circumstances do the mass media guide attention to certain issues and influence what we think about? How much influence do they have on policy makers in their choice of issues of political concern and action? In the past, the role of the media tended to be underestimated in policy making. However, the mass media have had a major influence over many years on governments' policy agendas through their ability to raise and shape, if not determine, issues and public opinion which, in turn, influence governments to respond. The arrival of the Internet in the 1990s made this process even more apparent, since the Internet has enabled the rapid mobilization and feedback of public opinion in ways that governments cannot easily predict or control, but which they may have to respond to in some way.

There are two basic types of media: print and electronic. They serve a range of vital functions: they are sources of information; they function as propaganda mechanisms; they are agents of socialization (transmitting a society's culture and instructing people in the values and norms of society) and they serve as agents of legitimacy, generating mass belief in, and acceptance of, dominant political and economic institutions such as democracy and capitalism. They can also criticize the way societies and governments operate, bringing new perspectives to the public.

The way the media function is affected by the political system. In many countries newspapers and television stations are entirely state-owned and censor themselves, fearing government reprisals for covering issues in an inappropriate way, thereby prejudicing their impartiality. In others, media are notionally independent of the state, but editors and journalists are intimidated, gaoled, expelled or worse. The Internet and satellite broadcasting are less easy for individual regimes to influence or undermine but are less accessible in poorer countries than television and radio which are easier to control. Even in liberal democracies, the mass media may be controlled in subtle ways. Governments, increasingly concerned about their image in the media, can favour certain more cooperative broadcasters over others, giving them exclusive news stories and advance warning of policy announcements to boost their viewer numbers in return for generally favourable coverage. Most mass media organizations in Western democracies are part of large conglomerates with a wide range of media interests in many countries. Some of the best known are owned by business magnates, such as Silvio Berlusconi and Rupert Murdoch, whose personal political values and commercial goals often shape the orientation of the news reporting and political commentary provided by their television channels and newspapers without the proprietors necessarily having to direct their journalists on a day-to-day basis. Most commercial media are also dependent to some degree on advertising. Taken together, the pattern of ownership and the requirements of advertisers tend to mean that in most countries the majority of newspapers and television stations adopt broadly right-of-centre, pro-capitalist, political positions. Advertisers and commercial interests can also, on occasions, influence the content of media directly, for example, through the sponsorship of newspapers and the placement of articles in the press apparently written by neutral journalists but intended to promote the industry's interests.

Despite being largely controlled by the state and major commercial interests, the media can, sometimes, put an issue on the policy agenda which researchers or interest groups unconnected with the state or business are trying to promote. Occasionally, they act like pressure groups by running campaigns on unjustly neglected issues. One of the most notable in the UK was *The Sunday Times'* successful campaign in the 1970s to win higher compensation for children with birth defects after their mothers had taken the tranquillizer, thalidomide. The newspaper's researchers succeeded in showing that the risk of congenital malformations had been foreseeable (Karpf 1988).

Campaigns can also be more blatantly populist and be designed to win readers such as the UK *Daily Mail's* campaign against speed cameras in the early 2000s. The campaign portrayed the research on injury reduction as severely flawed and, instead, appealed to the cynicism of the readers by focusing on the government revenue raised by the cameras in fines, much to the disappointment of public health experts trying to reduce traffic-related injuries and deaths.

Activity 4.8

Consider some campaigns run by the mass media in your country designed to get specific public health issues taken up by the government. What were the issues? How did the media present the issues? Do you think the media presented the issues fairly and responsibly? Was the issue an important one for health? Did the coverage influence the policy debate and help issues get onto the policy agenda? Did the media coverage have a positive or negative impact on the policy, in your view?

Feedback

Your answer will clearly depend on your example. But analysing an example in this way should help you understand the reasons why the 'story' unfolded in the way it did.

There have been calls for the mass media to become more responsible in their coverage of public health issues. Research in Britain on media coverage of health issues shows that the amount of news coverage of a topic is unrelated to the risk posed to the public health (Harrabin et al. 2003) and, indeed, the diseases with the lowest risk to population health receive the highest level of coverage, and vice versa. For example, coverage of vCJD or mad cow disease in humans bore no relationship to its extreme rarity. Yet, the same research showed that politicians change their priorities in response to media coverage rather than based on evidence of what was in the public interest.

Nevertheless, the extent of media influence on policy makers is open to question. First, policy makers have many different sources of information and can use the media themselves to draw attention to a particular issue. Often, the contents of government press releases will be reported verbatim by busy journalists. Second, it is difficult to separate different strands of influence on what gets onto the agenda. The media are both part of the process itself, not outside it, and they are not alone. Mostly, the media highlights movements that have started elsewhere – that is, they help to delineate an issue, but they do not necessarily create it.

Third, policy makers are less likely to be moved to action by a single media account. Concerted action by the press may make a difference, but in a competitive media environment, there is unlikely to be a unified view of an issue and the news media particularly are always looking for novelty.

Just as there are examples of the media inspiring policy shifts, so there are clear examples of politicians and their officials resisting media pressure to change policy.

So, there are no simple answers to questions such as: how much do the mass media influence public opinion and/or policy makers? The content of the policy issue, the political context and the process by which the debate unfolds and the policy issue is decided, all have a bearing on how influential the media will be.

In low income countries, the influence of the media on policy makers is less easy to discern. Journalists, editors, broadcasters and producers are members of the urban elite, and generally have close ties with policy makers in government. Where media are owned directly by government, there is unlikely to be much critical analysis of government policies. Policy circles are small in many low income countries, and those journalists who are perceived as threatening a political regime are often the first to be arrested when repression strikes. Although this is changing, the independence of the mass media remains vulnerable to political whim and to a weak capital base. For example, in high income countries consumer advertising revenue, which is not present in other countries, gives the mass media considerable financial independence of governments, but not necessarily independence from commercial interests.

The presence or absence of democracy also appears to be important in the influence of the media on agenda setting in low income countries. Sen (1983) compared the role of the media in reporting food shortages and famines in China and India since the Second World War and the impact on the governments' responses. In 1959–61, China suffered a massive famine due to crop failures. Between 14 and 16 million extra deaths occurred but the mass media remained silent. India, on the other hand, despite being a similarly poor country, had not experienced a famine since Independence in 1947 despite years with great food problems. Sen argued that India could not have famines because India, unlike China, was a democracy with a free press: 'Government cannot afford to fail to take prompt action when large-scale starvation threatens. Newspapers play an important part in this, in making the facts known and forcing the challenge to be faced. So does the pressure of opposition parties' (Sen 1983). In China, there were few ways of challenging the government to act to avoid the catastrophe and the famine could be kept hidden. Ironically, during the same period, communist China was far more committed to distributing food at public expense to guarantee some food for all than India. In normal times, this avoided the widespread malnourishment and non-acute hunger observed in India.

Summary

You have learnt how agenda setting is not a clear-cut part of the policy process. There are many actors involved and it is not necessarily dominated by government. The policy agenda may change at times of crisis or through 'politics-as-usual', but in both cases, certain factors will be important. A crisis will have to be perceived as such by the most influential policy elites, and they will have to believe that failure to act will make the situation worse. In politics-as-usual, many different reforms may compete for policy makers' attention and which one reaches the policy agenda will depend on a number of different factors, including who gains and who loses in the change. Timing is important, and issues may be around for a while before all three 'streams' come together, and an issue is propelled onto the policy agenda.

The media can be important for drawing attention to issues and forcing governments to act but this is more likely in relation to 'low politics' issues. On major, or 'high politics' topics (such as economic policy or threats to national security), the great majority of the media is likely to support the basic thrust of government policy, if the government is seen to be legitimate.

References

Berger PL and Luckman T (1975). *The Social Construction of Reality: A Treatise on the Sociology of Knowledge*. Harmondsworth: Penguin

Cobb RW and Elder CD (1983). *Participation in American Politics: The Dynamics of Agenda-Building*. Baltimore, MD: Johns Hopkins University Press

Grindle M and Thomas J (1991). *Public Choices and Policy Change*. Baltimore: Johns Hopkins Unversity Press

Hall P, Land H, Parker R and Webb A (1975). *Change, Choice and Conflict in Social Policy*. London: Heinemann

Harrabin R, Coote A and Allen J (2003). *Health in the News: Risk, Reporting and Media Attention*. London: Kings Fund

Hogwood B and Gunn L (1984). *Policy Analysis for the Real World*. Oxford: Oxford University Press

Karpf A (1988). *Doctoring the Media*. London: Routledge

Kingdon J (1984). *Agendas, Alternatives and Public Policies*. Boston: Little Brown & Co

Reich M (1994). Bangladesh pharmaceutical policy and politics. *Health Policy and Planning* 9: 130–43

Sen A (1983). The battle to get food. *New Society* 13 October: 54–7

5 Government and the policy process

Overview

The previous chapter showed how issues make their way onto the policy agenda through processes not necessarily controlled by government. This chapter focuses on the roles of government in the formulation and shaping of policy, and how much influence it has on the policy process. While policy formulation usually involves taking account of a wide variety of interests, albeit driven by the ideological assumptions of the government in power, the way this happens is very dependent on the type of government institutions or constitution of a country. You will look at the role of the institutions of government most frequently assumed to be directly involved in forming and carrying out policies: the legislature; the executive; the bureaucracy; and the judiciary. In terms of the framework for policy analysis introduced in Chapter 1, the focus in this chapter is on a particular set of official 'actors' within the policy process. In terms of the 'policy stages' model also discussed in Chapter 1, the main focus is on policy formulation with some reference to policy implementation.

Learning objectives

After working through this chapter, you will be better able to:

- **describe the main institutions involved in government policy making – the legislature, the executive, the bureaucracy and the judiciary – and their roles**
- **understand how they relate to one another differently in different types of government system**
- **understand the special characteristics of government policy making in the health sector**
- **understand how different parts of government (e.g. different ministries) and different levels (e.g. national, regional and local) require active coordination if policies are to be successful**
- **describe the organization of the health system of your country and be aware that the official chart of its organization may not reflect the true pattern of power and influence in the system**

Key terms

Bicameral/unicameral legislature In a unicameral legislature, there is only one 'house' or chamber, whereas in a bicameral legislature, there is a second or upper chamber, the role of which is to critique and check the quality of draft legislation promulgated by the lower house. Normally, only the lower house can determine whether draft legislation becomes law.

Bureaucracy A formal type of organisation involving hierarchy, impersonality, continuity and expertise.

Executive Leadership of a country (i.e. the president and/or prime minister and other ministers). The prime minister/president and senior ministers are often referred to as the cabinet.

Federal system The sub-national or provincial level of government is not subordinate to the national government but has substantial powers of its own which the national government cannot take away.

Judiciary Comprises judges and courts which are responsible for ensuring that the government of the day (the executive) acts according to the laws passed by the legislature.

Legislature Body that enacts the laws that govern a country and oversees the executive. It is normally democratically elected in order to represent the people of the country and commonly referred to as the parliament or assembly. Often there will be two chambers or 'houses' of parliament.

Parliamentary system The executive are also members of the legislature and are chosen on the basis that the majority of members of the legislature support them.

Presidential system The president or head of state is directly elected in a separate process from the election of members of the legislature.

Proportional representation Voting system which is designed to ensure as far as possible that the proportion of votes received by each political party equates to their share of the seats in the legislature.

Unitary system The lower levels of government are constitutionally subordinate to the national government. Lower levels of government receive their authority from central government.

Characterizing government systems

Two features of government systems have a major effect on the ability of states to make and implement policy: *autonomy* and *capacity* (Howlett and Ramesh 2003). In this context *autonomy* means the ability of government institutions to resist being captured by self-interested groups and to act fairly as an arbiter of social conflicts. The government system may not be neutral in a political sense (after all, it serves governments of different ideological complexions), but, if it is autonomous, it operates with some objective regard to improving the welfare of the whole country not just responding to and protecting the interests of sections of the community. *Capacity* refers to the ability of the government system to make and implement policy. It springs from the expertise, resources and coherence of the machinery of government. For example, it is essential that a government is able to pay its civil servants on time and keep corruption in check. At a more sophisticated level, it helps if individual ministries respect the fact that their decisions and behaviour can have major implications for other arms of government and refrain from self-interested actions. The different forms of government system have implications for the autonomy and capacity of government policy making.

Federal versus unitary systems

All governments operate at a variety of levels between the national and the local (for example, public health systems frequently have national and regional levels of administration). However, there is an important, basic distinction between *unitary* and *federal* systems which can be overlooked when thinking about policy change in health systems. In the former, there is a clear chain of command linking the different levels of government so that lower levels are strictly subordinate to higher levels. In France, for example, the national government has potentially all the decision making powers. It can delegate these powers to lower levels of government, but can also take these powers back. New Zealand, Japan and China are similar. Britain has a largely unitary system in which local government derives its powers from central government, but Scotland and Wales have recently been granted their own powers over most of their domestic affairs, including health services, under legislation passed by the national parliament in London. There are now elected bodies separate from the national parliament in Scotland and Wales.

In federal systems, there are at least two separate levels of government within the country with power shared between them. In other words, the sub-national level of government is not subordinate to the national level but enjoys a high level of freedom over those matters under its jurisdiction. Central government cannot remove these freedoms without consent which normally means rewriting the constitution of the country. For example, India, Brazil, Nigeria, the USA, Canada and Australia are all federal countries. In Canada, for instance, the health system is a responsibility of the provinces, not the federal government, though the latter contributes some of the funding for health services. This leads to lengthy negotiations and disputes between the two levels of government about who pays for what.

Indeed, federalism is widely regarded as a major reason for the relative inability of governments in these countries to bring about major, nation-wide policy changes in the health sector except when circumstances are highly favourable. A further complication is that federal and sub-national governments may be controlled by different political parties with different values and goals. Furthermore, elections at one or the other level rarely coincide, so lengthy negotiations can be disrupted by a change of government among any of the parties. So, typically, unitary government systems are associated with far more rapid policy change and less need to compromise when formulating policy. However, this does not necessarily mean that policies developed in this way will be implemented on the ground as their architects at national level intended (as you will see in Chapter 7). Even in unitary systems with relatively few constitutional obstacles to legislative change, the underlying conditions for fundamental system reform rarely occur. These are typically a combination of a government with a high level of authority (e.g. a strong parliamentary majority) and the political will to incur the risks of major change (i.e. reform must be sufficiently central to its policy agenda) (Tuohy 2004).

Relations between the legislature, executive and judiciary

Another feature of each country's government system affecting how public policy is formulated concerns the relations between the legislature, the executive and the judiciary. The *legislature* is the body which represents the people, enacts the laws that govern the people and oversees the *executive* which is the leadership of the country (i.e. the president and/or prime minister and other ministers). The *judiciary* is primarily responsible for ensuring that the government of the day acts within the laws passed by the legislature and adjudicates on the inevitable disputes that occur in the interpretation of laws in practice. Typically, in *parliamentary* systems, the executive is chosen by the legislature from among its members (i.e. ministers are members of the parliament or assembly) and remains in office as long as it has majority support among the legislators. Typically, in *presidential* systems, such as the USA, the executive is separate from the legislature, elected separately by the public and need not have the support of the majority of members of the legislature to govern.

These differences have major implications for the way in which policy is developed. In presidential systems, the executive (the president and senior colleagues) can propose policy but the approval of the legislature (the majority of whose members may not even be from the same political party) is required for the policy to become law. As a result, the US President, for example, frequently has to offer concessions to the legislature in one area of policy in return for support in another. In addition, members of the legislature can play an active part in designing and amending policies. This means that the policy development process is more open than in parliamentary systems with more room for interest groups to exert influence.

In parliamentary systems, while there may be some dispute and bargaining over policies within the governing political party, this usually takes place behind the scenes and the executive can normally rely on its majority in the legislature to obtain support for the measures it wishes to enact. Where the executive does not have an outright majority in the legislature, as happens more often in countries with systems of proportional representation where there may be a large number of political parties, it has to compromise in order to get policies through the legislature. This makes the policy process slower and more complex but not as difficult as policy making in presidential systems. Policy making is still ultimately centralized in the executive in parliamentary systems which usually allows more rapid and decisive action to be taken by the government.

Activity 5.1

As well as the separation of powers between the executive (the President and his staff) and the legislature (the two Houses of Congress), what else makes major policy change (e.g. a wholesale reform of the financing of the health care system) more difficult in the USA than in many other countries?

Feedback

The US system is also federal so the individual states will have to be persuaded to support any major change in domestic policy. This explains why Presidents of the USA tend to spend quite a lot of time and energy on defence and foreign policy where their power is less restricted and they can act on behalf of the entire nation.

The position of the judiciary also affects the government policy process. In federal systems and/or those based on a written constitution, often including a statement of human rights, there is typically an autonomous judiciary such as the US Supreme Court, charged with adjudicating in the case of disputes between the different tiers of government and with ensuring that the laws and actions of the government are consistent with the principles of the constitution. The US Supreme Court has frequently challenged the laws of individual states: in the 1950s, it enforced the civil liberties of black people by overturning legislation in the southern states which would have segregated schools between black and white pupils. In countries like Britain without a written constitution, though independent of government, the courts are more limited in what they can do to constrain the executive in the protection of the rights and liberties of individual citizens and, again, policy making is easier.

Activity 5.2

Imagine that you are a national Minister of Health wishing to introduce a major change into a health care system such as user fees for patients to use public hospitals. List the different considerations you would have to take into account if you were trying to introduce such legislation in a federal, presidential system versus a unitary, parliamentary system. Make two lists of factors.

Feedback

Your notes might look something like those presented in Table 5.1. You will immediately see the larger number and greater complexity of the considerations which the Minister of Health in a federal, presidential system will have to take into account compared with his counterpart in the unitary, parliamentary system. Note that Table 5.1 does not cover the implementation of the proposed changes, simply the ability of the minister and the government to get the reforms accepted and into law within the various legislative bodies. The officials and health professions at lower levels in both systems of government may not agree with parts of the changes, and may have considerable ability to resist or change the direction of policy. This is one of the central issues in policy implementation.

Having set out the roles of the various actors within the government system, you now need to consider their relative influence over the policy formulation process.

Table 5.1 Federal, presidential and unitary, parliamentary systems compared

Federal, presidential system	*Unitary, parliamentary system*
Which level of government is responsible for which aspects of health policy? Is this change within the jurisdiction of national government?	Has the intended reform been discussed in the governing political party? Is it in the election manifesto? What does the governing political party think about the intended reform? Is it broadly supportive? If not, are the majority of members of the legislature from the government party likely to be in support?
Does national government control the aspects of health policy most relevant to the proposed changes? For example, does national government control all the necessary resources to bring about the change?	Has the government got a majority in the legislature (parliament) to enact the changes? If not, can the government get sufficient votes from other parties in the ruling coalition?
Is the national legislature likely to support the changes? If not, what concessions might be made either in health or in other areas of policy to win the necessary support? Are these concessions worth making for this reform?	What concessions, if any, will be needed to get a majority in support of the reforms?
What are the odds of the proposed legislation passing through the national legislature without substantial amendment?	
If the government is dependent on the support of states or provinces to bring about the changes, what are the likely reactions of states or provinces to the reform? Which states or provinces have governments of the same political persuasion as the national government?	
What concessions to the states/provinces could the government make in health or other areas of policy without undermining its position with its supporters in order to obtain sufficient support for the health reforms, particularly from states/provinces governed by opposition parties? For example, will national government have to fund the changes in their entirety to have any chance of getting them accepted?	
What view are the courts likely to take to the reforms?	

Political parties

In liberal democracies (i.e. where people are free to set up political parties and put themselves forward for election without government interference), as opposed to one party states, political parties sit somewhere between wider societal actors such as pressure or interest groups and the institutions of government in that members of the executive and legislature are frequently drawn from one or another of the main political parties. Parties produce manifestos and policy documents on which they campaign at elections. So parties can directly affect the outcomes of elections and what follows. However, voters tend not to vote on the basis of specific policies, but are invited to support a broad package of measures designed to maximize the party's appeal. The detail of which policies reach the government agenda and how they are developed subsequently is outside the direct control of the party and the voters. Of course, a government in office has to be careful not to move too far away from what it promised its party members, supporters and the voters at the election, even if circumstances change, otherwise it will jeopardize its future support, but it is not required to follow party policy in every detail. Indeed, circumstances may change and ministers in office may find that turning manifesto promises into coherent policy is far more difficult technically and politically than they had envisaged while in opposition.

The evidence suggests that political parties have a modest direct effect on policy – their greatest contribution being at the early stages of policy identification – but a larger indirect effect through influencing the staffing of legislative and executive (and sometimes judicial) institutions.

In single party systems, the political party formulates all policies and it becomes the task of the government to find the best ways of implementing them. On the whole, elections in single-party systems do not provide voters with any real choices or policy alternatives, and criticism of the ruling party and its government are often mute or stifled (e.g. in Zimbabwe under President Robert Mugabe). In single-party regimes, the party can also intervene directly in policy. There is no clear-cut or simple separation between the party and the executive or legislature. Both the executive and the legislature can be criticized by the party to the extent that ministers and members of parliament can be removed for not responding with sufficient zeal to the party's views.

By contrast, in liberal democracies, once a political party wins power at an election, the government is in charge. Ministers can adapt party policy in the light of the political pressures placed upon them and the changing nature of the policy environment.

The role of the legislature

In the overwhelming majority of countries, the constitution states that the decisions of the legislature are the expression of the will of the people (popular sovereignty) and that the legislature is the highest decision making body. Most have three formal functions: (1) to represent the people; (2) to enact legislation; and (3) to oversee the executive (the prime minister or president and ministers). Legislatures in democracies are generally composed exclusively of elected members (deputies, senators, members of parliament). Three-fifths of the countries in the world have *unicameral* or single chamber legislatures; the rest have *bicameral* arrangements with two chambers or houses. Generally, the job of the upper house is to review and refine draft legislation and thereby contribute to better policy and law making. In presidential systems, as we saw earlier, the legislature has autonomy from the executive and, on occasions, can make policy. In parliamentary systems, the task of the legislature is primarily to hold the government to account to the public for its performance rather than to initiate policy. Legislators can identify problems in draft legislation and request changes.

In fact, in a range of different government systems, legislatures are increasingly regarded as bodies that rubber-stamp decisions taken elsewhere and even struggle to hold the executive to account. In a review of the literature on elections and parliaments in Africa, Healey and Robinson (1992) suggest that elected representatives are seldom more than marginal in the policy process, and in some countries are inhibited from criticizing proposed government policy by a history of detention without trial (e.g. Zimbabwe).

Activity 5.3

Why have national legislatures (i.e. parliaments and assemblies) become more marginal in policy making and in holding governments to account?

Feedback

Five main reasons are usually given for the gradual marginalization of legislatures. The relative importance of each depends on the country in question, but most are related directly or indirectly to the rising power of the executive:

1 Increasingly strong political party discipline, controlling the activities of members and reducing criticism of the executive.

2 The ability of the executive to use its powers of patronage (i.e. the ability to offer or withhold opportunities for promotion into ministerial and other positions) to control members of the legislature.

3 The shift of much political and policy debate from the parliamentary debating chamber to the mass media (e.g. to the set-piece television interview or debate between party leaders).

4 The expansion of government activities and delegation to a range of specialized agencies so that many decisions can be taken by bureaucrats without the need for new laws or legislative debate.

5 The increasing influence of supra-national bodies such as the European Union (EU) or the International Monetary Fund (IMF) that limit or remove issues from domestic legislative politics.

Although legislatures rarely propose new laws and struggle to fulfil their three main functions, they survive because they have great symbolic value, upholding the ideal of democratic representation of the public. Also, particularly in presidential systems, they can block the proposals of the executive by right. In parliamentary systems, legislators can scrutinize and delay legislation, but where a government has a parliamentary majority and reasonable party discipline, it will prevail over opponents. Only where there is no clear majority and the government is dependent on several smaller parties, do individual legislators have opportunities to shape policies directly. This is one of the arguments in favour of proportional representation.

If the legislature does not have a great deal of say in policy formulation, who does?

The influence of the executive

As you have seen, in most countries with multi-party systems, most of the power to make policy lies with the executive – the elected politicians who become prime minister or president and the ministers. This group is often called the 'cabinet'. The elected members of the executive are supported by the bureaucrats or civil servants who both advise ministers and take direction from them. There is debate about the relative influence on policy of elected officials and bureaucrats. It depends strongly on the country and the period studied as well as the nature of the policy issue at stake.

Compared with the legislature, the executive or cabinet has far greater constitutional, informational, financial and personnel resources. The cabinet has the authority to govern the country and has the ultimate authority to initiate and implement policies. Crucially, it can choose when to introduce draft laws to the legislature. In parliamentary systems, as long as the government has a majority support in the legislature, there are few limits on the power of the executive. In presidential systems, the executive has to convince the legislature to approve its proposed measures where these involve legislation. However, there are wide areas of policy where the executive has discretion, particularly in relation to defence, national security and foreign policy. Frequently, once the budget has been approved by the legislature, the executive has a great deal of control over the detail of how resources are used.

The role of the chief executive

If the executive is very powerful, does this power emanate from the collective decision making of the cabinet, or from the strength of the prime minister or president who occupies a position similar to the chief executive of a private corporation? In those low income countries where political leadership is personal and unaccountable – where constitutional checks on the executive rarely operate – most major policy decisions will be in the hands of the chief executive.

Sometimes, decision making is in the hands of a small group of ministers chosen from among the cabinet by the chief executive because they closely identify with the chief executive's goals and methods. There has been increasing discussion in parliamentary systems, especially Britain, about the more authoritarian style of decision making of prime ministers, starting with Margaret Thatcher, the Conservative prime minister in the 1980s. The Labour governments of Tony Blair after

1997 have similarly shown that the prime minister and his immediate staff are increasingly the key policy initiators, with the rest of the cabinet and the civil service relegated to managing the detail of implementation. Just as Margaret Thatcher launched a major review of the management and organization of the National Health Service in 1987 without consulting any of her cabinet colleagues during a television interview, so too Tony Blair made a major announcement on air. On the defensive regarding Britain's relatively low share of national income devoted to publicly financed health care, the prime minister announced that he intended to bring Britain's level of spending up to the EU average as a share of national income. This sudden, personal commitment led rapidly to a review of the sources and level of spending on the NHS and decisions to increase NHS spending to unprecedented levels over a five-year period (Wanless 2002). Other ministers and the civil service were faced with a *fait accompli*: whatever happened, there was going to be a major increase in NHS resources and capacity to end the long-standing criticism that many of the problems of the British NHS were simply due to under-investment (Secretary of State for Health 2000).

Individual political leadership does matter, even in the complex and inter-connected contemporary world which constrains national governments in many ways (as you will see in Chapter 8). One of the most striking examples of the impact of contrasting leadership decisions concerned government policy on HIV/AIDS in South Africa and Uganda in the late 1990s and early 2000s. Both countries had a very high prevalence of HIV/AIDS. In South Africa, President Thabo Mbeki denied the link between HIV and AIDS as part of a national political struggle over the control of information and resistance to Western dominance of science (Schneider 2002). His government refused to support the purchase of anti-retroviral drugs for the treatment of people with AIDS. In Uganda, President Yoweri Museveni was widely credited with a quite different policy of openly discussing HIV/AIDS and inviting all groups to help develop a national response to the epidemic. Although the wider political environment in Uganda particularly favoured such a stance (e.g. there was no major tourist industry to be harmed by openness), the President himself contributed decisively to the direction of policy (Parkhurst 2001).

The contribution of the bureaucracy

The appointed officials who administer the system of government are referred to as civil or public servants. Although referred to as 'servants' of the politicians, their role extends beyond simply serving to managing policy processes in many areas of policy. There are far too many functions for the executive to discharge more than a fraction of the highest profile ones, delegating many to bureaucrats to carry out in their name. Civil servants also have influence because of their expertise, knowledge and experience. While ministers and governments may come and go, most of the bureaucrats remain to maintain the system of government. Even in countries such as the USA and most Latin American countries where top civil servants change when the ruling government changes, most public servants' jobs are unaffected. In countries like Britain, New Zealand and Australia there is a strong tradition of civil service independence of politicians and neutrality. New governments and new ministers are clearly more dependent on their officials for information, if only until they are familiar with what is happening in their field of responsibility and with the detail of how the system of government works, but they may also be suspicious of officials who until recently had served a government led by their opponents and less likely to accept their views on policy options.

The power of the bureaucracy vis-à-vis politicians differs from country to country, over time and from policy sector to sector. In Korea, Japan, Singapore and France, the civil service has high status, a neutral professional ethos and a clear mandate to provide independent advice to politicians. After a long period of training, civil servants form a homogeneous, well-informed group and pursue a life-long career in government.

Activity 5.4

How does the civil service in your country compare with those discussed in the preceding paragraph? You might want to structure your answer by writing a few sentences in answer to the following questions:

- What is the social status of civil servants?
- How well is the civil service paid?
- What training do civil servants receive?
- How expert are they in different policy fields?
- Is being a civil servant a career or more like any other job?
- Does the civil service have a tradition of providing independent advice to ministers or is it more an extension of the executive?
- Do senior positions in the civil service change when the government changes?
- What are the implications of change or continuity for policy development?
- Are staff in the health care system part of the civil service or separate?
- How do you think your civil service could be improved, particularly in relation to the health system?

To answer these questions, you may have to do some research of your own. There may be a department of central government or an agency that controls the civil service or there may be descriptions in books on government in your country that discuss the civil service specifically.

Feedback

Looking around the world, it becomes apparent that countries like Korea with strong bureaucracies are exceptional. In many countries, particularly poorer ones, with corruption, low wages and lack of infrastructure, bureaucracies often do not have the capability to deal with the problems the country faces. In such settings, the executive and its political supporters tend to use the government machinery and policy to pursue their own interests, at the expense of the needs and well-being of the majority of the population. In other words, they lack the twin features of *autonomy* and *capacity* discussed earlier in the chapter.

Even in countries with a much better equipped civil service, the power of the bureaucracy depends on its internal organization within a particular sector. Thus, if in the health sector, there are a small number of institutions and a small number of officials in each body who have some decision making power independent of politicians, bureaucrats will tend to be influential in certain health policy processes. By contrast, if there are a large number of agencies each with some authority, no one group of officials is likely to be influential on a specific issue and politicians will most likely have more direct influence over a wider range of policy areas.

Similarly, the influence of the civil service on policy formation also depends on the extent to which it has a monopoly over advice reaching ministers. Thus in Britain, Australia and New Zealand where traditionally the civil service was the main source of advice to ministers, governments have acted in the past 25 years to widen the range of sources of advice to ministers, for example, by developing policy and strategy units within government staffed by a mixture of political advisers and handpicked civil servants, and by opening up civil service posts to outside applicants. In this way, the boundaries between the civil service and the political sphere together with other walks of life such as business and academia have been deliberately blurred, and political appointees have grown in number and influence within the government process.

Finally, the influence of the bureaucrats depends on the type of policy at issue. Major policies (macro economic policy, for example), and/or those with a high profile and ideological significance (i.e. 'high' politics) are more likely to be driven by the senior politicians. If the civil service opposes a policy direction, then, if the government persists, by definition, ministers will be leading and the civil service role will be confined to ensuring that the wishes of the government are implemented. By contrast, on issues of 'low politics' – dealing with problems relating to the day-to-day working of institutions – civil servants tend to have greater influence in shaping the issue and offering solutions.

The position of the Ministry of Health

The bureaucracy is not a seamless organization. It is divided into departments or ministries, as well as other agencies with specific functions. Indeed, specialization is a feature of bureaucracies. Each of these organizations will have its own interests and ways of operating. Most obviously, the Ministry of Finance is responsible for ensuring that resources are allocated between different ministries in line with government priorities whereas an individual ministry such as health is responsible for ensuring that the needs of their health sector is properly represented when decisions are made. Some conflict of view is inevitable as each ministry argues for what it regards as its proper share of the government's budget. In addition, different ministries relate to different 'policy communities' or 'policy networks' (i.e. more or less organized clusters of groups inside and outside government in a particular sector trying to influence government policy) which can vary in complexity and scale, thereby shaping the way ministries function. Furthermore, individual ministries are internally divided, often along functional, technical or policy lines. Thus, a Ministry of Health might have divisions relating to the main contours of the health system such as hospitals, primary health care and public health, as well as medical, nursing and other professional advisory departments which cut across these divisions. There are also likely to be regional or district levels of the ministry or separate health authorities which may not play a large part in policy identification and formulation, but are important for policy implementation, depending on the extent of decentralization in the government system (more on this in Chapter 7).

Ministries have differing status. Where in the informal hierarchy of ministries does the Ministry of Health usually sit? In low income countries, the Health Ministry is often seen as low down in the hierarchy, well behind the Ministries of Finance, Defence, Foreign Affairs, Industry, Planning and Education, despite having a relatively large budget because of the workforce, health centres and hospitals which it may pay for.

Activity 5.5

Why do you think that the Ministry of Health and health policy is often relatively low down the hierarchy of status and attention in low income countries? Do you think that this is always justifiable?

Feedback

Explanations for the low status include the fact that such countries frequently face very pressing economic problems, the solutions to which are generally seen as lying in reforming and stimulating the economy rather than developing the health system. The economists in dominant Ministries of Finance frequently regard spending on health as 'consumption' (i.e. current spending which produces only current benefits) and tend not to see it as 'investment' (i.e. spending now to produce a stream of benefits into the future) to which they give higher priority (Commission on Macroeconomics and Health 2001). Their approach traditionally has been to try to restrict consumption as far as possible in favour of investment in fields such as infrastructure (roads, harbours, drainage schemes) with a view to making longer-term economic gains. However, it is increasingly being recognized that wisely targeted spending on health improvement (e.g. HIV prevention and AIDS treatment in high prevalence countries) can be a worthwhile investment, especially in countries with low life expectancy, and should be seen as part of economic policy since a healthier workforce is highly likely to be more productive.

Despite these insights, it is still true to say that health issues tend to come to the attention of the cabinet only at times of crisis (see Chapter 4). Although there may be crises about epidemics of disease such as cholera, malaria, TB, AIDS or SARS, economic crises are more likely to force discussions about health issues such as how to pay for expensive medicines or new technologies against a background of falling government revenues. It is very common in such circumstances to see intensive discussion of proposals to introduce user fees into free clinics. Often, these fees are very unpopular, but more importantly, blanket fee increases tend to reduce access among the neediest groups in society.

Relations with other ministries

In all countries, not just those where the Ministry of Health is of low status, other ministries whose policies affect health tend to be absorbed with their own sectoral policy issues rather than concerned to contribute to a government-wide set of health policies. Thus departments responsible for sectors such as natural resources, agriculture and education, most notably, have their own goals to pursue and are accountable for meeting them. As a result, they may not give high priority to the human health implications of their decisions. Many countries set up inter-sectoral (cross-departmental) bodies in the 1970s for the development and implementation of health policy (e.g. a national health council in Sri Lanka) or across the whole of government (e.g. the Central Policy Review Staff in Britain) in response to a growing awareness of such problems. More recently, many countries have set up national committees or task forces in an attempt to respond to the HIV/AIDS epidemic in a coherent way across all relevant agencies of government. Despite these continuing efforts, most policies tend to be pursued sectorally, reflecting the over-riding structure of separate government ministries. Typically, ministries of agriculture continued to promote crops (e.g. tobacco) and forms of husbandry (e.g. intensive stock rearing) with the sole aim of maximizing profits without serious consideration of the potentially negative effects on health and nutrition. Many governments today continue to strive for more integrated or 'joined up' institutions and processes for policy formulation and implementation but fragmentation within the policy process is far easier to identify than to rectify. In many ways, it is perpetuated by other objectives such as raising the level of expertise within government which can lead to greater specialization and greater needs for better systems of coordination.

Activity 5.6

Which government policy decisions in your country would have been different if their health implications had been taken into account?

Feedback

Your answer will obviously be specific to your country and your experience. Typically, policies such as large environmental projects (e.g. dams or highways) are not thoroughly assessed for their health consequences either directly or indirectly. For example, better and faster roads, unless well engineered with a view to reducing pedestrian injuries and deaths, can have major adverse consequences, especially for children. Such effects are often not well understood or not weighed in the balance against other costs and benefits. If they were, policy decisions might be different. Another example of policy that might well have been different if the health implications had been taken into account relates to government subsidies for the production of tobacco in a number of low and middle income countries. The costs of the negative health effects of consuming locally produced tobacco can outweigh the economic gains from production and exports.

While health should not always be the predominant goal of government decisions since there are many other objectives that contribute to the well-being of populations and to better health (e.g. higher educational attainment), it is important for the full range of consequences of major policy decisions to be taken into account as far as possible. In the late 1990s, international agencies such as the Organisation for Economic Co-operation and Development (OECD) promoted a more 'outcomes-focused' approach as a way to encourage better coordination of the actions of different ministries and agencies, and greater attention to all the outcomes of policies. The idea is that all ministries should be required to show how they are contributing to improving the outcomes which the government values most, such as improving literacy and infant health, by the actions they take in their individual sectors. So, in principle, under such a system of reporting and accountability, the ministries of education and health should be more likely to take into account the inter-dependence of their activities since children's health is important for their educational attainment, and vice versa. Similarly, the ministry of transport would be required to report its contribution to child health by demonstrating that its road schemes were designed to protect pedestrians as well as ensure the smooth flow of traffic.

Professional versus other sources of advice

A notable feature of Ministries of Health lies in the relatively high status of their principal advisers. They employ and purchase technical advice from doctors, nurses, pharmacists and other professionals. In many countries, the divisional heads are mostly health professionals, particularly doctors. Potential conflict between high status professionals and other bureaucrats is clearly possible. If the Minister of Health is a doctor, there may be some dissonance between professional and other goals. For example, the minister may be reluctant to initiate reforms which threaten the clinical freedom of doctors. There may be a tendency in policy thinking to see medical care as the main means of health improvement to the neglect of public health measures such as immunization or better water supplies.

Activity 5.7

Now that you have read about the main institutions of government, prepare a description of the government system in your country. The following questions will help you organize your account:

1 How many political parties are there? How do elections work? Do the parties prepare manifestos setting out what they would like to do if they were to be elected to government? Were their views presented on television, radio or in the newspapers? Does the current government have its political party office separate from the government? Is the current government made up of one or more political parties?
2 Is the system of government unitary or federal, i.e. are there regions or provinces which have substantial freedom to organize their own affairs (e.g. in health services) or are all the main decisions taken at national level and simply carried out at lower levels?
3 Is the national legislature uni- or bicameral? Are all members elected or are some appointed? If so, who appoints them? How much influence does the legislature have compared with the executive (cabinet)? Can its members question or challenge the decisions of the president and/or prime minister?
4 Who makes up the executive in your country? If there is a president and a prime minister, what are their respective roles? Is the executive entirely separate from the

legislature or do members of the executive have to come from the legislature? How strong is the chief executive (president or prime minister) compared with other ministers in the executive?

5 What are the powers of the judiciary in relation to the actions of the executive and legislature? How independent are the judges of the governing party or parties? Is there a written constitution? Is it enforced by the courts?

6 Overall, what sort of government system would you say you have in your country? Refer to the types of political regimes described in Chapter 2.

Feedback

If you find that there are important gaps in your knowledge, you need to consult reference books and/or government publications to complete your description. The United Nations also publishes information on the government systems of countries around the world.

Activity 5.8

Now that you have an understanding of the wider government system in your country, it is time to sketch out the main organizations of government that comprise the health system. The following questions should help you structure your account:

1 Is there a Minister of Health at national level? What is the scope of his or her responsibilities? Is the Minister of Health in the cabinet? Is the post regarded as an attractive one for politicians?

2 Is there a national Ministry of Health? How does it relate to the minister and to the legislature? What are its responsibilities? Where do its resources come from? How is the ministry staffed (i.e. by generalists, specialists or a mix) and how is it organized internally? Is there a hierarchy of national, regional, district and local functions and activities in the ministry, or does the ministry just operate at national level (e.g. setting the general direction of policy)?

3 Are there other national organizations relevant to health policy? What does each do? How do these bodies relate either to the Minister or Ministry of Health?

4 If there are advisers or experts from international agencies involved at national level, what do they do and how do they relate to the Ministry of Health?

5 How is the health system organized below the national level?

6 How do you think each of the organizational features you have described above affects the way that health policy decisions are made and implemented in your country?

7 How does the wider government system which you summarized in the previous activity shape the way that the Ministry of Health and health system operate?

You will probably find it helpful to draw a diagram of how the different bodies relate to one another. This is known as an *organogram* or organizational chart. It is a convenient way of summarizing a lot of organizational information relatively simply. Typically, the chart shows lines of authority and accountability between different levels in a hierarchy.

Arrows can also be used to show how resources and information flow between bodies, as well as consultative and advisory relationships. Figure 5.1 is an example of an organizational chart for the health system of New Zealand.

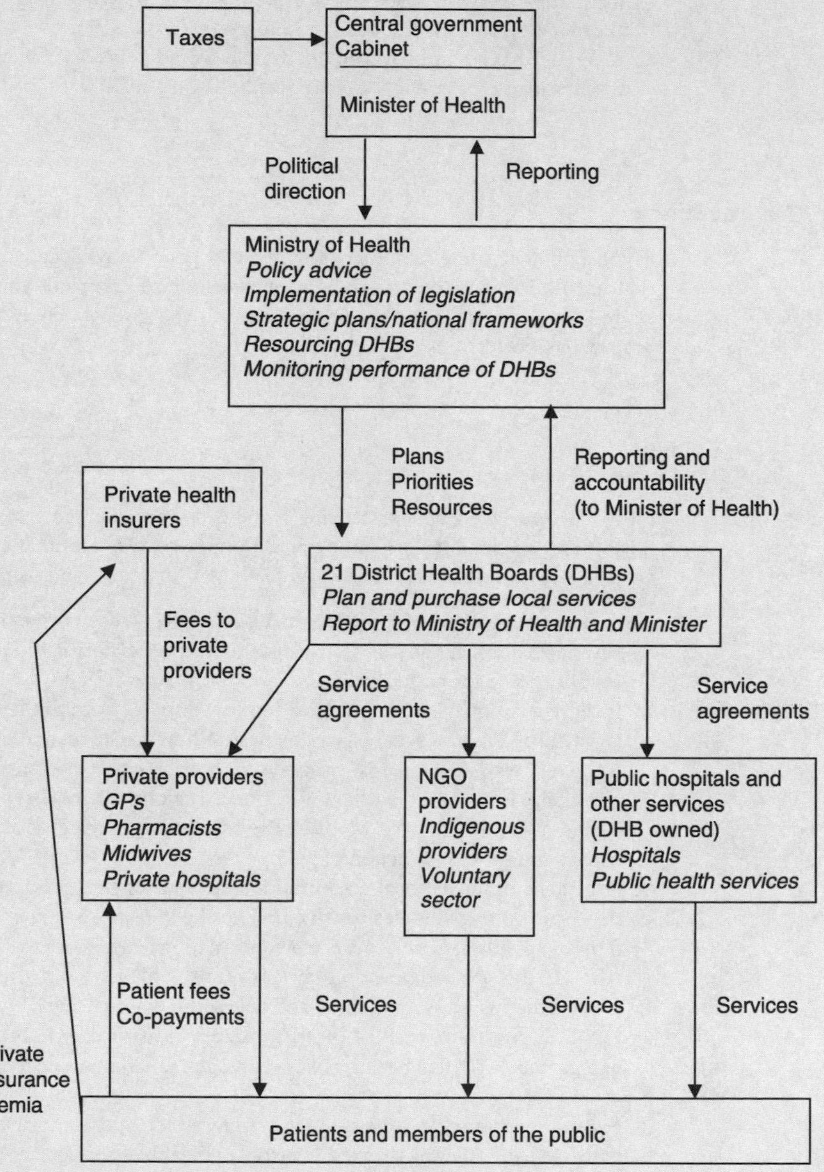

Figure 5.1 Organogram of New Zealand's health system, 2004

Source: Adapted from Ministry of Health (2004)

Feedback

Clearly your answer to these questions will depend on your country of choice.

It is important to be aware organizations charts are a highly abstract picture of the system and can be misleading. The way a system works in practice may not correspond very closely to the way it is presented formally on an organizational diagram. The organizational chart perhaps most closely reflects the rational model of the policy process (see Chapter 2). One of the aims of this book is to show that while this may be an aspiration, it is rarely an accurate depiction of the policy process. The previous chapter on how issues get onto the policy agenda and the following two chapters on the role of interest groups and on policy implementation show that the health policy process is strongly influenced by groups outside the formal decision making structure of the health system. In addition, the hierarchical, 'top-down' way in which systems are typically represented often fails to capture the way in which front-line staff can play a critical role in whether, and if so, how policies developed at higher levels are implemented.

Summary

Although most countries have legislatures which ostensibly make policy, their main function is normally one of debate and scrutiny of proposals coming from the executive. In most sectors of policy, the executive (ministers) and the bureaucracy (civil servants) usually have the resources and position to control what gets on to the policy agenda and is formulated into policy, with the legislators in a subsidiary role, particularly in parliamentary systems. Where politicians change frequently, a permanent bureaucracy may have very significant power in policy formulation, but, in general, politicians initiate the formulation of policies in areas of major political concern ('high' politics).

References

Commission on Macroeconomics and Health (2001). *Macroeconomics and Health: Investing in Health for Economic Development*. Report of the Commission on Macroeconomics and Health. Geneva: World Health Organisation

Healey J and Robinson M (1992). *Democracy, Governance and Economic Policy*. London: Overseas Development Institute

Howlett M and Ramesh M (2003). *Studying Public Policy: Policy Cycles and Policy Subsystems*. Don Mills, Ontario: Oxford University Press

Ministry of Health (2004). *The Health and Independence Report 2004: Director-General of Health's Report on the State of Public Health*. Wellington: Ministry of Health

OECD (1997). *In Search of Results: Performance Management Practices*. Paris: OECD

Parkhurst JO (2001). The crisis of AIDS and the politics of response: the case of Uganda. *International Relations* 15: 69–87

Schneider H (2002). On the fault-line: the politics of AIDS policy in contemporary South Africa. *African Studies* 61: 145–67

Secretary of State for Health (2000). *The NHS Plan: A Plan for Investment, a Plan for Reform*. Cm 4818-I. London: The Stationery Office

Tuohy CH (2004). Health care reform strategies in cross-national context: implications for primary care in Ontario. In Wilson R, Shortt SED and Dorland J (eds) *Implementing Primary Care Reform: Barriers and Facilitators*. Montreal and Kingston: McGill-Queen's University Press, pp. 73–96

Wanless D and Health Trends Review Team (2002). *Securing Our Future Health: Taking a Long-Term View*. London: HM Treasury

6 Interest groups and the policy process

Overview

The previous chapter focused on the institutions of government and how government policy makers are at the heart of the policy process. But neither politicians nor civil servants operate in a sealed system, especially not in well-functioning democracies. To use the terminology of the 'policy triangle' in Chapter 1, there are many other *actors* in the policy process. Governments often consult external groups to see what they think about issues and to obtain information. In turn, groups attempt to influence ministers and civil servants. In most countries, there are a growing number of interest or pressure groups that want to influence government thinking on policy or the provision of services. They use a range of tactics to get their voices heard including building relationships with those in power, mobilizing the media, setting up formal discussions or providing the political opposition with criticisms of government policy. Some interest groups are far more influential than others: in the health field, the medical profession is still the most significant interest outside government in most countries.

Learning objectives

After working through this chapter, you will be better able to:

- **explain what an interest or pressure group is**
- **classify the different types of interest or pressure groups**
- **describe the tactics used by different interest groups to get their voices heard**
- **appreciate the differential resources available to different sorts of interest groups**
- **identify how interest groups and government actors form around particular fields of policy**
- **account for the increasing prominence of civil society groups in public policy**

Key terms

Cause group Interest or pressure group whose main goal is to promote a particular issue or cause.

Civil society That part of society between the private sphere of the family or household and the sphere of government.

Civil society group Group or organization which is outside government and beyond the family/household. It may or may not be involved in public policy (e.g. sports clubs are civil society organizations, but not primarily pressure groups).

Discourse (epistemic) community Policy community marked by shared political values, and a shared understanding of a problem, its definition and its causes.

Insider group Interest groups who pursue a strategy designed to win themselves the status of legitimate participants in the policy process.

Interest (pressure) group Type of civil society group that attempts to influence the policy process to achieve specific goals.

Interest network Policy community based on some common material interest.

Iron triangle Small, stable and exclusive policy community usually involving executive agencies, legislative committees and interest groups (e.g. defence procurement).

Issue network Loose, unstable network comprising a large number of members and usually serving a consultative function.

Non-governmental organization (NGO) Originally, any not-for-profit organization outside government but increasingly used to refer to structured organizations providing services.

Outsider group Interest groups who have either failed to attain insider status or deliberately chosen a path of confrontation with government.

Peak (apex) association Interest group composed of, and usually representative of, other interest groups.

Policy community (sub-system) Relatively stable network of organizations and individuals involved in a recognizable part of wider public policy such as health policy. Within each of these fields, there will be identifiable sub-systems, such as for mental health policy, with their own policy community.

Sectional group Interest group whose main goal is to protect and enhance the interests of its members and/or the section of society it represents.

Social movement Loose grouping of individuals sharing certain views and attempting to influence others but without a formal organizational structure.

Introduction

In Chapter 2 you were introduced to the theory of pluralism, the view that power is widely dispersed throughout society such that no group holds absolute power. The pluralists were influential in drawing attention to the idea of the state arbitrating between competing interests as it develops policy. As a result, they focused on interest groups in order to explain how policy is shaped, arguing that, although there are elites, no elite dominates at all times. The sources of power such as information, expertise and money, are distributed non-cumulatively. While this may be true for routine matters of policy ('low politics'), pluralism has been criticized for not giving sufficient weight to the fact that major economic decisions, which are part of 'high politics', tend to be taken by a small elite in order to preserve the existing economic regime. In these circumstances, pluralism is clearly 'bounded' in that those interests wishing to replace a capitalist system of economic organization with a socialist one would not be invited to take part in the policy process. This chapter is principally concerned with the way interest groups attempt to influence routine matters of policy.

Pluralists have also been criticized for failing to recognize major differences between countries, particularly the fact that in many low income countries, there was little sign until comparatively recently of national interest groups putting pressure on governments and opening up the policy process to non-governmental influences. Traditionally, in these countries, extra-governmental influences have tended to derive from personal and family connections in which ministers and officials are expected to use their position to enhance the situation of members of their families or tribes. However, in the 1980s and 1990s there was growing evidence of interest group activity in such places. For example, the number of NGOs registered with the government of Nepal rose from 220 in 1990 to 1,210 in 1993. In Tunisia, there were 5,186 NGOs registered in 1991 compared with only 1,886 in 1988 (Hulme and Edwards 1997). In part, this growth was due to less authoritarian and elitist forms of government behaviour in a number of countries and, in part, it was due to a growing recognition by donor agencies of the useful role which organizations outside government could play in delivering services, in supporting policy and institutional reform, and in encouraging governments to be more accountable to their people. As a result, donors provided more funds to these organizations in low income countries. In the AIDS field, for example, Brazil received a substantial World Bank loan in 1992 which was used to make grants to 600 NGOs providing AIDS service organizations which, in turn, pressurized the government to provide universal access to anti-retroviral treatment and infection prophylaxis.

In high income countries, interest groups have long played a significant role in the political system, particularly worker and employer associations.

Activity 6.1

Before reading any further, take a few minutes to think about your understanding of what is meant by 'interest groups'. Write your own definition and a list of the groups that could come under the heading of 'interest groups' in relation to health policy.

Feedback

At its simplest, an 'interest group' promotes or represents a particular part of society (e.g. people suffering from blindness or manufacturers of pharmaceuticals) or stands for a particular cause (e.g. environmentalism or free trade). Different types of interest group are discussed later in the chapter.

Your list of 'interest groups' involved in health policy is likely to have contained organizations and groups such as those representing:

- staff, such as the medical, nursing and the allied health professions (e.g. physiotherapy, speech therapy)

- providers, such as hospital associations
- insurers such as sickness funds
- payers, such as employers' associations
- different groups of patients
- suppliers, such as pharmaceutical companies and medical equipment manufacturers

You may have wondered how different labels for organizations outside the formal system of government such as NGO, 'civic society group', 'interest group' and 'pressure group' related to one another. You will now try to clarify these different terms. Refer to the notes of your own definition as you go through this and modify them, if necessary.

Interest groups and civil society groups

'Interest group' is simply another term for 'pressure group'. While there are varying definitions of interest groups, most writers would agree on the following features:

- voluntary – people or organizations choose to join them
- aim to achieve some desired goals
- do not attempt to infiltrate the process of decision making to the extent of becoming part of the formal government process

Unlike political parties that are also voluntary and goal-oriented, pressure groups do not plan to take formal political power. Sometimes pressure groups evolve into political parties and then become involved in policy making from within government like the German Green Party which began life as an environmental pressure group, but most are organized groups outside government, even if some of them have very close relationships with government (as you will see in the discussion of 'policy communities' below).

Today it is common to describe interest groups as existing in *civil society*, meaning that they are located in the part of society that lies between the private space of the family or household and the public sphere of the government. Hence, the term 'civil society group' is sometimes used synonymously with interest group, though public policy issues can be very peripheral to the identity of some civil society groups (e.g. sports clubs will only very occasionally take a position on an issue of public policy when it risks impinging on their sporting activities, whereas other groups are constantly in campaigning mode). As a result, not all civil society groups are necessarily interest groups. Civil society organizations represent a wider range of organizations (Figure 6.1).

NGOs form the most familiar part of civil society. The term NGO originally referred to any not-for-profit organization outside government but more recently has taken on the more specific meaning of a relatively structured organization with a headquarters and paid staff working in fields such as client advocacy or service delivery, in many cases providing a service that might have been provided directly by the state at an earlier stage. Many NGOs retain a desire to influence public policy and can also act as pressure groups. Usually, 'civil society group' has positive connotations, implying that such groups are a sign of a vigorous, healthy, non-authoritarian society, whereas, for a politician or public official to call an organization a 'pressure group' can, on occasions, be a coded way of implying that

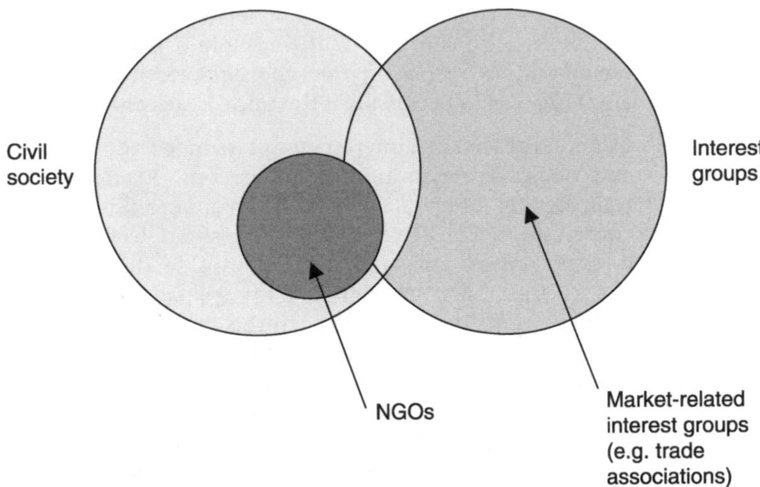

Figure 6.1 Civil society organizations, interest groups and NGOs

Note: Not to scale

it is narrowly focused, imbalanced in its point of view, illegitimate, or even a nuisance. However, not all civil society groups are necessarily good for society. For example, organized criminal gangs are part of civil society.

If not all civil society groups are necessarily to be seen as interest groups, then there is also some debate as to whether it is accurate to call *all* interest groups civil society groups. Some writers would exclude interest groups related to market activities (i.e. economic organizations such as trade associations) from civil society, arguing that civil society is 'a sphere located between the state and market: a buffer zone strong enough to keep both state and market in check, thereby preventing each from becoming too powerful and dominating' (Giddens 2001). Figure 6.1 is drawn from this perspective. Presumably, then, civil society lies in the social space not occupied by the family/household, the state and the market.

Interest groups may start simply as a group of people concerned about a particular issue with little or no formal organization. When a large number of such groups get involved with the same issue, sociologists talk of them as forming a '*social movement*'. For example, the series of popular protests against the British Labour government's policy of military intervention in Iraq in 2003 and 2004 was a loose, spontaneous linking of people to resist the direction of government policy. It had minimal organization and appeared to be coordinated in large part by the relaying of text messages between mobile phones. Had the anti-war movement developed a more formal set of structures, it would probably have fragmented into a number of different pressure groups with somewhat different goals.

Different types of interest groups

Political scientists are fond of classifying the great diversity of interest groups into a number of analytical types. Perhaps the most important distinction is between: *sectional* groups whose main goal is to protect and enhance the interests of their members and/or of the section of society they proclaim to stand for; and *cause* groups whose main goal is to promote a particular issue or cause and whose membership is open to anyone who supports the cause without necessarily having anything to gain personally if the cause is successful.

Examples of sectional interest groups include trade unions, employers' associations and bodies representing the professions. Examples of cause groups include campaigning groups such as those on abortion, human rights, environment and conservation. Crudely, sectional groups tend to stand for producer interests (e.g. doctors, nurses, etc.) and cause groups tend to stand for consumer interests (e.g. organizations campaigning for people suffering from particular diseases, or for patients' rights in general) though this distinction should not be exaggerated. For example, an organization representing disabled people is arguably both a sectional and a cause group. It promotes a cause, namely, improving the position of disabled people in society, but also stands for the self-interest of a section of society, namely, people with disabilities. Sometimes sectional groups can attract supporters who are concerned about an underlying principle rather having a personal stake in the presenting issue. For example, libertarians might join a sectional group devoted to protecting people's freedom to smoke tobacco in public places not because they wished to smoke, but because they believed that the state should not interfere with individual freedom except in very extreme circumstances.

Sectional groups

Sectional groups are usually able to bargain with governments because they typically provide a particular productive role in the economy. Their influence with government largely depends on how important government thinks this role is. On occasions, they can challenge government policy, if they do not like what governments propose. For example, well-organized trade unions, particularly in the public sector, can persuade their members to withdraw their labour, harming both the economy and the reputation of the government, as well as withdrawing their financial support for political parties (mostly parties on the political left). Obviously the power of interest groups such as trade unions depends on factors such as the structure of the economy (e.g. workers in a large number of small enterprises are far harder to organize than those in a small number of large firms), the structure of wage bargaining (in a more decentralized system, the power of unions is generally less than in more centralized systems), the number of unions, whether they are ideologically unified and how well funded they are. The media can be regarded as a special form of sectional interest with a particularly important role in agenda setting as well as in selling its services to maximize its profits.

In most sectors of policy, including health, producer interest groups tend to have the closest contacts with government and exercise the strongest influence, while consumer groups tend to have less influence, principally because their cooperation is less central to the implementation of policies. In health policy, the medical profession was traditionally regarded as occupying a dominant position not just in controlling the delivery of health care (particularly who is permitted to carry out which tasks), but also in shaping public health policy. In Western countries, physicians controlled and regulated their own training and day-to-day clinical work. The scope of practice of other health workers such as nurses depended on the consent of doctors and their role was seen primarily as supporting doctors rather than acting independently. In the eyes of the public, the medical profession was seen as the most authoritative source of advice on health-related matters whether at the individual, community or national levels. Health care systems tended to be organized in deference to the preferences of medical interest groups (e.g. systems of reimbursement in public systems that mirrored the fee-for-service arrangements in private practice). However, from the 1980s there was a significant, multi-pronged challenge to the medical profession's privileged status.

Activity 6.2

What have been the major challenges to the dominant position of doctors in health care and policy over the past 25 years?

Feedback

Your answer probably included a number of different challenges coming from different sources. Here are some of the challenges you may have identified:

- The so-called 'medical model' of disease which explains ill-health in terms of biological factors and the appropriate response in individual, curative terms was challenged by the 'primary care approach' which emphasized intersectoral action beyond the confines of individual treatment and of the health care system, and community involvement and control of health care facilities to make them more responsive to local needs.
- There was a growing recognition that patients themselves had expertise in relation to their own ill-health, particularly where this was chronic, that could contribute powerfully to better outcomes as long as it was recognized by doctors and patients were permitted to share responsibility with professionals.
- Nurses and other health care workers became better educated and governments moved to widen the range of clinical tasks they are permitted to undertake, sometimes at the expense of doctors.
- Governments attempted to control doctors' use of resources by imposing budget caps, limiting the range of drugs that they could prescribe, or restricting patient referral to the least cost or most efficient providers.
- Governments and insurers brought in stronger management and encouraged competition (e.g. between public hospitals and between public and private providers) in order to make medical services more responsive and efficient.
- Governments developed systems for assessing the quality of clinical care which were not under the direct control of the medical profession and promoted evidence-based medicine rather than an approach relying on precedent and individual clinical judgement.

All these challenges could be detected in government policies in Britain in the 1980s and 1990s. Governments not only introduced policies which were actively opposed by the medical establishment such as the 'internal market' in the NHS in 1991, they also contrived to split the profession, thereby weakening its ability to resist change. For example, in one strand of the internal market reforms of 1991, general practitioners were offered the opportunity of holding their own budgets for their patients' elective hospital care as well as for their pharmaceutical costs. A substantial minority were keen to do so, making it difficult for the doctors' trade union to sustain its opposition to the policy. Had the policy been imposed on all GPs, it would most likely have failed.

While it is undoubtedly true that medical interests have been challenged and have lost some influence in Western countries, this has mainly been a loss of some clinical autonomy and monopoly at the service delivery level. The knowledge and authority with which medical organizations speak is still a key resource enabling them to influence wider health policy (Johnson 1995).

In many low income countries, professional associations have not played such an important role in health policy (Walt 1994). In part, this is because most publicly paid-for health care and preventive activity is undertaken not by doctors but by nurses and community health workers in these settings. The medical profession largely serves the small urban elites through private practice. Doctors are influential in public health policy in such countries, but mainly as civil servants in the Ministry of Health as health ministers rather than through the medical associations.

Cause groups

Cause groups aim to promote an issue that is not necessarily specific to the members of the group themselves, although it can be. For example, disabled people or people living with AIDS may form a pressure group to shape policy directly related to themselves. On the other hand, people from all walks of life with a wide range of beliefs come together in organizations such as Greenpeace devoted to global conservation of species or Amnesty International which highlights human rights' abuses all over the world, or Médecins Sans Frontières (MSF) which is devoted to organizing humanitarian intervention in war zones.

It is generally assumed, somewhat naïvely, that cause groups arise spontaneously through the actions of unconnected individuals based on their beliefs. However, it is important to be aware that some pressure groups are actually 'front' groups which have been, and set up at arm's length from corporate interests as a way of getting their views into the civil society debate in a seemingly more persuasive way. The public relations arms of large corporations and trade associations reason that their messages are far more likely to be listened to by the public if they are articulated by apparently unconnected interest groups. Thus the Global Climate Coalition campaigned against the 1997 Kyoto Protocol to the UN Framework Convention on Climate Change, which limits the emission of greenhouse gases on scientific and social grounds, without it being immediately apparent to the casual observer that the Coalition was funded by the oil and motor industries. Similarly, the tobacco industry supports libertarian organizations in many countries devoted to promoting the human rights of smokers to smoke without hindrance from government regulation and the food and industry funds seemingly independent research bodies such as the International Life Sciences Institute and the World Sugar Research Organisation.

In the past 25 years in Western countries, membership of cause groups has risen and membership of political parties has tended to fall. Political scientists argue that this is a result of a growing disillusionment with conventional Left–Right party politics and with the seeming remoteness of representatives in a democratic system, especially among younger people. It is also a function of people's concern about large single issues such as environmental conservation that have not been given high priority by conventional political parties.

Activity 6.3

What are the main resources that interest groups have to bring about the change that they desire? Think of a range of different interest groups that you are familiar with and list their attributes and resources.

Feedback

The resources that interest groups can mobilize vary widely. Some of the resources you may have listed include:

- their members – the larger the number of members, all other things equal, the more influence an interest group is likely to have. Interest groups composed of other organizations, particularly where they are representative of these other associations (known as 'peak' or 'apex' associations), are particularly likely to have more influence and often draw on a wide range of skills, knowledge and contacts from within their constituent organizations.
- their level of funding and resources – funding affects all aspects of an interest group's activities such as the ability to hire professional staff to organize campaigns, prepare critiques of government policy, contribute to political parties, organize rallies and demonstrations, and so on. This explains, in large part, why health producer interest groups tend to be better organized than consumer groups since their members are often prepared to pay large subscriptions to ensure that their key economic interests are well represented.
- their knowledge about their area of concern – some of this information and understanding may be unavailable from any other source, for example, a government may be dependent on a commercial interest group for access to information about the financial impact of a proposed policy on its members
- their persuasive skills in building public support for particular positions or policies by stimulating activity by others, such as the mass media
- their contacts and relations with policy makers, officials, ministers, opposition parties and the media
- the sanctions, if any, at their disposal – these could range from embarrassing the government in international fora or the mass media to organizing consumer boycotts harming the domestic economy or protracted industrial action.

Strategies and relations to the state: 'insider' and 'outsider' groups

Interest groups can also be analysed in terms of how far they are recognized or legitimized by governments which, in turn, relates to their aims and their strategies. Grant (1984) identified two basic categories in this respect – *insider* and *outsider* groups. Insider groups are groups which are still not officially part of the machinery of government but are regarded as legitimate by government policy makers, are consulted regularly and are expected to play by the 'rules of the game'. For example, if they accept an invitation to sit on a government committee, they will respect the confidentiality of the discussions that take place there until ministers are ready to make a statement about the direction of policy. Insider groups thus become closely involved in testing policy ideas and in the development of their field. Typically, in health policy, producer groups such as medical and nursing associations expect to be consulted or directly involved in policy developments and frequently are, even if they do not always get their own way.

In the UK, the Association of the British Pharmaceutical Industry (ABPI) has insider status with the Department of Health on the grounds that the government is both concerned to promote the UK pharmaceutical industry and to ensure that safe and effective medicines are available at the earliest opportunity to patients. There are regular meetings between the industry, senior officials and ministers. The ABPI has also recruited retired civil servants to help it negotiate with government over drug regulation and prices.

Outsider groups, by contrast, are either organizations that reject a close involvement in government processes on strategic grounds or have been unable to gain a reputation as legitimate participants in the policy process. Perhaps the most high profile outsider groups in the contemporary health field are anti-abortion and anti-vivisection organizations because of the vehemence of their views and their reputation for taking direct action against clinics, laboratories and sometimes those who work in them. One of the best known direct action groups was BUGA UP (Billboard Utilising Graffitists Against Unhealthy Promotions). Founded in 1979 in Sydney, Australia, it was notorious (or celebrated, depending on your point of view) for illegally defacing outdoor advertising of unhealthy products, particularly tobacco and alcohol. Its tactic was to alter tobacco advertisements to provide a critical commentary on the industry's promotions. 'Anyhow, Have a Winfield' was changed to 'Anyhow, it's a Minefield' or 'Man how I hate Winfield'. When members of BUGA UP were charged, they defended themselves by arguing that their actions were essential to prevent a greater harm from occurring (Chapman 1996).

Interest groups may shift their strategies over time. For example, in its early stages Greenpeace favoured direct action as a way of drawing attention to conservation issues. Most notably it disrupted the activities of whaling vessels. More recently, Greenpeace has adopted a less flamboyant and less confrontational strategy through scientifically based advocacy. In the process, it has closer relations with governments, though is probably not regarded as a full insider group. Groups that shift their strategies or positions are known as *thresholder* groups. Studies of the evolution of policy in the HIV/AIDS field in the USA and Britain clearly show how outsider groups played a key role in the early stages of the epidemic in using their knowledge about the syndrome to pressurize governments to take the topic seriously. Some of these same organizations became more closely involved in both policy and service delivery as circumstances changed and were able to accept insider status. Often an outsider group becomes an insider group through taking responsibility for delivering services paid for by government or international donors. History may be repeating itself in low income countries where outsider groups such as the Treatment Action Group in South Africa have been highlighting what they see as drug company profiteering from AIDS drugs and pressurizing government to permit the import of cheaper generic substitutes.

Activity 6.4

Obtain information on a number of health-related interest groups (perhaps in a field of health that you are interested in) and try to work out what sorts of strategies they are using, their range of activities and whether they could be regarded as insider, outsider or thresholder groups.

Feedback

The stance of an organization will not always be apparent from their literature, but there are some clues you can look for. For example, the slogans of an organization give an indication of its stance towards government. If the organization is 'fighting' for animal rights, it is more likely to be an 'outsider' group than one that claims to be 'working' for animal rights. Similarly, an organization that lists its main activities as organizing demonstrations and mobilizing the media is highly likely to be pursuing an 'outsider' influencing strategy, while an organization that describes its participation in government committees and consultations, or its links to elected representatives is far more likely to be following an 'insider' track.

Functions of interest groups

Taken together, the different types of interest groups indicate the range of functions that they can fulfil in society. Peterson (1999) argues that interest groups provide the following seven functions in society:

1. Participation – given that elections in democracies are both an infrequent and a highly indirect way for citizens to involve themselves in public issues, interest groups provide an alternative way for voters to get involved in politics and register their opinions to politicians.
2. Representation – where policy makers take into account the views of a range of interest groups, this normally widens the range of opinion under consideration.
3. Political education – provide a way for members to learn about the political process, for example, if they become office holders in an interest group.
4. Motivation – interest groups can draw new issues to the attention of governments, provide more information, change the way governments view issues and even develop new policy options through their scientific and political activities.
5. Mobilization – interest groups build pressure for action and support for new policies (e.g. by stimulating media interest in a topic).
6. Monitoring – increasingly, interest groups are assessing the performance and behaviour of governments, thereby contributing to the public accountability of leaders, for example, by seeing whether political promises are implemented. They are also increasingly involved in holding private corporations to account as national governments struggle to deal with the power of transnational businesses.

7 Provision – interest groups can use their knowledge of a particular patient group or area of policy to deliver services with or without government funding (e.g. missionary societies).

Interest groups are also increasingly involved in conducting or commissioning scientific research, providing technical advice and using legal action or the threat of legal action against governments and trans-national corporations to promote their point of view and force change in policy. For example, national and international civil society organizations played an important part in the legal action against the South African government which forced the government to concede the principle that anti-retroviral drugs should be made available universally. It remains to be seen whether this will be fully implemented.

Activity 6.5

Taking the list of seven functions plus the ones mentioned in the paragraph immediately above, find examples of interest groups in your country that carry out each of these activities. You may find that some organizations carry out many of these functions and others focus on just one. You can get this information from libraries, information centres, the Ministry of Health, newspapers, websites, annual reports, and so on.

Feedback

Larger interest groups tend to have a wider range of functions and ways of operating. For example, Oxfam, the British-based international anti-poverty NGO describes itself as 'a development, advocacy and relief agency working to put an end to poverty worldwide'. Its activities cover 'motivation', 'mobilization', 'monitoring' and 'provision' according to Peterson's typology as well as 'representation' in some of the 70 countries it works in. Smaller NGOs tend to have more focused goals and activities. For example, the Fred Hollows Foundation, based in Australia is an NGO devoted to working with local blindness prevention agencies in 29 countries to reduce unnecessary and avoidable blindness, with a primary focus on cataract. Thus, as with many NGOs, its main function is 'provision', including training local staff to deliver services and developing high quality, low cost technologies for eye care. However, in its work with indigenous Australians, it has extended its role to include advocacy ('motivation' and 'mobilization').

Relations between interest groups and government

Political scientists have observed that when it comes to policy formulation (as opposed to getting an issue onto the agenda in the first place) in health the participants (actors) are usually individuals and organizations with an enduring interest and knowledge of the field, even if, conceivably, a far wider range of actors could be involved. Who is involved, for what reasons and how their relationships are structured have been the subjects of much research on what have been referred to at various times as 'issue networks', 'policy networks', 'policy communities' and 'policy sub-systems'. The terminology and classifications can be confusing and even contradictory.

One way of understanding the formal and informal relationships between government and non-government (interest group) actors is to identify the various *policy sub-systems* or *policy communities* in which they interact. At its simplest, a policy sub-system or policy community is a recognizable sub-division of public policy making. In health policy, for example, mental health policy formulation is distinctively different from policy on environmental health issues and involves different actors. Some sub-systems, known as 'Iron Triangles', are small, very stable and highly exclusive, three-way sets of relationships usually between politicians, bureaucrats and a commercial interest. In the case of defence procurement, the triangle is constituted by government, suppliers and end users in the military. Other sub-systems are typically larger (i.e. involving more entities), more fluid and with less clear boundaries (e.g. family policy). The challenges in the 1980s and 1990s to the dominant position of the medical profession in health policy in Britain led to a shift from a more to a less closed policy community with an increase in the number of, and space given to, groups representing users, although consumer groups remained relatively weaker than professional groups. Marsh and Rhodes (1992) distinguish between 'policy communities' which they see as highly integrated networks marked by stability of relationships, exclusive narrow interests and persistence over time, and 'issue networks' which they see as loosely interdependent, unstable networks comprising a large number of members and usually serving a consultative function in relation to policy development.

The main point about a policy community is that there is sustained interaction between the participants through a web of formal and informal relationships (Lewis, forthcoming). In health policy, organizations and individuals representing practitioners (health professionals), users, the public, researchers (from laboratory sciences to the social sciences), commentators (journalists and policy analysts), businesses (drug companies, medical equipment manufacturers), hospitals and clinics, insurers, government officials, politicians and international organizations will be involved to differing degrees depending on the issue at stake. Policy communities are not necessarily consensual networks. Increasingly, health policy communities in Western countries are marked by conflicts between a range of powerful interests representing providers, the community and government.

Within a policy sub-system or community, two sets of motivation guide the actions of groups involved in policy formulation: knowledge or expertise and material interest (Howlett and Ramesh 2003). Thus membership of a *discourse community* (sometimes known as an 'epistemic community') is defined by shared political values and a shared understanding of a problem, its definition and its causes, though usually marked by detailed disagreements about policy responses, whereas an *interest network* is based on some common material interest (this distinction parallels the earlier distinction between 'cause' and 'sectional' interest groups, respectively). Both discourse communities and interest networks operate in the health policy sub-system since both ideas and interests play a part in policy change. When discourse and interest networks are closely linked, stable and cohesive, the policy sub-system will be less amenable to new policy options. Shared understandings of the nature of the policy problem and the range of feasible responses are difficult to change once established.

Activity 6.6

Think of a 'policy community' or looser 'issue network' around a specific health policy issue in your own country. It could be focused on any public health issue such as whether or not condom use should be promoted to prevent HIV infection. List those interest groups known to be or likely to be critical of the current policies in your country and those likely to be supportive.

Feedback

Obviously your answer will depend on the policy network and issue you considered. If you chose the issue of condom use and HIV, your answer will reflect the precise arrangements for HIV/AIDS control in your country. It might include the following:

- in support of policies to increase condom use: Ministry of Health, national health promotion agency (if it exists), interest groups of people living with HIV/AIDS and their supporters, employers (possibly, if aware of the economic costs of AIDS)
- against policies to increase condom use: some religious groups, some international donors (i.e. those promoting abstinence), sections of the media (others may be supportive), certain professional associations

Which sorts of interest groups are most influential?

Among interest groups, business interests are generally the most powerful in most areas of public policy, followed by labour interest groups. This is because both capital and labour are vital to the economic production process. In capitalist societies, ownership of the means of production is concentrated in the hands of business corporations rather than the state. As a result, business has huge power vis-à-vis government, particularly in the current globally interconnected environment in which corporations can potentially shift their capital and production relatively easily between countries if their interests are being harmed by government policies.

As Chapter 3 showed, there is a wide range of industrial and commercial interests in the health policy community. Even in health care systems where most services are provided in publicly owned and managed institutions, there will be extensive links with private sector actors who bring new ideas and practices into the public sector. However, provider professionals and workers as well as governments have an important influence on policy in addition to business interests. In the case of governments, this is because of the large contribution of public finance and provision in most (particularly high income) countries. In the case of the doctors, this is because of the medical monopoly over a body of knowledge allied to the control that they are able to exert over the market for their services. Consumer and public interests are also increasingly listened to and responded to.

Through a study of successive hospital reforms in New York in the 1960s and 1970s, the sociologist Robert Alford argued that beneath the surface interplay of a wide range of interests in the health care arena in high income countries, lay three *structural* or fundamental interests that defined how health care politics operated:

- the *professional monopolists* – the doctors and to a lesser extent the other health professionals whose dominant interests are served by the existing economic, social and political structures of government and the health system
- the *corporate rationalizers* – those who challenge the professional monopolists by attempting to implement strategies such as rational planning of facilities, efficient methods of health care delivery and modern management methods over medical judgement. These can be private insurers, governments as payers, health plans, employers wanting to curb the cost of insuring their workers, commercial hospital chains, etc.
- the *equal health advocates* and *community health advocates* – the wide range of relatively repressed cause and sectional interest groups lobbying for patients' rights, fairer access to health care for poor and marginalized groups and more attention to be given to the views of patients and populations in health care decision making

In the 1970s, when Alford published his theory of structural interests, consumers and the public had relatively little voice in shaping health care policies but managers and planners were increasingly trying to assert greater control over how systems were financed and organized. However, the professionals, led by doctors, remained dominant. In the past 25 years, corporate rationalizers and patient and community health advocates have increased their influence in health care policy making in high income countries. However, it is generally accepted that professionals are still the most influential single group, despite some loss of professional autonomy at the level of clinical practice, due to the fact that their collective expertise and ways of thinking are still built into the institutions of health care (Johnson 1995). The *structuralist* approach is a useful way of understanding the broad contours of policy and who is likely to have the greatest influence. However, in order to understand the dynamics of particular policy decisions in particular contexts, it is necessary to analyse the contacts and interactions within the formal and informal networks that grow up around specific issues.

What impact do interest groups have?

It is increasingly apparent that interest groups such as patient organizations are playing a more influential role in health policy even in low income countries where they have traditionally been weak or absent. Of course, the extent of influence on policy from outside government and the immediate impact of party politics varies from place to place and from issue to issue. The history of the response to HIV/AIDS across the globe is noteworthy for the very high level of involvement and influence of interest groups or civil society organizations. 'Never before have civil society organizations – here defined as any group of individuals that is separate from government and business – done so much to contribute to the fight against a global health crisis, or been so included in the decisions made by policy makers' (Zuniga 2005, forthcoming). The HIV/AIDS history is also notable for the diversity of interest group activities, the large number of HIV/AIDS organizations involved (currently over 3,000 in 150 countries) and the shift of activism from the high to low income countries (Table 6.1).

Table 6.1 The history of the role of civil society groups in global policy to combat HIV/AIDS

Phase of activism	*Main activities*	*Main demands*	*Impact*
Early 1980s in US and Western countries: civil rights activism	Protest, lobbying and activism modelled on US black civil rights movement of 1960s	Protection of human and civil rights; PLWA are not to blame; inclusion of PLWA in policy process – inclusion and partnership	Traditional STI approach of isolation, surveillance, mandatory testing and strict contact notification replaced by rights based model promoted by WHO from 1987
Mid-/late-1980s in US and Western countries: aggressive, scientific activism	New more aggressive organizations such as ACTUP and TAG lobbying politicians; simultaneous street protests and scientific debates with government; AIDS pressure groups winning places on government committees	Government funding for treatment and price reductions for early ART	Access to effective treatment for PLWA; showed that new drugs did confer benefits and that early trials did not warrant denying treatment to PLWA; ensured that trials included women, minorities, etc.
1990s in US and Western countries: institutionalized and internalized activism	US/Western activist groups shrinking because of success; activists increasingly accepted and working within health policy system; established role of civil society group in provision	Ensuring that HIV/AIDS remains a policy and resource allocation priority in the West; attention should be given to HIV/AIDS in poorer countries	Increased awareness of distribution of HIV/AIDS globally
Later 1990s in low and middle income countries: growing activism	Overseas funding to raise awareness and educate people, and support civil society groups; explosion of civil society groups; North-South cooperation between civil society groups	Franker public discussion of HIV/AIDS, better leadership, concerted government responses, provision of AZT and treatment of co-infections	Notable impact in pioneer countries such as Uganda and Brazil; latter showed that ART could be provided in a middle income setting with good results and that comprehensive response could save health care costs
Late 1990s/early 2000s: global movement for treatment access	Period of advocacy sparked by successful civil society group protest and resistance to attempt by US/South African pharmas to prevent South African government from	Universal access to affordable treatment as a human right; HIV/AIDS to be seen as a development issue with major negative economic consequences	Civil society groups contributed to recognition that public health considerations had some weight alongside trade and intellectual property considerations in

	offering low cost, generic ART; growing international coalition of NGOs pushing for low cost ART by promoting production of generic drugs and pressurizing pharmas to reduce their prices in low income settings		World Trade Organisation; new funding initiatives (Global Fund to Fight AIDS, TB and Malaria, and US President's Plan for AIDS Relief); gradual roll-out of ART helped by lower drug prices in developing world

Sources: Seckinelgin (2002), Zuniga (2005)
Notes:
ACTUP = AIDS Coalition to Unleash Power
ART = Antiretroviral Therapy
AZT = Azidothymidine
PLWA = People living with AIDS
STI = sexually transmitted infection
TAG = treatment action group

Activity 6.7

Why has the HIV/AIDS policy arena attracted such a high level of civil society group involvement?

Feedback

A number of factors help to explain the high level of interest group activism, particularly in the early stages of the pandemic in high income countries which provided models for later activism in low and middle income countries:

- the demographic profile of the early affected population and most subsequent infections – HIV/AIDS tends to infect young adults and in countries like the UK, it affected a relatively affluent male homosexual population in cities
- HIV and even AIDS before therapy was available is not an immediate killer, allowing an opportunity for activism, unlike some other diseases
- spill-over from other social movements – in the USA and Western Europe, the most affected population group was homosexual men who had recent experience of the gay rights movement of the 1970s. They used some of the same civil rights strategies and refused to play the role of 'patients'. In low income countries subsequently, HIV/AIDS activism was inspired by and allied itself to wider social justice movements such as those for debt relief
- the slowness of the official response in high income countries. It took between two and four years, and sometimes longer, between the first diagnosis and the development of official awareness campaigns

Activity 6.8

Why do you think HIV/AIDS activism was less prominent in low income countries in the 1980s and early 1990s?

Feedback

There are a number of inter-related reasons for this phenomenon. You may have written down some or all of the following:

- a lack of data and, therefore, lack of awareness of the pandemic
- unresponsiveness of political leaderships, especially in undemocratic countries in Africa (which were more common in the 1980s)
- denial by governments and public opinion that AIDS was a Western, alien problem only affecting homosexuals
- the fact that HIV/AIDS in low income countries did not affect a cohesive, well-off group such as the male homosexual population in the USA but poor people who could easily be silenced and ignored
- other priorities competing for the attention of interest groups and health systems such as more immediately lethal diseases and malnutrition
- lack of donor interest and funding to NGOs in the area of HIV/AIDS

Activity 6.9

How would you characterize the evolution of the interest groups in the HIV/AIDS field from the early 1980s to the early twenty-first century from Table 6.1?

Feedback

Table 6.1 shows two main trends:

- a shift in interest group activity from advocacy (i.e. an 'outsider' stance) to involvement in policy and provision (i.e. an 'insider' stance), in some cases leading to advocacy organizations disappearing once their goals had been achieved
- a shift of the main focus of activism from the USA and other Western countries to low and middle income countries, stimulated by greater awareness of the global distribution of AIDS cases and international funding to interest groups in the South. This has been accompanied by cooperation and alliances between interest groups in the North and the South.

Is interest group participation a good thing in policy terms?

Up to now, the involvement of interest groups has been analysed without attempting to draw attention to its positive and negative consequences for policy making. Generally, in democratic societies, the involvement of organizations outside the government in policy processes is seen as a good thing. However, there are potential drawbacks.

Activity 6.10

List the possible positive and negative consequences of having a wide range of interest groups involved in the shaping of health policy.

Feedback

Your lists will probably have included some of the following possible advantages and drawbacks shown in Table 6.2.

Table 6.2 Possible advantages and drawbacks of interest groups being involved in shaping health policy

Potential advantages of 'open' policy processes	*Potential negative consequences of 'open' policy processes*
Wide range of views is brought to bear on a problem including a better appreciation of the possible impacts of policy on different groups	Difficult to reconcile conflicting and competing claims for attention and resources of different interest groups
Policy making process includes information that is not accessible to governments	Adds to complexity and time taken to reach decisions and to implement policies
Consultation and/or involvement of a range of interests gives policy greater legitimacy and support so that policy decisions may be more likely to be implemented	Concern to identify who different interest groups 'truly' represent and how accountable they are to their members or funders
New or emerging issues may be brought to governments' attention more rapidly than if process is very 'closed' allowing rapid response	Less well-resourced, less well-connected interests may still be disadvantaged by being overlooked or marginalized
	Interest groups may not be capable of providing the information or taking the responsibility allocated to them
	Activities of interest groups may not be transparent
	Proliferation of 'front' groups enables corporate interests to develop multiple, covert channels of influence
	Interest groups can be bigoted, self-interested, badly informed, abusive and intimidatory – being in civil society does not confer automatic virtue

Summary

There are many groups outside government that try to influence public policy on particular issues at various stages of the policy process. In some countries, there are many of these groups and they are strong; in other countries there are few non-governmental actors and their influence on policy makers is relatively limited. Until the 1990s, policy in low income countries was dominated by an elite closely affiliated with the government of the day. However, in the 1990s, in many low income countries the number of different groups and alliances of groups trying to influence government policies grew and governments increasingly came to recognize that they should listen. NGOs that had previously confined themselves to delivering services became more involved in policy advocacy. Most recently, alliances between interest groups in different countries, most notably between NGOs in high and low income settings, have become more prominent in their efforts to influence governments' policies in the health field.

Interest groups differ in the way they are treated by governments. Some are given high legitimacy, 'insider' status and are regularly consulted. Sectional groups often fall into this category because they are typically powerful and can employ sanctions if they do not approve of a government's policy. In contrast, cause groups may be highly regarded and consulted but have less recourse to sanctions. They may be perceived as 'outsider' groups or even deliberately pursue an 'outsider' strategy organizing demonstrations and ensuring a high level of media coverage in a bid to embarrass or put pressure on government.

References

Alford RR (1975). *Health Care Politics*. Chicago: University of Chicago Press

Chapman S (1996). Civil disobedience and tobacco control: the case of BUGA UP. Billboard Utilising Graffitists Against Unhealthy Promotions. *Tobacco Control* 5(3): 179–85

Giddens A (2001). Foreword. In Anheier H, Glasius M and Kaldor M (eds) *Global Civil Society*. Oxford: Oxford University Press, p. iii. Available at: http://www.lse.ac.uk/Depts/global/Yearbook/outline.htm

Grant W (1984). The role of pressure groups. In Borthwick R and Spence J (eds) *British Politics in Perspective*. Leicester: Leicester University Press

Howlett M and Ramesh M (2003). *Studying Public Policy: Policy Cycles and Policy Subsystems*. 2nd edn. Don Mills, Ontario: Oxford University Press

Hulme D and Edwards M (1997). *NGOs, States and Donors: Too Close for Comfort*. London: Macmillan

Johnson T (1995). Governmentality and the institutionalisation of expertise. In Johnson T, Larkin G and Saks M (eds) *Health Professions and the State in Europe*. London: Routledge: pp. 7–24

Lewis JM (2005). *Health Policy and Politics: Networks, Ideas and Power*. Melbourne: IP Communications.

Marsh D and Rhodes RAW (1992). Policy communities and issue networks: beyond typology. In Marsh D and Rhodes RAW (eds) *Policy Networks in British Government*. Oxford: Oxford University Press

Peterson MA (1999). Motivation, mobilisation and monitoring: the role of interest groups in health policy. *Journal of Health Politics, Policy and Law* 24: 416–20

Seckinelgin H (2002). Time to stop and think: HIV/AIDS, global civil society, and people's politics. In Anheier H, Glasius M and Kaldor M (eds) Global civil society 2002. Oxford:

Oxford University Press, pp. 109–36. Available at: http://www.lse.ac.uk/Depts/global/Yearbook/outline.htm

Walt G (1994). *Health Policy: An Introduction to Process and Power.* Johannesburg and London: Witwatersrand University Press and Zed Books

Zuniga J (2005). Civil society and the global battle against HIV/AIDS. In Beck E, Mays N, Whiteside A and Zuniga J (eds) *Dealing with the HIV Pandemic in the 21st Century: Health Systems' Responses, Past, Present and Future.* Oxford: Oxford University Press, forthcoming

7 Policy implementation

Overview

It will now be apparent that the policy process is complex and interactive: many groups and organizations at national and international levels try to influence what gets onto the policy agenda and how policies are formulated. Yet policy making does not come to an end once a course of action has been determined. It cannot be assumed that a policy will be implemented as intended since decision makers typically depend on others to see their policies turned into action. This chapter describes this process.

Learning objectives

After working through this chapter, you will be better able to:

- **contrast 'top-down' and 'bottom-up' theories of policy implementation**
- **understand other approaches to achieving policy implementation including those that attempt to synthesize insights from both 'top-down' and 'bottom-up' perspectives**
- **identify some of the tensions affecting implementation between international bodies and national governments, and between central and local authorities within countries**
- **describe some of the factors that facilitate or impede the implementation of centrally determined policies**

Key terms

Advocacy coalition Group within a policy sub-system distinguished by shared set of norms, beliefs and resources. Can include politicians, civil servants, members of interest groups, journalists and academics who share ideas about policy goals and to a lesser extent about solutions.

Bottom-up implementation Theory which recognizes the strong likelihood that those at subordinate levels will play an active part in the process of implementation, including having some discretion to reshape the dictates of higher levels in the system, thereby producing policy results which are different from those envisaged.

Implementation Process of turning a policy into practice.

Implementation gap Difference between what the policy architect intended and the end result of a policy.

Policy instrument One of the range of options at the disposal of the policy maker in order to give effect to a policy goal (e.g. privatization, regulation, etc.).

Principal–agent theory The relationship between principals (purchasers) and agents (providers), together with the contracts or agreements that enable the purchaser to specify what is to be provided and check that this has been accomplished.

Street-level bureaucrats Front-line staff involved in delivering public services to members of the public who have some discretion in how they apply the objectives and principles of policies handed down to them from central government.

Top-down implementation Theory which envisages clear division between policy formulation and implementation, and a largely linear, rational process of implementation in which subordinate levels of a policy system put into practice the intentions of higher levels based on the setting of objectives.

Transaction cost economics Theory that efficient production of goods and services depends on lowering the costs of transactions between buyers and sellers by removing as much uncertainty as possible on both sides and by maximizing the ability of the buyer to monitor and control transactions.

Introduction

Implementation has been defined as 'what happens between policy expectations and (perceived) policy results' (DeLeon 1999). Until the 1970s, policy scientists had tended to focus their attentions on agenda setting, policy formulation and decision making 'stages' of the policy process (see Chapter 1, for an overview of the 'stages', and Chapters 4, 5 and 6, for an account of agenda setting, and policy formulation within and outside government). While the notion of there being formal 'stages' is far from the messy reality of most policy processes, it remains a useful device for drawing attention to different activities and actors. The changes that followed policy decisions had been relatively neglected. However, it became increasingly apparent that many public policies had not worked out in practice as well as their proponents had hoped. A series of studies in the late 1960s of anti-poverty programmes, initially in the USA, led to an increasing focus by practitioners and analysts on showing the effects of policies and explaining why their consequences were often not as planned (Pressman and Wildavsky 1984).

Today, it is common to observe a 'gap' between what was planned and what occurred as a result of a policy. For example, there are numerous case studies of the impact of health policies 'imposed' by international donors on poor countries showing that they have had less than positive results for a range of reasons. For example, El Salvador received loans from the Inter-American Development Bank (IDB) to improve its health infrastructure. However, there was no concomitant closing of old facilities or improvement of existing, dilapidated facilities. As a result, the El Salvador Ministry of Health's maintenance and repair budget could not cope with maintaining the larger capital stock and facilities fell further into disrepair (Walt 1994). Much government reform is currently focused on trying to devise systems that increase the likelihood that governments' policies will be implemented in the way that ministers intended and that provide information on the impact of policies. For example, the Labour government in the UK in the late

1990s emphasized what it called 'delivery' by which it meant the imperative that policies should verifiably make a difference to people's lives. It set a series of quantitative targets with explicit achievement dates and held individual ministries and agencies accountable for their delivery. Similarly, the UN set its Millennium Development Goals in 2000 in order to focus the efforts of its own agencies and world governments on quantitative, timed targets to reduce poverty, malaria and AIDS, and increase access to education by 2015. Unfortunately, it looks unlikely that the goals will be met.

Activity 7.1

Why have programmes driven by overseas donors in low income countries been less successful than expected? What sorts of obstacles face ministries of health in implementing such programmes?

Feedback

The range of reasons has at various times included the following: limited systems in recipient countries to absorb the new resources, lack of government capacity in recipient countries to make good use of resources, the pressure to achieve quick and highly visible results driven by short funding cycles, the importation of alien policy models based on theories tested in other contexts (e.g. in Afghanistan, the World Bank reformed the health system by using its successful experience in Cambodia to introduce a purchaser–provider separation linked to performance-based contracting for services, regardless of the differences between the two countries), differences of view and operating procedures between donors and recipient countries, high costs imposed on recipients by donors' administrative requirements (e.g. the costs of having repeatedly to prepare proposals for fixed-term funding) and a failure to identify opposing interests and/or find ways of changing their positions.

Early theoretical models of policy implementation

'Top-down' approaches

'Top-down' approaches to understanding policy implementation are closely allied with the rational model of the entire policy process which sees it as a linear sequence of activities in which there is a clear division between policy formulation and policy execution. The former is seen as explicitly political and the latter as a largely technical, administrative or managerial activity. Policies set at a national or international level have to be communicated to subordinate levels (e.g. health authorities, hospitals, clinics) which are then charged with putting them into practice. The 'top-down' approach was developed from early studies of the 'implementation deficit' or 'gap' to provide policy makers with a better understanding of what systems they needed to put in place to minimize the 'gap' between aspiration and reality (that is, to make the process approximate more closely to the rational ideal). These studies were empirical but led to prescriptive conclusions. Thus, according to Pressman and Wildavsky (1984), the key to effective implementation lay in the ability to devise a system in which the causal links between setting goals and the successive actions designed to achieve them were clear and robust. Goals had to be clearly defined and widely understood, the necessary political, administrative, technical and financial resources had to be available, a chain of command had to be established from the centre to the periphery, and a communication and control system had to be in place to keep the whole system on course. Failure was caused by adopting the wrong strategy and using the wrong machinery.

Later 'top-down' theorists devised a list of six necessary and sufficient conditions for effective policy implementation (Sabatier and Mazmanian 1979), indicating that if these conditions were realized, policy should be implemented as intended:

- clear and logically consistent objectives
- adequate causal theory (i.e. a valid theory as to how particular actions would lead to the desired outcomes)
- an implementation process structured to enhance compliance by implementers (e.g. appropriate incentives and sanctions to influence subordinates in the required way)
- committed, skilful, implementing officials
- support from interest groups and legislature
- no changes in socio-economic conditions that undermine political support or the causal theory underlying the policy

Proponents of this approach argued that it could distinguish empirically between failed and successful implementation processes, and thereby provided useful guidance to policy makers. Its most obvious weakness was that the first condition was rarely fulfilled in that most public policies were found to have fuzzy, potentially inconsistent objectives. Other policy scientists were more critical still.

Activity 7.2

Given what you know already about policy in the health field, what criticisms would you level at the 'top-down' perspective on effective implementation? How good an explanation of policy implementation does it offer, in your opinion? How good a guide to policy implementation does it offer?

Feedback

The main criticisms of the 'top-down' approach are that:

- it exclusively adopted the perspective of central decision makers (those at the top of any hierarchy or directly involved in initial policy formulation) and neglected the role of other actors (e.g. NGOs, professional bodies, the private sector) and the contribution of other levels in the implementation process (e.g. regional health authorities and front-line staff)
- as an analytical approach, it risked over-estimating the impact of government action on a problem versus other factors
- it was difficult to apply in situations where there was no single, dominant policy or agency involved – in many fields, there are multiple policies in play and a complex array of agencies

- there was almost no likelihood that the preconditions for successful implementation set out by the 'top-downers' would be present
- its distinction between policy decisions and subsequent implementation was misleading and practically unhelpful since policies change as they are being implemented
- it did not explicitly take into account the impact on implementation of the extent of change required by a policy

In essence, the critics argued that the reality of policy implementation was messier and more complex than even the most sophisticated 'top-down' approach could cope with and that the practical advice it generated on reducing the 'gap' between expectation and reality was, therefore, largely irrelevant. To reinforce these points, Hogwood and Gunn (1984) drew up an even more demanding list of ten pre-conditions for what they termed 'perfect implementation' in order to show that the 'top-down' approach was unrealistic in most situations:

1. The circumstances external to the agency do not impose crippling constraints.
2. Adequate time and sufficient resources are available.
3. The required combination of resources is available.
4. The policy is based on a valid theory of cause and effect.
5. The relationship between cause and effect is direct.
6. Dependency relationships are minimal – in other words, the policy makers are not reliant on groups or organizations which are themselves inter-dependent.
7. There is an understanding of, and agreement on, objectives.
8. Tasks are fully specified in correct sequence.
9. Communication and coordination are perfect.
10. Those in authority can demand and obtain perfect compliance.

Since it was very unlikely that all ten pre-conditions would be present at the same time, critics of the 'top-down' approach argued that the approach was neither a good description of what happened in practice nor a helpful guide to improving implementation.

'Bottom-up' approaches

The 'bottom-up' view of the implementation process is that implementers often play an important function in implementation, not just as managers of policy handed down from above, but as active participants in a complex process that informs those higher up in the system, and that policy should be made with this insight in mind. Even in highly centralized systems, some power is usually granted to subordinate agencies and their staff. As a result, implementers may change the way a policy is implemented and in the process even redefine the objectives of the policy. One of the most influential studies in the development of the 'bottom-up' perspective on implementation was by Lipsky (1980) who studied the behaviour of what he termed 'street-level bureaucrats' in relation to their clients. 'Street-level bureaucrats' included front-line staff administering social welfare benefits, social workers, teachers, local government officials, doctors and nurses. He showed that even those working in the most rule-bound environments had some discretion in how they dealt with their clients and that staff such as doctors, social workers and teachers had high levels of discretion which enabled them to get round the dictates of central policy and reshape policy for their own ends.

Lipsky's work helped re-conceptualize the implementation process, particularly in the delivery of health and social services which is dependent on the actions of large numbers of professional staff, as a much more interactive, political process characterized by largely inescapable negotiation and conflict between interests and levels within policy systems. As a result, researchers began to focus their attention on the actors in the implementation process, their goals, their strategies, their activities and their links to one another. Interestingly, 'bottom-up' studies showed that even where the conditions specified as necessary by the 'top-down', rational model were in place (e.g. a good chain of command, well-defined objectives, ample resources, and a communication and monitoring system), policies could be implemented in ways that policy makers had not intended. Indeed, well-meaning policies could make things worse, for example, by increasing staff workload so that they had to develop undesirable coping strategies (Wetherley and Lipsky 1977).

Almost 30 years later, studies of 'street-level bureaucrats' still have relevance. For example, Walker and Gilson (2004) studied how nurses in a busy urban primary health care clinic in South Africa experienced and responded to the implementation of the 1996 national policy of free care (removal of user fees). They showed that while the nurses approved of the policy of improving access in principle, they were negative towards it in practice because of the way it exacerbated existing problems in their working environment and increased their workload, without increasing staffing levels and availability of drugs. They were also dissatisfied because they felt that they had not been included in the process of policy change. The nurses also believed that many patients abused the free system and some patients did not deserve free care because they were personally responsible for their own health problems. Such views were presumably at odds with the principles underlying the policy of free care and made nurses slow to grant free access to services to certain groups of patients.

Insights from the 'bottom-up' perspective on policy implementation have also guided a range of studies in health care systems of the way in which the relationships between central, regional and local agencies influence policy. The ability of the centre to control lower levels of the system varies widely and depends on factors such as where the funds come from and who controls them (e.g. the balance between central and local sources of funding), legislation (e.g. setting on which level of authority is responsible for which tasks), operating rules and the ability of the government to enforce these (e.g. through performance assessment, audit, incentives, etc.). Relationships between the centre and the periphery in health systems influence the fate of many policies. Sometimes, as the South African example above showed, policies are diverted to some degree during their implementation. At other times, they are entirely rejected. In New Zealand in the early 1990s, the government introduced user charges for hospital outpatients and inpatients in order, among other things, to remove the perceived incentive for patients to go to hospital rather than use primary care where they faced user charges. Whatever its intellectual merits, the policy was extremely unpopular among the public, patients, and the hospital managers and staff who had to collect the fees. The user charges were progressively withdrawn until they disappeared about two years after their introduction.

Activity 7.3

Write down in two columns the main differences between the 'top-down' and 'bottom-up' approaches to policy implementation. You might contrast the following aspects of the two approaches to implementation: initial focus; identification of major actors; view of the policy process; evaluative criteria, and overall focus.

Feedback

Your answer should have included some of the differences shown in Table 7.1. While the 'bottom-up' approach appeals to health care workers and middle-ranking officials because it brings their views and constraints on their actions into view, the approach raises as many questions as the 'top-down' perspective. One obvious question it raises is whether or not policy should be made predominantly from the top-down or bottom-up. Another question is how the divergence of views and goals between actors at different levels can or should be reconciled. Specifically, in a democracy how much influence should unelected professionals have in shaping the eventual consequences of policies determined by elected governments?

Table 7.1 'Top-down' and 'bottom-up' approaches to policy implementation

	Top-down approaches	*Bottom-up approaches*
Initial focus	Central government decision	Local implementation actors and networks
Identification of major actors	From top-down and starting with government	From bottom-up, including both government and non-government
View of the policy process	Largely rational process, proceeding from problem identification to policy formulation at higher levels to implementation at lower levels	Interactive process involving policy makers and implementers from various parts and levels of government and outside in which policy may change during implementation
Evaluative criteria	Extent of attainment of formal objectives rather than recognition of unintended consequences	Much less clear – possibly that policy process takes into account of local influences
Overall focus	Designing the system to achieve what central/top policy makers intend – focus on 'structure'	Recognition of strategic interaction among multiple actors in a policy network – focus on 'agency'

Source: Adapted and expanded from Sabatier (1986)

Activity 7.4

Write down any other drawbacks of the 'bottom-up' approach that you can think of.

Feedback

In addition to the value (normative) questions mentioned in the paragraph above, you could have listed:

- If there is no distinction analytically or in reality between 'policy' and 'implementation', then it is difficult to separate the influence of different levels of government and of elected politicians on policy decisions and consequences. This is important for democratic and bureaucratic accountability.
- If there are no separate decision points in the policy process, it becomes very difficult to undertake any evaluation of a particular policy's effects (as you will see in Chapter 9).
- The approach risks under-emphasizing the indirect influence of the centre in shaping the institutions in which lower level actors operate and in distributing the political resources they possess, including permitting them to be involved in shaping implementation.

This list of drawbacks is a reminder that it pays to be cautious when judging one theory superior to another in such a complex field as policy. Most theory in policy science inevitably simplifies the complexity of any particular set of circumstances in order to bring greater understanding.

Other ways of understanding policy implementation: beyond 'top-down' and 'bottom-up'

The approaches debated this far have largely been developed by political scientists and sociologists. However, management scientists and economists have also been drawn to trying to explain why 'top-down' and 'bottom-up' approaches leave gaps between intention and eventual outcome.

Principal–agent theory

From the principal–agent perspective, sub-optimal policy implementation is an inevitable result of the structure of the institutions of modern government in which decision makers ('principals') have to delegate responsibility for the implementation of their policies to their officials (e.g. civil servants in the Ministry of Health) and other 'agents' (e.g. managers, doctors and nurses in the health sector or private contractors) whom they only indirectly and incompletely control and who are difficult to monitor. These 'agents' have discretion in how they operate on behalf of political 'principals' and may not even see themselves as primarily engaged in making a reality of the wishes of these 'principals'. For example, even publicly employed doctors tend to see themselves as members of the medical profession first and foremost rather than as civil servants. Discretion opens up the potential for ineffective or inefficient translation of government intent into reality since 'agents' have their own views, ambitions, loyalties and resources which can hinder policy implementation. The inherent problem for politicians is to get the compliance of their officials and others who are contracted to deliver services at all levels. The more levels of hierarchy there are, the more principal–agent relations exist as each level is dependent on the next level below or beside it, and the more complex the task of controlling the process of implementation.

The amount of discretion and the complexity of the principal–agent relationships are, in turn, affected by:

- *the nature of the policy problem* – features such as macro versus sectoral or micro (i.e. scale of change required and size of the affected group), simple versus complex, ill-defined versus clear, many causes versus a single cause, highly politically sensitive versus neutral politically, requiring a short or long period before changes will become apparent, costly versus inexpensive. In general, long-term, ill-defined, inter-dependent (goals affected by other policies too), high profile problems affecting large numbers of people are far more difficult to deal with than short-term, specific issues with a single cause and a large technical component. Most public policy debate focuses on the former which are known, understandably, as 'wicked problems' or problems to which there is never likely to be an easy solution. A typical example would be how to simultaneously reduce the prevalence of illegal drug use in prisons while making existing drug use less hazardous to the health of prisoners (e.g. by providing clean syringes or sterilizing equipment). The risk is that the less risky drug misuse is made, the less likely it is that it will be reduced.
- *the context or circumstances surrounding the problem* – for example, the political situation, whether the economy is growing or not, the availability of resources and technological change
- *the organization of the machinery required to implement the policy* – most obviously this includes the number of formal and informal agencies involved in making the desired change and the skills and resources that have to be brought to bear.

As a result of these sorts of factors, officials who typically remain in post longer than politicians often become subject area experts and are able to exercise considerable discretion, for example, in how much they tell ministers and when. Politicians are thus often dependent on the goodwill of their officials to further their own interests and careers.

Activity 7.5

The three sets of factors listed above help explain why some policies are easier to implement than others. Take a health policy with which you are familiar and describe the nature of the problem, the context and the machinery required to implement the policy. Under each of the three headings, try to assess whether the factors you have listed are likely to be make implementation of the policy easier or more difficult.

Feedback

Your answer will clearly depend on the policy chosen. For example, if your chosen policy had simple technical features (e.g. introduction of a new drug), involved a marginal behavioural change (e.g. a minor change in dosage), could be implemented by one or a few actors (e.g. pharmacists only), had clear, non-conflicting objectives (e.g. better symptom control with no cost implications) and could be executed in a short period of time (e.g. drugs were easy to source and distribute), you would be lucky and you would be able to conclude that implementation would be relatively straightforward. Unfortunately, the majority of health policy issues and policies are more complex. Policy analysts are fond of contrasting the challenge of goals such as putting a man on the moon with the stock-in-trade of public policy such as reducing poverty. The former was carried out in a tightly organized, influential, well-resourced organization focused on a single goal with a clear end point. The latter is driven by a large number of causes, involves a wide range of agencies and actors and has inherently fuzzy objectives (Howlett and Ramesh 2003).

The insights of principal–agent and related theories such as transaction costs economics, which focuses on reducing the costs of relating buyers to sellers in markets and public services, led to a greater appreciation of the importance for policy implementation of the design of institutions and the choice of policy instruments in the knowledge that the 'top' needs to be able to monitor and control the 'street level' at reasonable cost. One aspect of this was a growing focus on the actual and implied *contracts* defining the relationships between principals and agents in order to ensure that the principal's objectives are followed by agents. So within the 'core' of central government, in the 1980s and 1990s, in a number of countries, the civil service was reformed to make more explicit what officials were expected to deliver to ministers in return for their salaries, and to put in place performance targets and performance indicators to assess whether their performance in meeting government objectives was improving or not.

In public services the conventional role of government as the direct provider of services was critically reviewed in many countries, with a view to improving the efficiency and responsiveness of services both to the objectives of ministers and the needs of consumers. The catch phrase of the reformers was that government should be 'steering not rowing' the ship of state (Osborne and Gaebler 1992), confining itself to what only it could do best. As a result, some services that had been directly provided in the public sector (e.g. by publicly owned hospitals) were contracted out to private for-profit or not-for-profit providers, thereby making the roles of purchaser and provider more explicit. Table 7.2 lays out the range of substantive

Table 7.2 The spectrum of substantive policy instruments

Family and community	Voluntary organizations	Private market	Information and exhortation	Subsidy	Tax and user charges	Regulation	Public enterprise	Direct provision
Voluntary action			Mixed voluntary and compulsory action				Compulsory action	
Law state involvement in production of services							*High state involvement*	

Source: Howlett and Ramesh (2003)

policy instruments available to government to ensure the delivery of goods and services, each entailing differing levels of government activity and degrees of compulsion. From the early 1980s, policy makers were encouraged to consider the potential of the whole range, in line with the preference in mainstream economics for markets over other approaches to producing goods and services and the fashionable economic theory that the self-interested behaviour of voters, politicians and bureaucrats tends to lead to an increase in taxation, public spending and government activity, often unnecessarily and inefficiently. From an economic point of view, the selection of instruments was seen as largely a technical exercise to improve the efficiency of public services.

Broadly, by the end of the 1990s, market, market-like (e.g. the separation of purchaser and providers within a publicly owned and financed health system) and voluntary instruments had become more prominent in many countries, leading to a more mixed set of policy instruments in sectors such as health. The supposition of reformers was that such arrangements would improve the implementation of centrally driven policy designed to improve the efficiency and effectiveness of public services.

As well as changes to instruments, there were also changes to the processes by which services were delivered, such as the trend to decentralize parts of the decision making function from central to local levels while reducing the number of tiers in the management hierarchy. In many jurisdictions, subordinate agents were given greater control over their own affairs on a day-to-day basis but remained accountable for the attainment of the government's key goals. The theory was that this would free agents to pursue the objectives of their principals, unfettered by unnecessary interference, and allow principals to judge the performance of their agents objectively and remove from agents the excuse that their poor performance was the result of inappropriate interventions by principals. These more autonomous entities are referred to as 'public firms' or 'public enterprises'. Since 1991, NHS hospitals in the UK have operated in this way as 'self-governing' bodies with some, limited freedom from direct ministerial control. In 2004, in England, better performing NHS hospitals were encouraged to apply for 'foundation status' which, in principle, gave them greater freedom to operate entrepreneurially and to keep the rewards of their good performance. Similar reforms have been pursued in low income countries such as Zambia where performance improvements were rewarded with greater freedom from government control (Bossert et al. 2003).

Taken together, these reactions to the perception that traditional ways of public administration had failed to deliver what governments needed came to be known as 'New Public Management (NPM)'. NPM rests (for it is still the dominant approach to public sector management worldwide) on economic critiques of policy implementation and the importation into the public sector of management techniques used in large private enterprises.

Activity 7.6

Extract the main elements of 'New Public Management' from what you have just read about principal–agent theory and related ideas.

Feedback

NPM is a hybrid of different intellectual influences and practical experience, and emphasizes different things in different countries, but the following elements are commonly seen as distinctive in NPM:

- clarification of roles and responsibilities for effective policy implementation by separating 'political' (i.e. advising ministers on policy direction) from 'executive' (i.e. service delivery) functions within the government machinery. For example, this has led to governments setting up agencies to run public services at arm's length from central government (e.g. courts, prisons and health services) with greater operational freedom and attempting to slim down central government ministries providing policy advice
- separation of 'purchase' from 'provision' within public services in order to allow the contracting out of services to the private sector if this is regarded as superior to in-house, public provision, or the establishment of more independent public providers (e.g. turning UK NHS hospitals into 'foundation trusts' at arm's length from direct government control)
- focus on performance assessment and incentives to improve 'value for money' and to ensure that services deliver what policy makers intended
- setting standards of service which citizens as consumers can expect to be delivered

Towards a synthesis of 'top-down' and 'bottom-up' perspectives?

While economists tended to see the choice of the best policy instrument to implement a policy as a technical exercise and were keen to recommend approaches, political scientists studied how governments behaved and with what consequences. For example, Linder and Peters (1989) identified the following factors as playing a critical role in shaping the policy implementation choices of governments:

- *Features of policy instruments* – some instruments are intrinsically more demanding technically and politically to use. They vary on at least four dimensions: resource intensiveness; targeting; political risk; and degree of coerciveness. Ripley and Franklin (1982) suggested that distributive policies (i.e. allocating public funds to different groups) tended to be relatively easy to implement, regulatory policies (e.g. allowing nurses to prescribe drugs previously restricted to doctors) were moderately difficult, and redistributive policies (i.e. policies involving the re-allocation of income or opportunities between socio-economic groups) were very difficult to implement since there were obvious losers from the last category of policy, whereas the costs of the first category were spread across the population less visibly.
- *Policy style and political culture* – in different countries and different policy fields, participants and the public were accustomed to, for instance, different degrees of government control and/or provision. Policies departing from these traditions were more difficult to implement.
- *Organizational culture* – the past operating experience and ways of doing things of the implementing organizations, linked to point 2.
- *Context of the problem* – the timing (e.g. in relation to how well the economy was performing), the range of actors involved, the likely public reaction, etc.

- *Administrative decision makers' subjective preferences* – based on their background, professional affiliations, training, cognitive style and so on.

These factors highlight two general sets of variables affecting policy implementation, namely, the *extent of government capacity* and, therefore, its ability to intervene, and the *complexity of the particular policy field* it is attempting to influence. Attempts to reconcile the 'top-down' and 'bottom-up' approaches have focused on the interplay between these two sets of variables. Crudely, 'top-down' theory provides the focus on government capacity, whereas 'bottom-up' theory offers the focus on sub-system complexity since the former emphasizes how institutional design and socio-economic conditions (context) constrain and shape the process of implementation and the latter emphasizes how the beliefs of participants, their relationships and networks, and inter-organizational dynamics shape and constrain implementation. The best-known attempt to bring together these different strands of theory and research was developed by Sabatier and various colleagues (Sabatier and Jenkins-Smith 1993).

The policy sub-system or advocacy coalition framework

Sabatier's framework is a general approach to understanding the policy process since it rejects the idea of separating 'implementation' from other parts as unrealistic and misleading. Instead, policy change is seen as a continuous process that takes place within policy sub-systems bounded by relatively stable limits and shaped by major external events. Within the sub-system (e.g. mental health policy), 'communities' of actors interact over considerable periods of time. The actors include all those who play a part in the generation, dissemination and evaluation of policy ideas. Sabatier does not include the public in any policy sub-system on the grounds that ordinary people do not have the time or inclination to be direct participants.

The large number of actors and networks within each sub-system are organized into a smaller number of '*advocacy coalitions*', in conflict with one another. Each competes for influence over government institutions. An 'advocacy coalition' is a group distinguished by a distinct set of norms, beliefs and resources, and can include politicians, civil servants, members of civil society organizations, researchers, journalists and others. Advocacy coalitions are defined by their *ideas* rather than by the exercise of self-interested power (see Chapter 9 for more on their role in bringing ideas from research to bear on policy). Within advocacy coalitions there is a high level of agreement on fundamental policy positions and objectives, though there may be more debate about the precise means to achieve these objectives (the concept has much in common with that of a discourse community discussed in the previous chapter). Sabatier argues that the fundamental (or 'core') norms and beliefs of an advocacy coalition change relatively infrequently and in response to major changes in the external environment such as shifts in macroeconomic conditions or the replacement of one political regime by another. Otherwise, less fundamental, 'normal' policy changes occur as a result of policy-oriented learning in the interaction between advocacy coalitions within the policy sub-system.

The final element in Sabatier's model is to identify the existence of so-called '*policy brokers*', that is actors concerned with finding feasible compromises between the positions advocated by the multiplicity of coalitions. 'Brokers' may be civil servants experienced in a particular sub-system or bodies designed to produce agreement, such as committees of inquiry.

Subsequent empirical work has shown that the advocacy coalition model works fairly well in explaining policy change over a decade in relatively open, decentralized, federal, pluralistic political systems such as the USA, but works less well in political systems such as Britain's which are more closed and where there is less interplay between advocacy coalitions. It has also been little used in the context of low income countries where policy making has been traditionally even more closed and elitist. Looking at its utility in specific policy sub-systems, it appears to fit well with sub-systems such as HIV/AIDS policy and other aspects of public health where government typically has to try to reach agreement among conflicting advocacy coalitions, but is far less applicable to the policy sub-systems of 'high politics' such as defence and foreign policy (e.g. decisions to go to war) where policy decisions are normally made within a small and tightly defined elite since the national interest as a whole may be perceived to be at stake.

There a number of different approaches to understanding implementation which transcend the contrast between 'top-down' and 'bottom-up' approaches. Through the concept of 'advocacy coalitions', Sabatier's has the virtue of highlighting the possibility that many of the most important conflicts in policy cut across the simple divide between policy makers and those formally charged with putting policy into practice.

What help to policy makers are the different approaches to policy implementation?

Most of the research discussed in this chapter was not directly devoted to providing practical advice for policy makers, though some fairly simple messages emerge. For example, there is little doubt that policies which are designed to be incremental (with small behavioural change), can be delivered through a simple structure involving few actors and have the support of front-line staff are more likely to succeed than those that are not. However, this is no great help to those charged with bringing about radical policy change in complex systems where conflicts of fact and opinion abound.

Grindle and Thomas (1991) encourage policy makers, whoever they are, to carefully analyse their political, financial, managerial and technical resources and work out how they may be mobilized as well as those of their likely opponents before making decisions about how to bring about change. The key message from their approach is a reminder that the political aspects of the policy sub-system are just as important as aspects of government capacity such as the quality of the technical advice available. Where governments lack capacity and the sub-system is complex, involving a large number of inter-dependent actors, the advice from this perspective might be to use subsidies to encourage particular forms of behaviour rather than attempt direct provision. For example, rather than attempting to employ primary care doctors, the government might subsidize the cost of patients' visits to private doctors.

Given the range of frameworks for analysing policy implementation, each of which has something valuable to offer, Elmore (1985) argues that thoughtful policy makers should use a variety of approaches to analyse their situation simultaneously, both 'bottom-up' and 'top-down'. A key skill is the ability to map the participants ('stakeholders' in modern jargon), their situations, their perspectives, their values, their strategies, their desired outcomes and their ability to delay, obstruct, overturn or help policy implementation (see Chapter 10 for more on this).

As a broad generalization, in the various health policy sub-systems, most governments are ambitious (they want to make a significant impact), but the sub-systems are complex and governments have relatively modest levels of direct control over many of the key actors, for example, they are highly dependent on a range of influential professional groups. This suggests that persuasion and bargaining will often be important parts of any strategy of implementation.

Drawing these threads of advice together, Walt (1998) sets out a strategy for planning and managing the implementation of change in the health sector which is summarized in Table 7.3.

Table 7.3 Strategy for planning and managing the implementation of change

Area or aspect of implementation	*Type of action or analysis*
Macro-analysis of the ease with which policy change can be implemented	Analyse conditions for facilitating change and, where possible, make adjustments to simplify, i.e. one agency, clear goals, single objective, simple technical features, marginal change, short duration, visible benefits, clear costs
Making values underlying the policy explicit	Identify values underlying policy decisions. If values of key interests conflict with policy, support will have to be mobilized and costs minimized
Stakeholder analysis	Review interest groups (and individuals) likely to resist or promote change in policy at national and institutional levels; plan how to mobilize support by consensus building or rallying coalitions of support
Analysis of financial, technical and managerial resources available and required	Consider costs and benefits of overseas funds (if relevant); assess likely self-interested behaviour within the system; review incentives and sanctions to change behaviour; review need for training, new information systems or other supports to policy change
Building strategic implementation process	Involve planners and managers in analysis of how to execute policy; identify networks of supporters of policy change including 'champions'; manage uncertainty; promote public awareness; institute mechanisms for consultation, monitoring and 'fine tuning' of policy

Source: Adapted from Walt (1998)

Summary

Implementation cannot be seen as a separate part of a sequential policy process in which political debate and decisions take place among politicians and civil servants, and managers and administrators at a lower level implement these decisions. It is best viewed as a mostly complex, interactive process in which a wide range of actors influence both the direction of travel as well as the way that given policies are executed, within the constraints of existing institutions. Implementation is a political process shaped by government capacity and system complexity. Experience suggests that this basic insight from the social sciences of the interplay of actors (agency) and institutions (structure) is still imperfectly built into plans for putting policy into practice.

To avoid the gap between policy expectation and reality, policy makers should develop a strategy for implementation that explicitly takes account of financial, managerial and technical aspects of the policy (capacity) and the anticipated resistance and support from all the actors in the sub-system within and outside government.

References

Bossert T, Bona Chita M and Bowser D (2003). Decentralization in Zambia: resource allocation and district performance. *Health Policy and Planning* 18: 357–69

DeLeon P (1999). The missing link revisited: contemporary implementation research. *Policy Studies Review* 16: 311–38

Elmore R (1985). Forward and backward mapping. In Hanf K and Toonen T (eds) *Policy Implementation in Federal and Unitary Systems*. Dordrecht: Martinus Nijhoff

Grindle M and Thomas J (1991). *Public Choices and Policy Change*. Baltimore, MD: Johns Hopkins University Press

Hogwood B and Gunn L (1984). *Policy Analysis for the Real World*. Oxford: Oxford University Press

Howlett M and Ramesh M (2003). *Studying Public Policy: Policy Cycles and Policy Subsystems*. Don Mills, Ontario: Oxford University Press

Linder SH and Peters BG (1989). Instruments of government: perceptions and contexts. *Journal of Public Policy* 9: 35–58

Lipsky M (1980). *Street Level Bureaucracy: Dilemmas of the Individual in Public Services*. New York: Russell Sage Foundation

Osborne DE and Gaebler TA (1992). *Reinventing Government: How the Entrepreneurial Spirit is Transforming the Public Sector*. Reading, MA: Addison-Wesley

Pressman JL and Wildavsky A (1984). *Implementation*. 3rd edn. Berkeley, CA: University of California Press

Ripley R and Franklin G (1982) *Bureaucracy and Policy Implementation*. Homewood, IL: Dorsey

Sabatier PA (1986). Top-down and bottom-up approaches to implementation research: a critical analysis and suggested synthesis. *Journal of Public Policy* 6: 21–48

Sabatier PA and Jenkins-Smith HC (1993). *Policy Change and Learning: An Advocacy Coalition Approach*. Boulder, CO: Westview Press

Sabatier PA and Mazmanian DA (1979). The conditions of effective implementations: a guide to accomplishing policy objectives. *Policy Analysis* 5: 481–504

Walker L and Gilson L (2004). 'We are bitter but we are satisfied': nurses as street-level bureaucrats in South Africa. *Social Science and Medicine* 59: 1251–61

Walt G (1994). *Health Policy: An Introduction to Process and Power*. Johannesburg and London: University of the Witswatersrand Press and Zed Books

Walt G (1998). Implementing health care reform: a framework for discussion. In Saltman RB, Figueras J and Sakellarides C (eds) *Critical Challenges for Health Care Reform in Europe*. Buckingham: Open University Press, pp. 365–84

Wetherley R and Lipsky M (1977). Street-level bureaucrats and institutional innovation: implementing special education reform. *Harvard Educational Review* 47: 171–97

8 Globalizing the policy process

Overview

In this chapter you will learn about the global dimensions of the health policy process. First you will consider why globalization has intensified the need for states and other national level policy actors to cooperate internationally, then identify actors who seek to develop health policies at the global level and those who operate internationally to influence policy at the national health level and finally consider policy transfer between the global and national levels.

Learning objectives

After working through this chapter, you will be better able to:

- **explain what is meant by globalization**
- **appreciate how globalization impacts on health policy**
- **understand why states cooperate to address health problems and why they increasingly do so with non-state actors**
- **identify a range of actors which operate globally in the area of health policy making**

Key terms

Global civil society Civil society groups which are global in their aims, communication or organization.

Global public goods Goods which are undersupplied by markets, inefficiently produced by individual states, and which have benefits which are strongly universal.

Globalization Complex set of processes which increase interconnectedness and inter-dependencies between countries and people.

Introduction

Most of this book has treated policy making in the national context, although one set of contextual factors highlighted in Chapter 1 were those that were described as 'international' or 'global'. International factors were treated as 'exogenous' to domestic policy making. With the intensification of global integration, these global factors are playing an increasingly prominent role in national policy making.

Few countries or health policies are immune from global influences. You have seen that health policies, even in high income countries, are subject to pressures from transnational corporations, for example, in relation to second-hand smoke. National policies are also subject to international trade rules, for example, the challenge by the Canadian government of the French ban on the importation of Canadian asbestos on alleged health grounds. High income countries also voluntarily adopt policies so as to coordinate action to address global health threats, for example, on border controls to combat infectious diseases, such as Severe Acute Respiratory Syndrome. Similarly, and arguably to a much greater extent, health policies in low income countries are subject to external forces. Policy conditions may be set by donor organizations on ministries of health in return for access to loans. Policies may also be established in response to pressure from global social movements, for example, South Africa's decision to provide treatment for persons infected with HIV. Moreover, implementation of policies, such as childhood immunization programmes, may be dependent on support from global public–private partnerships such as the Global Alliance for Vaccines and Immunizations. While national policies have always been subject to external influences, globalization has amplified and multiplied them.

For health policy analysts a key question relates to how globalization affects policy making. This can be broken down into three concerns. First, how do global interactions facilitate the transfer of policies among countries and organizations? Second, who influences the transfer of policies? Third, how has globalization shaped the content of health policy? This chapter addresses these questions – but doing so requires that you first have some background knowledge on globalization and an overview of how governments have traditionally cooperated in health.

Globalization

The term globalization is ubiquitous and used in many different ways. Views are polarized on whether or not globalization is a good thing and, because the term is used in different ways, some dispute the very existence of the phenomenon. You can distinguish five ways the term globalization is used. First, globalization is associated with the increasing volume, intensity and extensiveness of cross-border movement of goods, people, ideas, finances, or infectious pathogens (internationalization). Second, globalization sometimes refers to the removal of barriers to trade which have made greater movement possible (liberalization). Alternatively, some associate globalization with the trend towards a homogenization of cultures (universalization) or of a convergence around Western, modern and particularly US values and policies (McDonaldization). While some might rightly question whether or not these trends are new or unprecedented, most agree that they are taking place on a greater scale and with greater intensity than ever before. As a result, there is increasing inter-dependence among countries.

Jan Scholte (2000) argues that what is novel about the contemporary world is the reconfiguration of 'social space' and specifically the emergence of 'supraterritorial' or 'transworld' geography. While 'territorial' space (villages and countries) remains important to people and policy makers, what has changed is that people and organizations have increasing connections to others in ways that transcend territorial boundaries. For example, people can have loyalties, identities and interests that go beyond an allegiance to the nation–state, linked to values, religion, ethnicity or even sexual identity. Moreover, technologies seemingly compress both time and space. Not only do people and things travel much further, much faster and much more frequently, at times they do so in ways that defy territorial boundaries. Problems can occur everywhere and nowhere. For example, a virus can almost simultaneously infect millions of computers irrespective of their physical location. Millions of currency transactions take place in 'cyberspace' on a daily basis. These examples illustrate a particular dimension of globalization that is new.

Globalization is said to have spatial, temporal and cognitive dimensions (Lee et al. 2002). The spatial dimensions have already been alluded to (we are increasingly 'overcoming' distance) as have the temporal ones (the world has become faster). The cognitive element concerns the thought processes that shape perceptions of events and phenomenon. The spread of communication technologies conditions how ideas, values, beliefs, identities and even interests are produced and reproduced. For some, globalization is producing a global village in which all villagers share aspirations and interests whereas others see Western-inspired values, particularly consumerism and individualism, coming to dominate.

Activity 8.1

Provide an example of the five meanings of globalization.

Feedback

- internationalization – more people flying around the world; the ability to buy 'seasonal' fruits all year around
- liberalization – removal of protection for domestic production of cigarettes
- universalization – same shops and same brand found around the world or the same words used (Internet, STOP)
- McDonaldization – Starbucks in Beijing and Burma
- superterritoriality – buying airline tickets over the Internet from a third country

To fully appreciate the health policy implications of globalization, it is necessary to understand some of the ways that globalization impacts on health.

Globalization and health

The impact of globalization on health is most evident in the area of infectious diseases. Microbes can now find their way to multiple destinations across the world in less than 24 hours. The SARS outbreak in 2003 spread rapidly from China to neighbouring countries and on to places such as Canada. Not only did the virus cause illness and death, it was estimated to have cost Asian economies US$30 billion and the economy of Toronto US$30 million per day at its peak. In 1990, a ship pumping its bilge in a Peruvian harbour spread cholera throughout Latin America causing 4,000 deaths and 400,000 infections in the first year and considerable costs in terms of lost trade and travel. This was part of the seventh cholera epidemic which spread more quickly than the preceding six. In 2003 and 2004, polio spread from Nigeria to 12 polio-free countries in Central, West and Southern Africa. These outbreaks demonstrate that if an epidemic is not detected or contained by a national health system, it can rapidly become a health threat in other parts of the world because of globalization.

It is not only infectious diseases that benefit from globalization. The global production, distribution and marketing of foods, for example, carry with them health risks linked to unhealthy diets. Behaviours may also be prone to globalization in relation to road traffic accidents, sedentarism, smoking, use of alcohol, the sex trade, and so on. Globalization can also affect the ability of the health care system to respond to health threats. One pressing example relates to health workers. High income countries which cannot meet the demand for health workers domestically tend to recruit workers from poorer countries. The Philippines and India have responded to this global demand by training workers for export. Other countries, such as South Africa and Nigeria, have been losing health workers by default rather than design as they are unable to retain staff due to poor working conditions. As a result of significant global flows of health workers, over 50 countries have shortages of staff which entail that essential health services, such as emergency obstetrics, are not provided.

Activity 8.2

Most health issues and problems are affected in one way or another, often both positively and negatively, by forces associated with globalization. Select a health issue or problem with which you are familiar and attempt to identify the transnational dimensions of the determinants of the problem.

Feedback

You will have first identified the determinants of the health issue. Subsequently, you would need to think about how globalization (in its many guises) may have impacted on the determinant. Take, for example, the incidence of sexually transmitted infections (STIs) in Bangladesh. Arguably, the most important determinants are the position of women, access to treatment for infected persons, and human mobility. Globalization has likely impacted on each of these determinants in different ways. For example, trade liberalization and other factors have resulted in a large movements of workers to and from the Gulf States as well as busy overland trucking routes among India, Bangladesh, Nepal and Burma. This has facilitated a booming sex industry with attendant consequences for STI rates. Trade liberalization and increased foreign investment have resulted in the development of a very large clothing industry in urban areas which has largely employed women. This has improved the bargaining position of women considerably in general and perhaps in relation to sexual relationships which may slow the spread of STIs.

It is important to consider that countries, peoples and problems are differentially integrated. Some countries in Sub-Saharan Africa are not as well integrated into the global economy, for example, as are India and China. Nonetheless, as a result of globalization, most countries will not be able to directly control all the determinants of ill-health and will therefore have to cooperate with other actors outside of their borders to protect the health of those within them.

Traditional inter-state cooperation for health

States have always been concerned about the spread of disease over their borders. For example, as early as the fourteenth century, the city–state of Venice forcibly quarantined ships which were suspected of carrying plague-infected rats. The practice spread to other ports. These early initiatives paved the way for more formal international agreements in the nineteenth century which aimed to control the spread of infectious disease through restrictions on trade. These, in turn, resulted in the International Health Regulations (IHR) which were accepted by all members of WHO in 1969. The regulations provide norms, standards and best practice to prevent the international spread of disease but equally importantly require states to report on a number of infectious diseases. The regulations provide a useful illustration of how states have cooperated to address common problems. The IHR also, however, illustrate the limits of such cooperation. In particular, although states were obliged to report to WHO, many often did not, and there was nothing that WHO could do about the lack of compliance.

States may cooperate in many ways, both formally and informally. You will now learn about the formal arrangements that have been established to facilitate cooperation, focusing particularly on multilateral organizations.

The United Nations

The United Nations (UN) system was established at the end of the Second World War to maintain peace and security and to save further generations from the scourge of war. At the heart of the system was the sovereign nation–state which could take up membership in the various UN organizations (such as WHO, UNICEF). The organizations were established to promote exchange and contact among member states and to cooperate to resolve common problems. Member states dictate the policies of the organizations with little interaction with non-governmental bodies. Thus, within the UN system, governments, particularly governments of high income countries, were able to influence international health policy. Yet, as you will see, UN organizations are also, to varying degrees, able to influence national policy.

WHO was founded in 1948 as the UN's specialized health agency with a mandate to lead and coordinate international health activities. Presently, most nation–states (192) belong to WHO and non-voting 'associate membership' allows 193 NGOs in 'official relations' to participate in the governance of the organization. WHO is governed through the World Health Assembly (WHA). Composed of representatives of member states, typically Ministers of Health, the WHA meets annually to approve the Organisation's programme and budget and to make international health policy decisions. WHO's Constitution grants the WHA the authority 'to adopt conventions or agreements with respect to any matter within the competence of the Organisation'. Decisions are made on the basis of one vote per member and are binding on all members unless they opt out in writing. The Constitution does not, however, provide for sanctions for failure to comply with regulations. In practice, most of the decisions are expressed as non-binding recommendations, in particular, as technical guidelines, which states may adopt or dismiss depending on their perceived relevance and national politics.

The WHA is advised by an Executive Board which facilitates the work of the Assembly and gives effect to its decisions and policies. The Secretariat is led by an elected Director-General, who is supported by 3,500 experts and support staff working at headquarters in Geneva, in six regional offices and in many country offices. Collectively, they attempt to fulfil the following functions (WHO 2003):

- articulating consistent, ethical and evidence-based policy and advocacy positions
- managing information by assessing trends and comparing performance; setting the agenda for, and stimulating research and development
- catalysing change through technical and policy support, in ways that stimulate cooperation and action and help to build sustainable national and inter-country capacity
- negotiating and sustaining national and global partnerships
- setting, validating, monitoring and pursuing the proper implementation of norms and standards
- stimulating the development and testing of new technologies, tools and guidelines for disease control, risk reduction, health care management, and service delivery

Among these functions, WHO is best respected for the technical norms and standards developed by its extensive networks of experts and its technical advice to members. While WHO may provide the technical basis for health policies around the world, it has virtually no ability to 'impose' these policies on sovereign states – its influence rests on its technical authority.

Other organizations within the UN system also have some responsibility for health. These include the World Bank, the United Nations Children's Fund (UNICEF), the UN Programme on HIV/AIDS (UNAIDS), the UN Development Programme, the Food and Agricultural Organisation (FAO), the World Food Programme and the UN Fund for Drug Abuse and Control. Unsurprisingly, as these organizations matured and grew in size, they began not only to serve their members' needs (i.e. to provide a platform for information sharing and collaboration) but to pursue their own organizational interests in policy debates at both the national and international levels. In this process, UN organizations became actors in their own right; often competing with each other and pursuing different health policy alternatives. For example, the 1980s were marked by a major conflict between WHO and UNICEF over the interpretation of primary health care policy. WHO took the position that a multi-sectoral and preventive approach that improved water and sanitation, literacy, nutrition and was based on mass participation was required to improve health in poor countries. In contrast, UNICEF advocated focusing activity on a few narrow health care interventions that had proved cost-effective and implementing them through vertical programmes (e.g. childhood immunization). Although this public quarrel was short-lived, it points to differences between organizations over policies which they promote to member states.

Another UN organization with significant influence in health policy is the World Bank. The Bank has a mandate to provide financial capital to assist in the reconstruction and development of member states. Unlike other UN organizations which make decisions on the basis of one country–one vote, voting rights in the World Bank are linked to capital subscriptions of its members. As a result, the Bank has often been perceived as a tool of high income countries. The Bank entered the health field through lending for population programmes in the 1960s, began lending for health services in the 1980s and by the late 1980s led international health policy focusing on financing reforms. By the end of the century, it was the largest external financier of health development in low and middle income countries. Its influence derived not just from the loans it disbursed but also from the perceived neutrality and authority of its economic analysis, and its relationships with powerful finance ministries in borrowing countries. In effect, acceptance of policy conditions associated with health sector loans (which may have been resisted by health officials) could be linked to Bank support for projects in energy or industrial sectors which other ministries cared deeply about. Although the Bank's policies have been contested, most donors, industry and governments have supported them in general.

The World Trade Organisation

The most significant addition to the international architecture emerged in 1995 with the founding of the World Trade Organisation (WTO). The WTO administers and enforces a series of international trade agreements – with the goal of facilitating trade. These global ground rules for trade can impact on health directly through access to medicines, trade in health services or flows of health workers, and indirectly through exposure to consumption and environmental risks that arise from trade. Domestic policies dealing with these issues have become more constrained as a result of the WTO agreements because, by joining the organization, states commit themselves (with no reservations allowed) to alter their policies and statutes to conform with the principles and procedures established in all the WTO agreements.

The WTO Trade Policy Review Body conducts periodic surveys of member government's policies to ensure that they are WTO consistent. Alleged violations can also be notified to the WTO by other member states. Panels of experts review the alleged violations and their decisions, including the need to amend laws to make them WTO-compliant, are binding on member states.

A number of the WTO agreements have implications for health policy. TRIPS, or the Agreement on Trade Related Intellectual Property Rights, has had the highest profile among the treaties in international health policy circles because of its impact on policies concerned with generic drug production and trade. Yet the Agreement on Technical Barriers to Trade, the Agreement on the Application of Sanitary and Phytosanitary Measures, the General Agreement on Trade in Services have all been invoked to challenge the health policies of member states when other governments fear that they serve to protect domestic industries instead of protecting health.

Bilateral cooperation

Bilateral relationships (that is, government to government) including cooperation and assistance, are as old as the notion of nation–states. Bilateral organizations including the United States Agency for International Development (USAID), the UK Department for International Development (DfID), the Swedish International Development Agency (SIDA), play roles at the international, regional and national levels. They are often major financiers of health programmes in low income countries and of health programmes of UN organizations. Bilateral cooperation often involves a political dimension and these organizations may use their support to pursue a variety of objectives (diplomatic, commercial, strategic) within the UN system and recipient countries. For example, UK bilateral support often favours Britain's ex-colonies; while a large proportion of US bilateral assistance is earmarked for Israel and Egypt, and that of Japan for South-East Asian countries.

Activity 8.3

List five to seven examples of multilateral and bilateral organizations that operate in your own country.

Feedback

Clearly your list will depend on the country chosen but is likely to include several of the UN organizations discussed above.

You have learned that states have a long history of collaboration in relation to health and that they have established a variety of institutions to this end. The impetus for such collaboration has been varied. Some states have clubbed together so as to create global public goods; goods which markets will not produce and governments cannot efficiently produce on their own but have benefits which are universal (e.g. eradicating polio, developing an AIDS vaccine, research on public health issues). At times, cooperation has been more altruistic – perhaps because of shortcomings or lack of resources in other states (e.g. through humanitarian or development cooperation arrangements). Cooperation has also arisen for reasons of enlightened or naked self-interest (e.g. shore up surveillance in low income countries to reduce threat of bio-terrorism in high income ones). At times, 'cooperation' resulting in policy change has been achieved due to threat or coercion, e.g. during 'mopping up' campaigns to achieve universal immunization or as a result of trade sanctions imposed through the WTO regime. Whatever the impetus for interaction, domestic policy processes are not hermetically sealed from international processes; international actors are often actively engaged in national policy making.

Modern cooperation in global health

So far, collaboration has been discussed in the context of formal interaction among states and among states and the international system. Yet, two of the features of the contemporary global health landscape are the emergence of many non-state actors and emergence of policy through informal mechanisms. Both of these developments will now be considered.

Particular emphasis is placed on global civil society, transnational corporations and global public–private partnerships. The aim is to demonstrate that these actors actively participate in international and national health policy processes.

Global civil society

There has been a spectacular proliferation of global civil society groups over the past 50 years; from 1,117 international associations registered with the Union of International Associations in 1956 to over 16,500 in 1998 (UIA 1998). Lester Salamon (1994) argued that a global 'associational revolution' is underway that will be as 'significant to the latter 20th century as the rise of the nation–state was to the latter 19th'.

Global civil society encompasses a diverse set of actors targeting a diverse set of issues. For example, there are global civil society organizations active in:

- reproductive health – such as the International Women's Health Coalition
- trade agreements – such as Health Action International (a coalition of 150 NGOs from 70 countries)
- rights of people with AIDS – for example, the International Community of Women Living with HIV/AIDS which claims to represent 19 million HIV-positive women
- ethical standards in humanitarian relief – for example, the SPHERE Project
- landmines – for example, the International Campaign to Ban Landmines is coordinated by a committee of 13 organizations but bringing together over 1,300 groups from over 90 countries

Global civil society constitutes a heterogeneous lot, from a group of people linked together via the Internet to communicate a shared vision across national frontiers to organizations which have vast amounts of political assets. One civil society organization has eclipsed the World Bank in many important respects as the epicentre of global health. The Bill and Melinda Gates Foundation was established in 2000 and is now a central actor in international health. The Foundation, with an endowment of over US$27 billion (in 2005), disburses over US$500 million per year on health in developing countries.

Although the Foundation is led by Bill Gates Sr. and Patty Stonesifer, and run by a small executive staff, Bill Gates (the world's richest man) and his wife Melinda are actively engaged in the strategic direction of the Foundation and in grant-making operations. They wield considerable influence over health policy and priority setting in international health as a result of the magnitude of resources at the disposal of the Foundation.

The Foundation has played a catalytic role in changing the organizational landscape in international health. Whereas the other major financier of health development, the World Bank, largely provides loans to governments, the Foundation has mainly supported non-governmental organizations, particularly public–private partnerships with grants. Indeed, one of the most striking features of the Foundation is the number of global public–private partnerships and alliances that it has engineered, incubated and supported financially as well as providing staff to sit on many of their governing bodies. For example, the Foundation played a central role in conceiving the Global Alliance for Vaccines and Immunizations, the Foundation for New Innovative Diagnostics, and the Global Alliance for Improved Nutrition, among others. While the Foundation's support has been critical in financing research, development and product access for a range of neglected conditions, arguably equally important has been its success in getting public and private sector actors to collaborate on policy projects.

The Foundation has been involved in health policy in other ways as well. Through its grant making it has supported evidence-based policy making (see Chapter 9). For example, it has provided US$20 million to help African academies of science to strengthen their ability to provide evidence-based advice to inform government policy making. It has also supported the establishment of a Global Health Policy Research Network whose working groups produce highly influential analytical reports.

Funding provided by the Foundation acts to set priorities in international health by default as governments, non-governmental organizations and international organizations gravitate to where the action is. Moreover, as a result of large investments in international health activities, the Foundation has easy access to influential decision makers at all levels.

Like their national counterparts, civil society organizations play a range of roles in the policy process – either influencing formal international organizations (such as the World Bank) or influencing debates at the national level. They adopt similar strategies: some as insider groups, through global policy communities and issue networks as in the case of Médecins Sans Frontières (MSF) on principles for humanitarian interventions in conflict zones; some as outsider groups which use confrontational tactics such as shareholder activism or organize consumer boycotts against transnational corporations; and some act as thresholder groups which shift between the two positions. For example, MSF was part of a wider issue network working with WHO, UNAIDS and other groups to increase access to HIV/AIDS drugs but was also a member of a network of activist groups using confrontational tactics to lower prices among other demands.

In Chapter 6 you learned that civil society often performs critical roles in the policy process, including participation, representation, and political education and that individual civil society organizations can be identified which motivate (draw attention to new issues), mobilize (build pressure and support), and monitor (assess behaviour of states and corporations and ensure implementation) in respect of particular issues and policies. Partially as a result of improved global communications, global civil society plays the same roles at either the sub-national, national and international levels.

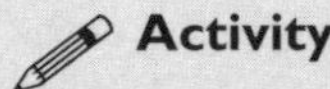

Activity 8.4

As you read the following account of the role of global civil society by Jeff Collin and colleagues (2002), make notes and draw a two- or three-sentence conclusion on the functions it performs at different political levels.

Civil society and the Framework Convention on Tobacco Control

In May 2003 the text of the Framework Convention on Tobacco Control (FCTC) was agreed after almost four years of negotiation by the member states of WHO. The process was highly contested and often polarized with industry pitted against public health activists and scientists and both sides seeking to influence the negotiating position of member states'. While the text provides the basis for national legislation among ratifying countries, the process highlights the important role that global civil society can play in international health forums and its limits as well. Interested NGOs with 'consultative status' at WHO participated formally, but in a circumscribed manner (i.e. no voting), in the negotiation process – but were able to use this status to lobby official delegations. Moreover, many NGOs pressed WHO to accelerate the process by which international NGOs enter into official relations with the Organisation – and a decision was made to provide official relations for the purposes of the FCTC process. Second, WHO hosted public hearings in relation to the Convention at which many civil society organizations provided testimony and written statements. Third, civil society groups, such as Campaign for Tobacco Free Kids and ASH, provided an educative function – organizing seminars, preparing briefings for delegates on diverse technical aspects of the Convention, publishing reports on technical issues, and issuing a daily news bulletin on the proceedings. A fourth, and perhaps unique, role involved acting as the public health conscience during the negotiations. For example, some NGOs drew attention to the obstructionist positions of some member states and industry tactics – often in a colorful manner such as awarding an Orchid Award to the delegation that they deemed had made the most positive contribution on the previous day and the Dirty Ashtray award to the most destructive. Fifth, individuals working for civil society organizations were, on some occasions, able to participate directly in the negotiations through their inclusion in national delegations. Over the course of the negotiations, global civil society organizations became a more powerful lobbying force through the formation of a Framework Convention Alliance which sought to improve communication between groups directly involved in systematically outreaching to smaller groups in developing countries. By the end of the negotiations over 180 NGOs from over 70 countries were members. The Alliance thus provided a bridge to national level actions which involved lobbying, letter writing, policy discussions, advocacy campaigns and press conferences before and after meetings.

Feedback

There is general agreement that civil society provided critical inputs into the FCTC process which influenced the content of the Agreement through a variety of approaches. Yet there were limits to its influence. For example, the final negotiations were restricted to member states – thus, effectively restricting the direct inputs of civil society. Perhaps more importantly, the transnational tobacco companies have a larger amount of political resources that they can deploy to block the implementation of the Convention.

Keck and Sikkink (1998) have drawn attention to the advocacy role that global civil society networks and coalitions play in world politics in diverse areas such as policies on breast milk substitutes and female genital mutilation. Such coalitions aim to change the procedures, policies and behaviour of states and international organizations through persuasion and socialization – by engaging with and becoming members of larger policy community on specific issues. The power of such coalitions stems from their information, ideas and strategies to 'alter the information and value contexts within which states make policies'. In Chapter 6 you learned about the role of advocacy coalitions in altering perceptions of interests through discursive and other tactics in relation to HIV/AIDS. Groups such as the Treatment Action Campaign (largely national) and ACTUP (global) have redefined the agenda and altered the perspectives of corporations (e.g. to lower the cost of drugs, drop lawsuits against governments wanting to implement TRIPS, etc.) and successfully invoked policy responses at the national and international levels (Seckinelgin 2003).

The growth of global civil society has been embraced for a number of reasons. For some it is welcomed due to the declining capacity of some states to manage policy domains – such as health. For others, it is a means to improve the policy process – by bringing new ideas and expertise into the process, by reducing conflict, improving communication or transparency. For others, civil society involvement provides the means to democratize the international system – to give voice to those affected by policy decisions thereby making these policies more responsive. Civil society is also thought to engage people as global citizens and to 'globalize from below'. Others equate civil society as pursuing humane forms of governance; providing a counterweight to the influence of the commercial sector. Despite these promises, there are others who are less sanguine.

Activity 8.5

You have read some of the positive reasons for welcoming the growth of global civil society. What criticisms do you think have been made of global groups?

Feedback

Your list may include:

- *Legitimacy of 'global' groups* may be questioned by North–South imbalances with most funds and members coming from the North and setting the agenda. Fewer than 15 per cent of the NGOs accredited to the UN were based in the South.
- *Concerns about elitism.* While global civil society is often thought to represent the grass roots in practice, some organizations are described as 'astroturf' in that they draw their membership from southern elites.
- *Lack of democratic credentials.* Many organizations have not considered the depth of participation of constituencies nor how to manage consultation.

- *Lack of transparency.* Many groups fail to identify clearly who they are, what their objectives are, where their funds originate, nor how they make decisions. Some are fronts for industry and would be better described as being part of the market.
- *'Uncivil' civil society.* Global civil society is a catch-all phrase for a diverse group of entities. Transborder criminal syndicates and pro-racist groups both have a place in this sector.

Transnational corporations

In Chapter 3 you learned about the heterogeneous character of the commercial sector and the ways that the sector wields influence in domestic health policy debates. The commercial sector, particularly transnational corporations (TNCs), commercial associations and peak associations, also pursue their interests through the international system. In 1998, the Secretary General of the International Chamber of Commerce (ICC) wrote that 'Business believes that the rules of the game for the market economy, previously laid down almost exclusively by national governments, must be applied globally if they are to be effective. For that global framework of rules, business looks to the United Nations and its agencies' (Cattaui 1998). The ICC was particularly interested in the WTO fostering rules for business 'with the proviso that they must pay closer attention to the contribution of business'. The then President made clear that 'We want neither to be the secret girlfriend of the WTO nor should the ICC have to enter the World Trade Organisation through the servants entrance' (Maucher 1998). As a result, the ICC embarked on a systematic dialogue with the UN and a multi-pronged strategy to influence UN decision making – including an overt attempt to agree a framework for such input. The activities resulted in a joint UN–ICC statement on common interests as well as a 'Global Compact' of shared values and principles which linked large TNCs with the UN without the shackles of formal prescriptive rules or a binding legal framework.

While the Global Compact is a highly visible, tangible and controversial expression of the interaction of the commercial sector with the international system, other avenues have also been utilized. The following illustrative list of the ways that the commercial sector exercises its influence in relation to inter-governmental organizations and their work should alert you to the need to include this group of actors in health policy analysis:

- influence on inter-governmental organizations such as WHO, for example, industry roundtables with the Director General, involvement in expert advisory and working groups, staff from industry assume temporary positions; and covert infiltration
- delaying the introduction of international legal instruments
- blocking the adoption of an international instrument, for example, the sugar industry mobilized significant opposition to the international dietary guidelines proposed by FAO/WHO in 2003 (Waxman A 2004)
- influencing the content of international agreements, for example, Philip Morris successfully lobbied the US administration to adopt a particular position on the text of the FCTC (Waxman H 2004)
- challenging the competence and mandate of an international organization to

develop norms in a particular policy area, for example, the food industry opposed and attempted to circumscribe the extent to which WHO can address the obesity epidemic (Waxman 2004)

This list reveals that the commercial sector is actively involved in international organizations – organizations which started life as tools to facilitate inter-country cooperation. The following case study provides an in-depth look at industry involvement in the development of global trade rules.

Activity 8.6

As you read through the case study on intellectual property rights (IPR) consider the following questions, making notes as you go along.

1 Why does industry want binding as opposed to voluntary rules governing IPR?
2 Why does industry seek global rules?
3 Why did the American administration support the Intellectual Property Committee?
4 Why are these trade rules important for public health?

The globalization of intellectual property

Sell (2003) provides a fascinating account of industry influence on the development of an inter-governmental agreement on IPRs that is virtually global in scope. The impetus for global rules arose from the concern among certain industries that weak intellectual property protection outside the US was 'piracy' and represented a huge loss and threat to further investment in knowledge creation. As a result, the Chief Executive Officers (CEO) of 12 US-based TNCs (in chemicals, information, entertainment, and pharmaceuticals) established the Intellectual Property Committee (IPC) to pursue stronger and world-wide protection of IPR. The Committee was formed in 1986, just prior to the launch of the Uruguay Round of trade negotiations which culminated in the establishment of the WTO.

The Committee worked as an informal network. Its goals were to protect IPR through trade law. The Committee began by framing the issue – linking inadequate protection to the US balance of payments deficit. Based on these economic arguments, its considerable technical expertise, and links to administration officials, it was able to win the support of the US administration to its cause. The IPC then set about convincing its industry counterparts in Japan, Canada and Europe of the logic of its strategy (linking IPR to trade law) and gained their support to put the issue on the agenda of the Uruguay negotiations. The IPC commissioned a trade lawyer to draft a treaty which would protect industry interests. This draft was adopted by the US administration as 'reflecting its views' and came to serve as the negotiating document in Uruguay. The IPC was able to position one of its members, the CEO of Pfizer, as an adviser to the US delegation. Although India and Brazil attempted to stall negotiations and to drop IPR from the round, economic sanctions brought them into line. As a result, the Agreement on Trade Related Intellectual Property Rights (TRIPS) emerged and according to industry, 'The IPC got 95% of what it wanted.'

As a WTO agreement, TRIPS has a particularly powerful enforcement mechanism and is likely to have profound implications for public health. The Agreement obliges countries that had hitherto failed to protect product or process patents to make provisions for doing so and in particular to set the patent period at 20 years. Industry argues that monopoly protection is required to encourage investment in R&D. Critics are concerned that this will place unnecessary restrictions on the use of generic products, inevitably increase drug costs, and erect barriers to scientific innovation.

Feedback

1 Industry wanted binding rules so that all firms would have to comply. Voluntary schemes often result in piecemeal compliance.

2 Industry wanted global rules as they didn't want countries to be allowed to opt out.

3 The US administration is thought to have supported the IPC for a number of reasons. First, the administration accepted the framing of the problem and the magnitude of the problem as estimated by industry. Second, industry provided unique expertise in the area which the US government did not have. Third, these industries provide a great deal of campaign finance and invest heavily in lobbying.

4 The public health impact might be positive and negative. There will likely be more private investment in health R&D. Yet, the availability of these advances might be limited to those able to pay.

As you learned in Chapter 3, the commercial sector influences domestic health policy in a variety of ways and can be a force for positive or negative change. You will recall that the commercial sector also develops private health policy initiatives without the involvement of the public sector. For example, it has developed numerous codes of conduct that are global in scope. Companies also establish alternative mechanisms when public systems fail in ways that affect their profitability. For example, in response to heavy losses incurred as a result of the SARS outbreak in 2003, a group of investment banks, insurance companies and airlines began discussions to establish a fund that would help reduce the risk of global epidemics by strengthening national and global surveillance and response capabilities.

Global public–private health partnerships

One of the features of the globalizing world is the tendency of actors from distinct sectors and levels to work collectively as policy communities and issue networks on policy projects as described in Chapter 6. One of the most visible forms of collaborative efforts (albeit at the formalized end of the spectrum) in the health sector is the multitude of public–private partnerships (PPPs) which have been launched since the mid-1990s. While the PPP label has been applied to wide range of cooperative endeavours, most bring together disparate actors from public, commercial and civil society organizations who agree on shared goals and objectives and commit their organizations (sometimes numbering in the hundreds as is the case with the Global Partnership to Stop TB) to working together to achieve them. Some partnerships develop independent legal identities, such as the International AIDS Vaccine Alliance, whereas others are housed in existing multilateral or non-governmental organizations, such as Roll Back Malaria and the Global Alliance for Vaccines and Immunizations in WHO and UNICEF respectively.

PPPs assume a range of functions. Some undertake R&D for health products, for example, the Medicines for Malaria Venture raises funds from the public sector and foundations which it uses to leverage the involvement of pharmaceutical and biotechnology companies to focus on producing malaria vaccines for use in low income countries. Others aim to increase access to existing products among populations which could otherwise not afford them. The International Trachoma Initiative, for example, channels an antibiotic donated by Pfizer to countries which use it as part of a public health approach to controlling trachoma. A small number of PPPs mobilize and channel funds for specific diseases or interventions, while some operate primarily in advocacy mode, such as the International Partnership for Microbicides. In the course of their work, many PPPs develop policies, norms and standards that may have previously been developed by governments or intergovernmental organizations and most actively seek to set agendas, influence the priority given to health issues, and become involved in policy formulation or implementation by national governments and international organizations.

From a policy perspective, what makes PPPs noteworthy is that fact that they have come to represent important actors in global and national health policy arenas – as even partnerships hosted by other organizations (e.g. STOP TB) will assume distinct identities and pursue specific objectives. Their influence often stems from the range of political resources at their disposal which gives them an edge over organizations working independently or mono-sectorally, for example, political access and savvy, multiple sources of knowledge and perspectives relating to many facets of a policy process, as well as breadth and depth of skills ranging from research capacity to product distribution to marketing techniques. Their power is also a function of their ability to unite a number of important policy actors behind a particular position; actors who may have pursued competing policy alternatives or not been mobilized at all on a particular policy issue. Consequently, PPPs have become powerful advocates for particular health issues and policy responses.

Activity 8.7

Closer relationships between public and private sectors, including through partnerships, while welcomed by most have drawn criticism from some quarters. Write down four or five reasons which may explain critics' misgivings of PPP as they relate to health policy making.

Feedback

Your response may have included any of the following points, most of which are more or less valid at least some of the time:

- PPPs may further fragment the international health architecture and make policy coordination among organizations even more difficult.
- PPPs increase the influence of the private sector in public policy making processes which may result in policies which are beneficial to private interests at the expense of public interests.
- Following on from the previous point, there are concerns that decision making in PPPs

may be subject to conflicts of interest. Although many PPPs develop technical norms and standards, very few have mechanisms for managing real, apparent or potential conflicts of this nature.

- Through association with public sector actors, PPPs may enhance the legitimacy of socially irresponsible companies (what critics term 'blue wash').
- Private involvement may skew priority setting in international health towards issues and interventions which may, from a public health perspective, be questionable. PPPs have tended to be product-focused (often curative) and deal with communicable as opposed to non-communicable diseases. Addressing non-communicable diseases is both more difficult and may directly affect the interests of commercial lobbies (i.e. food and beverage, alcohol).
- PPPs may distort policy agendas at the national level. PPPs behave as other international actors in that they pursue particular policy objectives – they are just another actor.
- Decision making in PPPs is dominated by a northern elite which stands in contrast to decision making in many UN organizations (i.e. one country; one vote). Moreover, representatives from the South tend also to be elites.

Although critics have raised valid concerns about public–private partnerships, in an increasingly integrated world it is natural that policy is increasingly made through policy communities and issue networks. These open up new sites for actors to pursue policy goals and in so doing add further complexity to the health policy arena.

Globalizing the policy process

In Chapter 6, the concept of an 'iron triangle' was introduced – the idea that three broad sets of actors are active in the policy process at the national level (i.e. elected officials, bureaucrats, and non-governmental interest groups – particularly the commercial sector). The changes described in this chapter suggest that policy has an increasing global dimension and specifically that global and international actors often play important roles. Cerny coined the term 'golden pentangles' to reflect these changes to the policy process (2001). While domestic bureaucrats, elected officials and interest groups remain influential, they have been joined on the one hand by formal and institutionalized activities of international organizations (e.g. the World Bank, the World Trade Organisation, the G8, etc.) – the fourth side of the pentangle – and less formal, often networked, entities (e.g. public–private partnerships) and transnational civil society and market activities on the other – the fifth side. Depending on the issue, any or all five categories of actors may be involved and one or more sets may dominate. The image of the pentangle is useful to policy analysts in that it draws attention to the range of interests that may be active and the complexity of any policy process. For governments, particularly those in low and middle income countries, managing this cacophony of inputs in the political system is a difficult business.

Ministries of health in low income countries face an increasing number of actors in the policy process in addition to managing numerous bilateral relationships with diverse donor organizations – often in the context of discrete projects. In the early 1990s it became clear that the demands placed on many ministries by donors who pursued different priorities and demanded separate and parallel project accounting mechanisms were overwhelming and even undermining limited capacity and making it a challenge to formulate coherent and consistent policy in the sector. As a result, a broad consensus emerged on the need for improved coordination and efforts were placed on establishing 'sector-wide approaches' (SWAPs). These involved articulating an agreed policy framework and medium-term expenditure plan. All external donors were expected to operate within the framework, only to finance activities contained in the plan (preferably through a common pool and ideally intermingled with domestic funds) and to accept consolidated government reports.

Given the politics of development cooperation, success with SWAPs was mixed; many donors continued to fund off-plan, externally designed projects which were poorly harmonized and subject to burdensome and complex reporting and accounting practices – often for purposes of attribution. In countries where progress was made, these gains were often threatened by the arrival of new global public–private partnerships. Many countries now host over 20 health PPPs which often operate as vertical programmes with parallel systems – thus pulling the ministry in differing directions as they compete for attention and priority. As a result, there have been renewed and high profile pleas for coherence at the country level. Similarly, it has been recognized that country-level coordination needs to be supported by global-level coordination. The most prominent manifestation are the Millennium Development Goals (MDGs) agreed in 2000 by 189 countries, with the support of the International Monetary Fund (IMF) and the World Bank, the Organisation for Economic Cooperation and Development (OECD), and the G8 and G20 countries. The eight MDGs have specific targets and include verifiable indicators against which progress is to be measured and to which all actors are to be committed.

Activity 8.8

Why has it been so challenging to coordinate efforts at the country level? Give two or three reasons.

Feedback

Your answer should have discussed the fact that different actors pursue different interests. Often these interests are difficult to reconcile. Bilateral donor organizations may pursue diplomatic or commercial interests in addition to health and humanitarian objectives through development cooperation and these may be at odds with priorities established through a consultative process within another country. As you learned above, international organizations pursue distinct and multiple objectives as well. All organizations, including public–private partnerships, will compete to get their issues onto the policy agenda and to see that they receive attention. Hence, there will always be a political as well as a technical dimension to coordination with external agencies attempting to set agendas and get national counterparts to implement their preferred policy alternatives.

The pentangle model raises questions of whether or not the addition of new categories of actors leads to greater pluralism and whether or not increased interaction leads to the consideration of a wider range of policy alternatives. There is no one answer to these questions as it will depend on the policy and context. The few empirical studies in the health sector suggest that although some areas have included a greater range of groups, decisions tend to be dominated by communities of policy elites often representing a narrow range of organizations, albeit from public, civic and for-profits sectors (i.e. elite pluralism).

As for the question of whether or not globalization increases the range of policy options under consideration, it would appear that policy agenda setting and formulation are marked by increasing convergence – particularly in relation to the health sector reforms outlined in Chapter 3. Yet the transfer of policies from country to country – often through international intermediaries (such as global partnerships or international organizations) – which results in convergence is not a straightforward process. Explicit cross-border and cross-sector lesson learning (e.g. through study tours) or the provisions of incentives (e.g. loans, grants) does not automatically lead to policy transfer and change. Often the processes are long and drawn out and involve different organizations and networks at various stages.

Summary

In this chapter you have learned that globalization is a multifaceted set of processes that increase integration and inter-dependence among countries. Integration and inter-dependence have given rise to the need for multilayered and multi-sector policy making (above and below the state as well as between public and private sectors). State sovereignty over health has generally, albeit differentially, diminished. Yet the state retains a central regulatory role even if it has to pursue policy through conflict and collaboration with an increasing number of other actors at various levels through policy communities.

References

Cattaui MS (1998). *Business Partnership Forged on a Global Economy*. ICC Press Release. 6 February, 1998. Paris: International Chambers of Commerce

Cerny P (2001). From 'iron triangles' to 'golden pentangles'? Globalizing the policy process. *Global Governance* 7(4): 397–410

Collin J, Lee K and Bissell K (2002). The Framework Convention on Tobacco Control: the politics of global health governance. *Third World Quarterly* 23(2): 265–82

Keck ME and Sikkink KI (1998). *Activists Beyond Borders*. Ithaca, NY: Cornell University Press

Lee K, Fustukian S and Buse K (2002). An introduction to global health policy. In Lee K, Buse K and Fustukian S (eds) *Health Policy in a Globalizing World*. Cambridge: Cambridge University Press, pp. 3–17

Maucher HO (1998). *The Geneva Business Declaration*. Geneva: ICC

Salamon LM (1994). The rise of the non-profit sector. *Foreign Affairs* 73(4): 109–22

Scholte JA (2000). *Globalisation: A Critical Introduction*. Houndsmill: Palgrave

Seckinelgin H (2003). Time to stop and think: HIV/AIDS, global civil society and peoples' politics. In Kaldor M, Anheier HK and Glasius M (eds) *Global Civil Society Yearbook 2003*. Oxford: Oxford University Press, pp. 114–27

Sell S (2003). *Private Power, Public Law: The Globalisation of Intellectual Property*. Cambridge: Cambridge University Press

UIA (1998). *Yearbook of International Associations*. Vol. 1. Organisational descriptions. Union of International Associations. London: UIA

Waxman A (2004). The WHO global strategy on diet, physical activity and health: the controversy on sugar. *Development* 47(2): 75–82

Waxman HA (2004). Politics of international health in the Bush administration. *Development* 47(2): 24–8

WHO (2003). *Overview of WHO*. Geneva: WHO

9 Research, evaluation and policy

Overview

This chapter looks at how and in what circumstances the findings from research and evaluation are used in the policy process. In terms of the now familiar device of seeing the policy process as a 'policy cycle', evaluation is commonly portrayed as the fourth and final phase (is the policy effective?), but it is also, in principle, the beginning of another cycle (if the policy is not delivering what was intended, what needs to change or should it be abandoned?). Research can contribute to policy in other ways and at other stages in the policy cycle (e.g. helping define the nature of problems in the first stage and thereby getting issues on the policy agenda). This chapter explores different models of the nature of the relationship between researchers and decision makers, and some of the steps that both are encouraged to take to improve the 'fit' between research and policy decisions. Although the idea that researchers and policy makers inhabit different cultural worlds explains a great deal of the difficulties of communication between the two, studies of the policy process reveal that the principal divide is between different 'policy communities' or 'advocacy coalitions' which often involve both researchers and policy makers, competing for ascendancy in particular policy areas.

Learning objectives

After working through this chapter you will be better able to:

- **define 'evidence', 'research' and 'evaluation', and the different ways 'evidence' may be used in the policy process**
- **contrast different models of the relationship between research and policy, and their links to general perspectives on the policy process**
- **identify some of the barriers to research uptake by policy makers and reasons why the relationship between research findings and policy decisions is rarely, if ever, direct and linear**
- **set out some of the strategies that researchers and policy makers are increasingly using in an attempt to close the 'gap' between research findings and policy decisions, and assess their likelihood of success**
- **critique the 'two communities' conceptualization of researchers and policy makers**

Key terms

Audit Review of performance usually judged against criteria and standards.

Dissemination Process by which research findings are made known to key audiences, including policy makers.

Evaluation Research designed specifically to assess the operation and/or impact of a programme or policy in order to determine whether the programme or policy is worth pursuing further.

Evidence Any form of knowledge, including, but not confined to research, of sufficient quality to be used to inform decisions.

Evidence-based medicine Movement within medicine and related professions to base clinical practice on the most rigorous scientific basis, principally informed by the results of randomized controlled trials of effectiveness of interventions.

Evidence-based policy Movement within public policy to give evidence greater weight in shaping policy decisions.

Formative evaluation Evaluation designed to assess how a programme or policy is being implemented with a view to modifying or developing the programme or policy in order to improve its implementation.

Knowledge transfer Strategy incorporating a variety of 'linkage' and 'exchange' activities designed to reduce the social, cultural and technical 'gap' between researchers and the policy community.

Monitoring Routine collection of data on an activity usually against a plan or contract.

Research Systematic activity designed to generate rigorous new knowledge and relate it to existing knowledge in order to improve understanding of the physical or social world.

Summative evaluation Evaluation designed to produce an overall verdict on a policy or programme in terms of the balance of costs and benefits.

Introduction

This chapter focuses on how research and evaluation may affect policy through introducing new ways of seeing the world, new techniques for improving health, or reasons for changing existing policies. The policy process is a 'policy cycle' with three stages: (1) agenda setting; (2) policy formulation; and (3) policy implementation. Evaluation is sometimes considered the fourth stage in the policy cycle. *Research* is a systematic process for generating new knowledge and relating it to existing knowledge in order to improve understanding about the natural and social world. It uses a wide variety of methods, theories and assumptions about what counts as valid knowledge. 'Applied' research takes new knowledge from 'basic' research and tries to apply it to solving practical problems.

Health research spans both basic (e.g. laboratory-based) and applied (e.g. health services) research and covers a wide range of disciplines including laboratory sciences, epidemiology, economics, anthropology, sociology and management science. This book is informed principally by theories and evidence from political science and policy analysis which also contribute to health research.

For some people, 'evaluation' is distinct from research, but since evaluations use research methods, it makes sense simply to see them as one goal of research, defined as: 'any scientifically based activity undertaken to assess the operation and impact of [public] policies and the action programmes introduced to implement those policies' (Rossi and Wright 1979). It is common to make a distinction between *formative* and *summative* evaluations. The former is best thought of as an evaluation designed to contribute directly to assisting those responsible for a programme to shape the programme while it is being designed or implemented. Formative evaluations generally take place during the early stages of a programme and focus on activities and processes with a view to providing advice directly to the policy makers that can be used to modify and develop the programme. By contrast, summative evaluations are designed to try to provide a verdict on a policy or programme. In other words, they focus on measuring the impact or outcome and the extent to which a programme has met its objectives. They tend to produce their findings later on and to use quantitative methods. Formative evaluations tend to use qualitative methods such as observation and semi-structured interviews.

Evaluations are seen as particularly policy-relevant forms of research since they are normally commissioned by decision makers or funders to assess whether or not policies or programmes are going well and to what effect. Within the conventional device of the 'policy cycle', evaluation is portrayed as an important fourth and final stage to see if a policy has been effective. However, since policy is a continuous process, it makes just as much sense to see evaluation as contributing to the first stage in another policy cycle in which a problem is identified with the status quo requiring policy attention.

Policy makers have access to forms of 'evidence' other than scientific research. Research is usually distinguished from *audit* which examines the extent to which a process or activity corresponds to pre-determined standards or criteria of performance (e.g. checking that the facilities and staffing at a clinic are adequate to deliver babies safely). It is also distinguished from *monitoring* which constitutes the continuous, routine collection of data on an activity (such as staffing levels) to ensure that everything is going according to plan. For a government, focus groups and/or stakeholder analysis (which you will learn about in Chapter 10) can be seen as a form of monitoring. Both audit and monitoring may be used to inform policy as well as information from other sources such as opinion polls and community consultations. As a result, *evidence*, from the point of view of a policy maker, is likely to be a broader concept than knowledge derived from research.

Yet there has been a notable intellectual movement which started in the early 1990s – *evidence-based medicine* – which advocates the greater and more direct use of research evidence in clinical practice decisions, in particular, promoting the application of the findings of systematic reviews of randomized controlled trials. In the latter part of the 1990s, the movement broadened into a call for *evidence-based policy*. Proponents wish to give research evidence greater weight than other considerations in shaping policy decisions. Others have a more modest goal, defining evidence-based policy making as 'the integration of experience, judgement and expertise with the best available external evidence from systematic research' (Davies 1999). Both formulations of evidence-based policy can be seen as a reaction to politics driven entirely by conviction.

How does research and evaluation influence policy?

Slogans such as evidence-based policy and the related catch-phrase coined in government in the UK of 'what counts is what works' assume a particular relationship between research findings and policy decisions, namely, that ideally there should be a direct, relatively rapid relationship. This is known as the *engineering* model in which either a problem is identified by policy makers and 'solved' by researchers or new knowledge (e.g. of a previously unidentified health risk) leads to policy change. It is another formulation of the rational, linear approach to policy development outlined in Chapter 2 which argues that policy choices should be made in the light of what works well. Just as there have been many criticisms of the rational model of policy making, so too the engineering model of the links between research and policy has been extensively critiqued. One problem is that there are relatively few empirical examples of a direct link between a particular set of research results and a policy change. Harrison (2001) identifies at least seven conditions that would have to be met for the perfect implementation of research in clinical practice and similar conditions would be required for health policies:

- the existence of comprehensive, authoritative statements based on systematic reviews of research evidence
- the ability of such statements to provide a direct guide to decision making in specific circumstances
- knowledge of such statements by all relevant actors
- adequate resources (e.g. time) to act upon the authoritative statements of evidence
- sufficient incentive to apply the evidence
- absence of substantial disincentives (material or non-material) to apply the evidence
- an implementation chain sufficiently short to ensure a good likelihood of compliance with the implications of the evidence

Another difficulty with the model is the way it assumes that research precedes the policy solution to a pre-defined problem when there are plenty of examples of policy solutions being promoted and implemented without it being clear which policy problem they are supposed to be a response to. For example, many people argue that the vogue for privatization and contracting out of public services in low income countries was a solution in search of a problem, ill-suited to circumstances in many such settings.

Despite this, the rational, linear model of the relation between research and policy still tends to inform the day-to-day working assumptions of many researchers and policy makers. As Lomas (2000a) puts it, tongue in cheek, 'The research-policy arena is assumed to be a retail store in which researchers are busy filling shelves of a shop front with a comprehensive set of all possible relevant studies that a decision maker might some day drop by to purchase.'

Studies of the complex way in which policy is made in practice led to a different more indirect conceptualization of the relationship between research and policy, and to the recognition that research conclusions can be 'used' in a wide variety of different ways by policy makers. Researchers observed that new knowledge and insights appeared to percolate through the political environment like water falling on limestone: the water is absorbed, disappears into multiple channels and then emerges unexpectedly some time later elsewhere. Weiss (1979) suggested that it was more accurate to term this process one of *enlightenment*. Concepts and ideas derived from research filtered into the policy networks that shaped the policy process in a particular field and had a cumulative, indirect effect rather than an immediate, direct effect on policy (for instance, it took seven years from the publication of the crucial research on smoking and lung cancer before the UK Ministry of Health began to take its implications seriously and many more years before the first restrictions on advertising of cigarettes were introduced). Under this model, the primary impact of research and researchers is at the level of ideas and ways of thinking about problems which are taken up by others rather than in providing specific answers to specific policy puzzles. 'Research is considered less as problem solving than as a process of argument or debate to create concern and set the agenda' (Black 2001).

Activity 9.1

Compare and contrast the engineering (or problem-solving) model of how research may influence policy with the enlightenment model. Think of some of the limitations of each approach.

Feedback

Your answer is likely to have included the points given in Table 9.1.

Table 9.1 Differences between the 'engineering' and 'enlightenment' models of how research influences policy

Engineering or problem-solving model	*Enlightenment model*
Sees relationship between research and policy as rational and sequential	Sees relationship as indirect and not necessarily logical or neat
A problem exists because basic research has identified it	Problems are not always recognized, or at least not immediately
Applied research is undertaken to help solve the problem	There may be a considerable period of time between research and its impact on policy. Much research develops new ways of thinking rather than solutions to specific problems
Research is then applied to helping solve the policy problem. Research produces a preferred policy solution	The way in which research influences policy is complex and hidden. Policy makers may not want to act on results
Rarely or never describes how the relationship between research and policy works in practice	How research influences policy is indirectly via a 'black box', the functioning of which is hidden rather than explained

Other researchers saw the use of research in entirely political terms as an instrument to be used by government and powerful interest groups to promote their causes. This *strategic* model views research as ammunition to support pre-determined positions or to delay or obstruct politically uncomfortable decisions (Weiss 1979). There is certainly empirical support for this somewhat cynical view of the nature of politics and the use of research. A classic recurrent example of the strategic use of research is for a government to argue that no decision can be made on a contentious issue without further research and analysis and to appoint a commission of enquiry taking several years to do the necessary work. The effect of this action is to take the issue off the policy agenda. With any luck, a different set of ministers will be in office when the awkward report arrives from the commission.

An example of the interpretation and use of research findings in public health that can be interpreted in 'strategic' terms relates to the decline in HIV seroprevalence in Uganda in the 1990s. While the totality of the epidemiological evidence indicated an improvement in the situation, commentary and discussion were dominated by the 'headline' figures of a huge reduction from 30 per cent to 10 per cent in seroprevalance between 1992 and 1996. Parkhurst (2002) argues that this selective, perhaps deliberately uncritical, interpretation of the evidence was the product of pressure on international donors from the international community to show the success of the global anti-AIDS effort and a desire on the part of the Ugandan government to present its HIV/AIDS programme in the best possible light. Another attraction of the Ugandan story was that it provided an international role model of a government that had taken HIV/AIDS seriously with very positive results.

A less cynical model of the relation between research and policy, drawing on some of the same political insights, is the *elective affinity* model. This theory holds that a policy community is more likely to react positively to research findings and insights if its members have participated in the research process in some way, if the findings are disseminated at the right time in relation to the decision making process and if the implications of the findings coincide with the values and beliefs of the policy audience (Short 1997). Essentially, this approach emphasizes the importance of ideological compatibility between the researchers and the policy makers at a particular point in time as well as the extent of contact between researchers and policy makers (see the development of 'linkage', below, as a way of increasing the likelihood that research will be used for policy). It indicates that research that introduces new thinking and challenges the status quo will be ignored unless it fits in with dominant policy makers' ideology. If it does not fit, the research may play an 'enlightenment' role over a much longer period of time with much more uncertain consequences.

While all these models, apart from the engineering model, rightly see research and evaluation as only one input to a complex policy process, they implicitly support the view that researchers and policy makers are each relatively homogeneous groups with similar views and distinctly different from one another. In fact, a notion of *two communities* of research and policy underlies not only many theories of the relationship, but also much of the practical thinking about how the relationship can and should be improved. The two communities model emphasizes the idea that researchers and policy makers live in different cultures based on different assumptions about what is important and how the world works.

Activity 9.2

As a demonstration of the two communities hypothesis, list the main differences you can think of between, say, university researchers and government officials in terms of the type of activities they engage in, their attitudes to research, who they are accountable to, their priorities, how they build their careers and obtain their rewards, their training and knowledge base, the organizational constraints they face, and so on.

Feedback

Your table might look something like Table 9.2.

Table 9.2 The 'two communities' model of researchers and policy makers

	University researchers	*Government officials*
Work	Discrete, planned research projects using explicit, scientific methods designed to produce unambiguous, generalizable results (knowledge focused); usually highly specialized in research areas and knowledge	Continuous, unplanned flow of tasks involving negotiation and compromise between interests and goals, assessment of practical feasibility of policies and advice on specific decisions (decision focused). Often required to work on a range of different issues simultaneously
Attitudes to research	Justified by its contribution to valid knowledge; research findings lead to need for further investigations	Only one of many inputs to their work; justified by its relevance and practical utility (e.g. in decision making); some scepticism of findings versus their own experience
Accountability	To scientific peers primarily, but also to funders	To politicians primarily, but also the public, indirectly
Priorities	Expansion of research opportunities and influence of experts in the world	Maintaining a system of 'good governance' and satisfying politicians
Careers/rewards	Built largely on publication in peer-reviewed scientific journals and peer recognition rather than practical impact	Built on successful management of complex political processes rather than use of research findings for policy
Training and knowledge base	High level of training, usually specialized within a single discipline; little knowledge about policy making	Often, though not always, generalists expected to be flexible; little or no scientific training
Organizational constraints	Relatively few (except resources); high level of discretion, e.g. in choice of research focus	Embedded in large, interdependent bureaucracies and working within political limits, often to short timescales
Values/orientation	Place high value on independence of thought and action; belief in unbiased search for generalizable knowledge	Oriented to providing high quality advice, but attuned to a particular context and specific decisions

Barriers to the use of research

As you were completing your table, you probably began to think about the various factors that are likely to intervene in the process of translating research into policy or act as barriers in that process. The two communities perspective focuses attention on barriers relating to the different questions that researchers and policy makers may be interested in answering, as well as problems associated with the translation, dissemination and communication of research findings. However, there are more fundamental obstacles that relate more directly to the nature of public policy and politics.

Political and ideological factors

You should by now be familiar with the notion that 'policy' is a process that takes place in a particular context influenced by the values and interests of the participants. As a result, politics and ideology inevitably affect the way that research is used. For example, who initiates and undertakes evaluation, and why it is wanted, are likely to influence how far it is used by policy makers. In low income countries, evaluations of public health programmes are mostly a requirement of external donors, ostensibly as the basis for decisions about whether funding should be continued or not. They tend to be undertaken by foreign experts commissioned by the donors. As a result, the evaluations are less likely to be taken seriously by national governments or those working in the programmes, irrespective of the technical quality of the analysis they contain, even if they do influence the decisions of donors. In general, it is safe to assume that the validity and reliability of a piece of research may be necessary for it to have any chance of influencing policy but these characteristics alone are not sufficient to guarantee its influence.

Political and ideological context matters in the interpretation and use of research evidence. In the later 1990s, the President of South Africa, Thabo Mbeki, controversially rejected the orthodox scientific view that the HIV virus was causally linked to AIDS and espoused the position of a small minority of dissident scientists. Thereby, he called into question the view that AIDS is a viral infection spread mainly by sexual contact.

Activity 9.3

Why do you think President Mbeki was attracted to the dissident scientific position on the link between HIV and AIDS?

Feedback

You may have suggested one or more of the following reasons:

1 It enabled him to play down what he took to be a racist insinuation that the high prevalence of AIDS in South Africa was the result of the sexual behaviour of black South Africans and black Africans in general.

2 It enabled him to assert the right of the elected government to decide not only who had the right to speak about AIDS and determine the appropriate response, but even who had the right to define what the HIV/AIDS problem was.

3 It enabled him to support indigenous science against a Western orthodoxy based largely, but not exclusively, on research from outside Africa.

4 It enabled the new post-apartheid state and African National Congress government to identify themselves as leaders in Africa in the resistance against the dominance of bio-medical research by former colonial and other wealthy countries.

Of course, it is not just politicians whose approach to, and use of, research can be shaped by ideology. Research requires resources and researchers have to apply to public and private sources of funds to support their projects. In turn, public and private funding bodies influence which sorts of research will be undertaken and which researchers will be selected to do the research. Globally, the share of total health research funding from governments has been falling even though total spending has been rising in real terms. By 2001 it was 44 per cent of the total (as against 47 per cent in 1998) with 48 per cent coming from the for-profit private sector and 8 per cent from the private not-for-profit sector (Global Forum on Health Research 2004a). The rising share of private for-profit spending is most likely a reflection of the rising cost of bringing new pharmaceuticals to market. The high cost of developing these new drugs means that companies will invest in products targeted at the most lucrative markets in high income countries. Research needed by low and middle income countries will be a much lower priority.

In the early 1990s around 75 per cent of pharmaceutical companies' research funds went to university researchers who are, by and large, interested in disseminating the findings of their research widely. By 2000, this proportion had fallen to 34 per cent with the rest accounted for by in-house research or research in private institutes linked to the industry or to advertisers (Petersen 2002). Even if there is no direct interference in privately funded research undertaken outside universities, it is clear that the incentive on such researchers is to produce findings that maintain a flow of funds from their sponsors. For example, while the data collected are likely to be used by the sponsoring companies, they are less likely to be made publicly available. The results are also likely to be interpreted in ways that are broadly supportive of the pharmaceutical industry and that avoid criticisms of the effectiveness of new drugs.

Another factor in private funding of research is the subsequent control which ownership of the research findings gives to the funder, thereby reducing the odds of wider use of the research. For example, Boots, a leading British pharmaceutical company, funded research on the effectiveness of its drug, Syntharoid, after small-scale tests had suggested it might be better than alternative drugs. Although more definitive research showed no benefits, Boots was able to hire other researchers to re-analyse and interpret the data, as well as to prevent publication of the findings for a further seven years during which time it was able to sell the drug successfully (Rampton and Stauber 2001).

In addition, both funders and researchers are influenced by prevailing social, economic and cultural trends. For example, a combination of economic retrenchment in the face of weak economic growth and a dominant free market ideology in many Western countries in the 1980s led to an increasing convergence of view between researchers, funders and policy makers in what Fox (1990) called the *economizing model* of research in health and other sectors. By this he meant a focus on efficiency and value-for-money which were associated with free market institutions and the dominance of ways of thinking derived from economics. In this way, the nature of the research available for use was shaped by the prevailing climate.

Cutting across public and private interests, and ideological shifts, the impact of research on policy in the health field is shaped by the interests of different countries with very different economic resources in supporting research on health problems relevant to their settings. About US$106 billion was spent globally on health research in 2004, of which roughly 10 per cent was spent on the problems facing low income countries which account for 90 per cent of the global burden of disease (measured in terms of disability-adjusted life years) (Global Forum for Health Research 2004a). This has been described as the '10/90 gap' by those pressing for a more equal distribution of global research effort. Thus one reason why poorer countries make less use of research than they might is related simply to the fact that there is so little basic and applied research on many of the health problems they exclusively face. For example, of the 1,233 drugs that reached the global market between 1975 and 1997, only 13 (1 per cent) were for use in combating tropical infections which primarily affect the poor (Global Forum for Health Research 2004b).

Policy and scientific uncertainty

Particularly in the case of policy or programme evaluations, interpreting and using the findings can be difficult for two reasons: the goals of the original programme are often deliberately broad and open to interpretation; and the effects are likely to be small in relation to all the other influences on the outcome(s) of interest. Indeed, it is now generally accepted that the better designed the evaluation, the smaller the effect it is likely to demonstrate. It can be difficult for policy makers to know whether the fact that an evaluation fails to show a programme achieving the results intended is due to the intrinsic methodological difficulty of disentangling the specific contribution of the programme from other factors, or whether the programme has genuinely failed to meet its objectives. This is particularly likely in relation to policies designed to tackle long-standing, complex, multi-causal problems such as child poverty or poor health in early life. These tend to be the most important programmes attracting a high degree of public interest and debate.

If there is little agreement as to what the main goals of a programme are and how progress towards them should be measured, then an evaluation is open to a variety of interpretations in policy terms. For example, a programme may improve equity but harm efficiency, yet it is unlikely that the programme's goals would be laid out in such a way as to describe the precise weight which should be given to each of the objectives of improving equity and raising efficiency.

Another point of contention surrounding the interpretation and use of research relates to its generalizability and relevance to a particular policy context. Faced with research from elsewhere that does not support their policy line, policy makers tend to play down the relevance to the research. By contrast, scientists tend to emphasize the generalizability of their findings to a wider range of settings.

Different conceptions of risk

Individual conceptions of risk also shape the way that evidence influences health policies. People's perceptions of the likelihood of harm from environmental hazards generally exceed their perceptions of the risks of harm caused by alcohol, tobacco or poor diets, in spite of the fact that far more people are at risk of disease from the latter group than the former.

The mass media reinforce these perceptions by tending to focus on the dramatic, the rare and the new, thereby highlighting some pieces of research ahead of others and potentially putting politicians under pressure to act in the absence of good evidence. For example, in the UK in 2002–3, media coverage of the reported potential risk of autism associated with receiving the combined measles, mumps and rubella (MMR) vaccination was huge. In the MMR case, the risk was extremely small and subsequent research indicated that there was no link between autism and MMR vaccine. Unfortunately, during what turned into a media scare, many parents chose not to have their children vaccinated, thereby exposing them to other, greater health risks. Media coverage led to high levels of public anxiety and pressure on government to act to reduce risks to health. This was before a systematic review of all the evidence had shown that the link between autism and MMR was almost certainly non-existent. The government resisted the pressure to change its childhood immunization policy even though this was unpopular at the time.

Perceived utility of research

Today, researchers of all kinds, but particularly social scientists, are far more willing than in the past to try to make their research potentially useful. Their ability to do so partly depends on the kinds of information generated by their research. Weiss (1991) identified three basic forms of output from research, generated to differing degrees by different research styles:

- data and findings
- ideas and criticism – these spring from the findings and typify the enlightenment model of how research influences policy
- arguments for action – these derive from the findings and the ideas generated by the research but extend the role of the researcher into advocacy

Each is likely to be perceived as useful in different circumstances. Weiss argues that apparently objective data and findings are likely to be most useful when a clear problem has been recognized by all actors and there is a consensus about the range of feasible policy responses. The role of research is then to help decide which option to go for.

Ideas and criticism appear to be most useful in an open, pluralistic policy system distinguished by a number of different policy networks in stable communication with one another when there is uncertainty about the nature of the policy problem (or, indeed, whether one exists worthy of attention) and where there is a wide range of possible responses.

Research as argument may be used when there is a high degree of conflict over an issue. It has to be promoted in an explicitly political way if it is to have an impact.

Its use depends on the lobbying skills of the researchers and whether the key policy audiences agree with its values and goals. If they do not, the research will be ignored. Thus, this is a high risk strategy for researchers since, unlike simply letting the research percolate into policy and practice, it requires researchers to abandon their customary status as disinterested experts and enter the rough-and-tumble of political argument.

Timing

Another factor as to whether or not research is used in policy making is timing. Decision makers often criticize researchers for taking too long when they are facing pressure to act. Sometimes, researchers have an influence because their findings happen to appear at just the right time in a policy development process, but it is difficult to predict this and build it into the plan of a research project. There may be a trade-off between the timeliness and the quality of research which is particularly apparent to the researchers. However, high quality is no guarantee that policy makers will take notice of research when it suits them. The first reasonably rigorous estimate of the number of deaths associated with the 2003 invasion of Iraq by the USA, the UK and their allies published in the *Lancet* (Roberts et al. 2004) was treated extremely sceptically by ministers on both sides of the Atlantic principally because its central estimate differed so much from previous much lower estimates of casualties, despite its superior methods.

Communication and reputation

The above study of deaths in Iraq shows clearly that the ease with which a piece of research can be communicated has a bearing on its use for policy purposes. The more complex, opaque and indeterminate the results and presentation of findings, the less likely, all other things being equal, they are to be taken notice of and accepted. On the other hand, no matter how well research is communicated, if it proposes radical structural change to institutions and society, it is much more likely to be ignored. The perceived quality of the research together with the reputation of the researchers and the institution where they are based also affect the attention that research will receive from policy makers.

The political and media reaction to the Iraq mortality study demonstrated all of these considerations. The fact that the researchers appropriately presented their results as a range of estimates (including some estimates lower than the previous estimates produced using an entirely different method) with differing probabilities of being correct confused some and enabled others conveniently to portray the estimates as 'soft' compared with the previous estimates. Yet, the researchers were highly reputed scientists from the prestigious Johns Hopkins School of Public Health in the USA, among other institutions, so their findings were difficult to ignore entirely. Finally, the timing of the publication played its part in how the research was received. The paper appeared just before the US Presidential elections of 2004 in which the Iraq war was a central issue between the Democratic challenger and the Republican incumbent. The *Lancet* and the researchers were criticized for fast-tracking the research to publication for political reasons. Yet as conscientious scientists they presumably believed that the sooner their much higher estimate was in the public domain, the better for informed decisions about the future prosecution of the war.

Activity 9.4

For each of the potential obstacles to research being accepted and used by policy makers, identify one or two possible ways of overcoming each of them.

Feedback

The main ways of overcoming potential obstacles are given in following paragraphs. Add to your list as you read about them.

Improving the relationship between research and policy

Since the mid-1990s in the health field, there has been an explosion of interest in using the insights from the different models of the research–policy relationship discussed above, especially the idea of the two communities, to try to reduce the barriers to the use of research in policy making and health system management in line with the goal of 'evidence-based policy'. In the early stages of this movement, the emphasis was simply on improving the flow of information to policy makers through better *dissemination* of research findings (e.g. researchers were encouraged to produce user-friendly summaries of their research findings and to try to draw out the policy and practical implications of their work). This emphasis was consistent with improving the functioning of the engineering model of research and policy. To this was added an emphasis on improving the *diffusion* of ideas and insights from research to policy, derived from the evidence on how innovations diffuse within different sectors of the economy (Rogers 1995). This had much in common with the enlightenment view of research–policy relations. The focus then shifted to more active strategies of '*knowledge transfer*' (Denis and Lomas 2003).

Practical steps and advice inspired by the two communities hypothesis to reduce the 'gap' between research and policy

Table 9.3 summarizes the practical steps which researchers and policy makers have been encouraged to take in order to improve dissemination and diffusion of research into practice.

Linkage and exchange model of health research transfer

The steps outlined in Table 9.3 tend to emphasize better communication and translation of research findings, but offer little by way of a response to the political and ideological barriers discussed earlier. Perhaps the most sophisticated practical

Table 9.3 Practical steps advocated to reduce the 'gap' between research and policy

Steps to be taken by researchers	*Steps to be taken by policy makers*
Provide a range of different types of research reports including newsletters, executive summaries, short policy papers, etc., all written in an accessible, jargon-free style and easily available (e.g. by hiring a scientific journalist to translate research reports into lay terms or training researchers in accessible writing style)	Set up formal communication channels and advisory mechanisms involving researchers and policy makers to identify researchable questions, develop research designs and plan dissemination and use of findings, jointly
Put on conferences, seminars, briefings and practical workshops to disseminate research findings and educate policy makers about research	
Produce interim reports to ensure that findings are timely	
Include specific policy implications in research reports	Ensure that all major policies and programmes have evaluations built into their budgets and implementation plans rather than seeing evaluation as an optional extra
Identify opinion leaders and innovators, and ensure that they understand the implications of research findings	
Undertake systematic reviews of research findings on policy-relevant questions to enable policy makers to access information more easily	Publish the findings of all public programme evaluations and view evaluation as an opportunity for policy learning
Keep in close contact with potential policy makers throughout the research process	Commission research and evaluation directly and consider having additional in-house research capacity
Design studies to maximize their policy relevance and utility (e.g. ensure that trials are of interventions feasible in a wide range of settings)	Establish intermediate institutions designed to review research and determine its policy and management implications (e.g. the National Institute for Clinical Excellence in England and Wales which advises patients, health professionals and the NHS on current 'best practice' derived from robust evidence syntheses)
Use a range of research methods, including 'action-research' (i.e. participative, practically-oriented, non-exploitative research which directly involves the subjects of research at all stages with a view to producing new knowledge that empowers people to improve their situation) and other innovative methods	Provide more opportunities for the public and civil society organizations to learn about the nature of research, to be able to ask questions of researchers and policy makers concerning the use of research and to participate more actively in the policy process from an informed position
Choose research topics that are important for future policy	Encourage the mass media to improve the quality of their reporting and interpretation of research findings and their policy implications through devoting more time and effort to media briefing

approach to improving research utilization is that developed by Lomas (2000b) through the Canadian Health Services Research Foundation (CHSRF). This approach recognizes the interactive nature of policy development and focuses on mutual exchange and the joint creation of knowledge between policy makers and researchers. Using a variety of 'cross-boundary' techniques, researchers and policy makers are encouraged to work together to plan and develop research projects. They remain in direct contact throughout the life of projects as well as working on longer-term programmes of research. The objectives are to grow the research literacy of decision makers, enhance the relevance and utility of the research undertaken, increase the policy and managerial awareness and experience of researchers and increase the likelihood that the knowledge from research will be successfully transferred and translated into appropriate action. The CHSRF sees a crucial new role for various forms of 'knowledge broker' whose activities span the boundaries of different organizations in the worlds of research, and policy and management.

Informed by insights from policy science, the 'linkage and exchange' approach sees policy not as a series of discrete decisions or products but as a continuous process taking place in a context that includes the institutions of government and an array of stakeholders or interest groups organized into coalitions of stable groups, all shaped by prevailing beliefs, values and ideologies.

Although a large part of the CHSRF approach is informed directly by the 'two communities' idea, it does recognize that policy makers, at least, are *not* homogeneous. The approach encourages researchers to identify the different target groups among decision makers for their work and to use appropriate strategies for each. The 'linkage and exchange' approach is being tested in a series of experiments with some encouraging results (Denis and Lomas 2003). However, as Gibson (2003) points out, the approach still tends to see the problem of knowledge transfer and evidence-based policy making as relating to the *separation* between two worlds, hence the interest in notions of brokerage. This fails to take into account the degree of conflict *between* researchers and policy makers, and the *alliances* between subgroups of both. For example, most academic disciplines are notable for controversies and disputes between rival groups of researchers and theorists. This is even more so in fields of enquiry occupied by different disciplines, each of which brings a range of perspectives to bear on each substantive topic. To the contrary, the 'knowledge transfer' approach still shies away from explicitly recognizing the inherently political nature of the policy process as demonstrated in the preceding chapters of this book.

Beyond the two communities: are policy communities, policy networks and advocacy coalitions a better representation of reality?

Rather than seeing resistance to research being between the research world and the policy world, contemporary perspectives on the policy process from political science would locate the barriers to the uptake of research for policy as lying between groups which involve both researchers and others more closely involved with the policy process (in Chapter 7 you learnt about the general theories of the policy process).

Policy networks and policy communities

Conceiving of the policy process in terms of *policy networks* and *policy communities* focuses attention on the pattern of formal and informal relationships that shape policy agenda setting, formulation, decisions, implementation and evaluation in an area of policy. Research can be involved in each of these activities. Rhodes (1988) identifies a continuum between fields of policy which are characterized by policy communities which have stable and restricted memberships and those which feature policy networks that are much looser, less stable and less exclusive sets of interests. Where a particular policy area sits on the continuum between tight and loose groups, the degree of integration shapes the way in which policy is made in that area and the way in which research evidence is considered by members of the network or community. The looser the policy network, the more divergent are the views represented and the wider the range of different types of research that are likely to be used by those advocating different policy lines (Nutley and Webb 2000). The key point is that the divide between policy networks and communities is not based on the distinction between whether people are researchers or policy makers.

The advocacy coalition framework

As you learnt in Chapter 7 the *advocacy coalition* framework sees each area of public policy as occupied by networks and communities of actors interacting with varying degrees of intensity over time. Rather than pitting researchers against bureaucrats or politicians, advocacy coalitions comprise a diverse range of actors including politicians, civil servants, pressure groups, journalists, academics, think tanks and others. Each advocacy coalition interprets and uses research to advance its policy goals in different ways.

Implications of these theories for ways of enhancing the impact of research on policy

Gibson (2003) concludes that theories of the policy process that abandon the two communities perspective have a number of implications for those who wish to increase the impact of research on policy:

1 Researchers who wish to influence policy must analyse the policy area politically to identify the advocacy coalitions and their core values and beliefs about the nature of the policy problem, its causes and potential solutions.
2 Researchers must be engaged directly with advocacy coalitions or policy communities if they wish to have influence rather than focusing exclusively on managing the boundary between research and policy activities.
3 Research evidence owes its influence in the policy process to its ability to be turned into arguments and advocacy by actors in the policy process rather than its ability to reveal an uncontested 'truth'.
4 A strategy to enhance the role of research in policy is as much about influencing values and beliefs, and producing good arguments as it is about improving the knowledge base and its transmission.

Summary

You have learnt how researchers and research are only one among a wide variety of influences on policy processes. Yet, there is no doubt that the policy making process is influenced by research: research can help define a phenomenon as a policy problem potentially worthy of attention and research provides 'enlightenment' with many ideas affecting policy makers indirectly and over long periods of time. This is facilitated by the links between policy makers and researchers, the role of the media, timing and how the research is communicated. There are also many impediments to research being acted upon, including political and ideological factors, policy uncertainty, uncertainty about scientific findings, the perceived utility of research and how easy it is to communicate. There is considerable enthusiasm at present for using a variety of brokerage and knowledge exchange mechanisms to improve the productivity of the relationship between researchers and policy makers.

The idea that researchers and policy makers comprise two culturally distinct 'communities' is potentially misleading. Neither group is homogeneous and there are areas of common ground shared by some researchers and some policy makers. Sub-sets of researchers and policy makers participate together in competing 'advocacy coalitions' or 'policy networks' around issues. This perspective suggests that research enters policy as much through influencing political argument as through the transmission of knowledge. This indicates that recent efforts to use techniques of 'linkage' and 'exchange' to bridge the supposed 'gap' between research and policy are unlikely to succeed as much as their proponents would like.

References

Black N (2001). Evidence based policy: proceed with care. *British Medical Journal* 323: 275–8

Davies PT (1999). What is evidence-based education? *British Journal of Educational Studies* 47: 108–21

Denis JL and Lomas J (eds) (2003). Researcher:decision maker partnerships. *Journal of Health Services Research & Policy* 8 (suppl 2)

Fox DM (1990). Health policy and the politics of research in the United States. *Journal of Health Politics, Policy and Law* 15: 481–99

Gibson B (2003). Beyond 'two communities'. In Lin V and Gibson B (eds) *Evidence-Based Health Policy: Problems and Possibilities*. Melbourne: Oxford University Press, pp. 18–32

Global Forum for Health Research (2004a). *Monitoring Financial Flows for Health Research*. Geneva: Global Forum for Health Research, www.globalforumhealth.org/, accessed 08/11/2004

Global Forum for Health Research (2004b). *The 10/90 Report on Health Research 2003–2004*. Geneva: Global Forum for Health Research, www.globalforumhealth.org/, accessed 08/11/2004

Harrison S (2001). Implementing the results of research and development in clinical and managerial practice. In Baker MR and Kirk S (eds) *Research and Development for the NHS: Evidence, Evaluation and Effectiveness*. Abingdon: Radcliffe Medical Press

Lomas J (2000a). Connecting research and policy. *Isuma: Canadian Journal of Policy Research* 1: 140–4

Lomas J (2000b). Using linkage and exchange to move research into policy at a Canadian Foundation. *Health Affairs* 19: 236–40

Nutley S and Webb J (2000). Evidence and the policy process. In Davies HTO, Nutley SM and

Smith PC (eds) *What Works? Evidence-Based Policy and Practice in Public Services*. Bristol: The Policy Press, pp. 13–41

Parkhurst J (2002). The Ugandan success story? Evidence and claims of HIV-1 prevention. *Lancet* 360: 78–80

Petersen M (2002). Madison Ave. plays growing role in drug research. *New York Times* Online www.nyt.com

Rampton S and Stauber J (2001). *Trust Us, We're Experts: How Industry Manipulates Science and Gambles with Your Future*. New York: Putnam

Rhodes RAW (1988). *Beyond Westminster: The Sub-Central Governments of Britain*. London: Unwin Hyman

Roberts L, Lafta R, Garfield R, Khudhairi J and Burnham G (2004). Mortality before and after the 2003 invasion of Iraq: cluster sample survey. *Lancet*. Published online 29 October 2004, available on: http://image.thelancet.com/extras/04art10342web.pdf

Rogers EM (1995). *Diffusion of Innovations*. 4th edn: New York: The Free Press

Rossi P and Wright S (1979). Evaluation research: an assessment of theory, practice and politics. In Pollitt C, Lewis L, Negro J and Pattern J (eds) *Public Policy in Theory and Practice*. London: Hodder and Stoughton

Sabatier PA and Jenkins-Smith HC (1993). *Policy Change and Learning: An Advocacy Coalition Approach*. Boulder, CO: Westview Press

Schneider H (2002). On the fault line: the politics of AIDS policy in contemporary South Africa. *African Studies* 61: 145–67

Short S (1997). Elective affinities: research and health policy development. In Gardner H (ed.) *Health Policy in Australia*. Melbourne: Oxford University Press

Weiss CH (1979). The many meanings of research utilization. *Public Administration Review* 39: 426–31

Weiss CH (1991). Policy research: data, ideas or arguments? In Wagner P et al. (eds) *Social Sciences and Modern States*. Cambridge: Cambridge University Press

10 Doing policy analysis

Overview

In this chapter you will be introduced to a political approach to policy analysis and a range of tools for gathering, organizing and analysing health policy data. The chapter aims to assist you to develop better political strategies to bring about health reform in your professional life.

Learning objectives

After working through this chapter you will be better able to:

- **undertake retrospective and prospective policy analysis**
- **identify policy actors, assess their political resources, and current positions on a given policy**
- **develop successful political strategies to manage policy change**
- **gather and present data for policy analysis**

Key terms

Analysis Separating a problem into its constituent parts so as to better understand its whole.

Stakeholder An individual or group with a substantive interest in an issue, including those with some role in making a decision or its execution. Used synonymously with actor and interest group.

Introduction

By now you will appreciate that policy change is political, dynamic and highly complex. Policy change in the health sector is particularly challenging because health systems are technically complex; changing one part of the system invariably affects other parts and many different actors. Experience with health sector reform suggests that the costs of reform often fall on powerful and well-organized groups (e.g. doctors and drug companies) while the benefits are often intended for widely dispersed and disadvantaged groups with little political clout. Achieving successful policy reform is, therefore, often difficult.

After reiterating the way that policy analysis can be used, this chapter introduces you to tools that are employed in policy analysis, primarily to improve the prospects of successful policy change. Tools permit you to gather, use and apply knowledge in more systematic ways. You will be introduced first to stakeholder analysis. Identifying actors is at the centre of the policy triangle and therefore considerable emphasis is placed on this method. The chapter then presents an approach to developing political strategies, guidance for gathering evidence for analysis, as well as some suggestions for using the policy triangle to present the results of the analysis. The chapter concludes with some thoughts on the ethics of policy analysis. The chapter does not deal with rational-comprehensive approaches to policy analysis, such as applied economic techniques, because of their technical as opposed to political orientation (Weimer and Vining 1999).

Retrospective and prospective policy analysis

In Chapter 1 you learned that there are two types of policy analysis; these were characterized as analysis *of* policy and analysis *for* policy. Analysis of policy tends to be retrospective and descriptive. Analysis of policy looks back at why or how a policy made its way onto the agenda, its content, and whether or not and why it has achieved its goals (e.g. a summative evaluation). For example, disappointing results with health sector reform in some countries have prompted the World Bank to undertake analysis of past reform processes to diagnose the political dimensions of the problem. Analysis *of* policy comprises the bulk of this book.

Analysis *for* policy tends to be prospective. It is usually carried out to inform the formulation of a policy (e.g. a formative evaluation) or anticipate how a policy might fare if introduced (e.g. how other actors might respond to the proposed changes). Typically, analysis for policy will be undertaken, or sponsored, by interested parties to assess the prospects and manage the politics of policy change in a way that meets their goals. At times such analysis will result in the decision to abandon a particular course of action due to its poor political feasibility.

It is likely that you will want to use what you have learned from this book to undertake analysis for policy – to increase the chances that your plans are brought to fruition. Having read the preceding chapters you will appreciate that an astute policy reformer will engage in prospective analysis at all stages of the policy cycle – from problem identification, through formulation, implementation and evaluation – as each of these stages are subject to the flow of political events. Hence, successful policy change depends on continuous and systematic political analysis (Roberts et al. 2004).

Analysis in the early stages of policy making, particularly in problem definition and agenda setting, are particularly important. It was argued in Chapter 4 that epidemiological or economic facts do not simply speak for themselves in setting priorities but will be used or not depending on political processes. The role of the media in agenda setting was highlighted as critical to raising and framing problems in public debates and in policy circles. Similarly, policy entrepreneurs actively promote particular problems and solutions and wait for windows of opportunity to get issues onto the agenda and ensure a policy response (Kingdon 1995).

If you want to successfully influence policy outcomes, you will need to:

- engage in framing problems

- understand how agendas are set
- learn to recognize political opportunities
- understand how to manipulate political processes to encourage wider acceptance of your definition and proposed solution
- understand the positions, interests and power of other interested parties (including the media) based on the distribution of costs and benefits of the proposed policy
- adapt your solutions to make them more politically feasible

Undertaking these tasks constitutes analysis *for* policy, and will provide the basis for developing political strategies to manage policy change. While such analysis may enhance your success in influencing policy outcomes, they cannot guarantee such outcomes – for that depends on many factors beyond your control.

Stakeholder analysis

Irrespective of whether or not analysis is retrospective or prospective, it will be based on an analysis of stakeholders. Stakeholders include those individuals and groups with an interest in an issue or policy, those who might be affected by a policy, and those who may play a role in relation to making or implementing the policy – in other words, actors in the policy process. Although a variety of approaches to stakeholder analysis have been described (Varvasovszky and Brugha 2000), three distinct activities can be identified (Roberts et al. 2004). These are: (1) identifying the policy actors; (2) assessing their political resources; and (3) understanding their position and interests with respect to the issue.

Identifying stakeholders

A number of chapters in this book have focused on the range of stakeholders in health policy – from those inside government to the spectrum of interest groups in civil society and the private sector. Stakeholders will be specific to the particular policy and the context within which it is being discussed. Identifying stakeholders who are, or might become, involved in a particular policy process, requires the judgement of the analyst. For example, recognizing groups within organizations which may hold different interests (e.g. does one treat the Ministry of Health as one actor or are there different groups within it with differing interests?). The idea is to discover independent actors who wield considerable influence while keeping the number sufficiently small to make the analysis manageable.

To compile a list of stakeholders, you will need to think about the implications of the content of the proposed policy. Relevant actors will include those who are likely to be affected by the policy either positively or negatively and those who might take action or could be mobilized to do so. Particular importance needs to be devoted to individuals or organizations which can either block policy adoption (often leaders of political parties, heads of agencies, etc.) or implementation (often bureaucrats but other groups as well).

Activity 10.1

Choose a health policy with which you are familiar. Using the above guidelines identify 15–20 individuals or groups who have an interest in the issue or a role to play in adopting or implementing the policy.

Feedback

Health sector reform often involves the following types of groups, some of which you may have identified as having a stake in the issue you are analysing (Reich 1996): consumer organizations (e.g. patient groups); producer groups (nurses, doctors, pharmaceutical companies); economic groups (workers who may be affected, industries, companies with health insurance schemes); and ideological groups (single issue campaign organizations, political parties).

Assessing power

The second step in a stakeholder analysis consists of assessing the power of each actor. You learned in Chapters 2 and 6 that political resources take many forms but can be divided into tangible (e.g. votes, finance, infrastructure, members) and intangible resources (expertise and legitimacy in the policy issue, access to media and political decision makers). Access to these resources increases stakeholders' influence in the policy process. For example, groups with a developed organization and infrastructure will often have more power than groups which have yet to organize themselves. Similarly, doctors have relevant expertise and are, therefore, often viewed as legitimate, are often organized into long-standing professional organizations, and, because they usually have high status, frequently have access to financial resources and decision makers. As a result of these political resources, doctors are usually characterized as a group with considerable political power on health policy issues. Pharmaceutical companies have great expertise, considerable finance, but often limited legitimacy in civil society. The type of strategy any group will employ in wielding their power will depend on the nature of the political resources at their disposal. The context will often condition the value that any particular resources in terms of its influence. To take an extreme example, where corruption is rife, finance becomes a very useful political resource to buy policy decisions.

Activity 10.2

Select ten of the stakeholders you identified in Activity 10.1. For each, make an inventory of the major resources at their disposal. Differentiate between tangible and intangible resources. Given these political assets, characterize each of your stakeholders as having high, medium or low power.

Feedback

Clearly your inventory will depend on the stakeholders you select. An example serves to illustrate, e.g. patient groups (medium power):

- tangible resources, e.g. large number of members; electoral votes
- intangible resources, e.g. access to media; public sympathy and support

Assessing interests, position and commitment

Each actor's interests, position and commitment to a particular policy issue will determine how actors will deploy their political resources. Assessing these attributes constitutes the third and final stage in a stakeholder analysis.

You learned about interest groups in Chapter 6 – here we are concerned not just with so-called cause and sectional interest groups, but the 'interests' of any relevant actor in a particular policy issue. Interests are those which benefit an individual or group (as distinct from wants or preferences). Often it is the expected economic effect of a policy on an actor's interests which plays an over-riding role in determining their position on a policy. Determining what these interests are can be complex. At times, actors may conceal their real interests for tactical purposes, at times because they are illegal (e.g. illicit payment for referrals). At other times, interests may be difficult to discern because the policy content may be fuzzy or there may be a number of variants of the policy under discussion. For example, a Minister of Health may be committed to a policy of contracting out publicly funded service delivery to non-state organizations. Doctors employed in the public sector who practise privately may not be sure whether or not to support such a policy unless they have assurances that they will be eligible to compete for contracts with NGOs or private practitioners and or have assurances that their employment in the public sector will not be compromised by the new policy – details that the minister may not wish to elaborate upon until s/he undertakes a stakeholder analysis.

Activity 10.3

Select any five of the stakeholders you have identified in Activity 10.2 and list their interests in relation to the above policy. Seek to reveal what they would stand to gain or lose from policy change.

Feedback

Often the financial or economic impacts of policy change constitute central interests. In the example of a policy to contract out publicly financed services, public sector doctors might perceive their interests at risk if they think that the policy's aim is to reduce their number (i.e. they could lose their job) or if they fear that one outcome of such a policy would be to increase competition that they face in their private practices (i.e. limiting the amount they can earn by practising illegally). Yet other interests might also be perceived to be under threat. For example, the potential loss of a public sector position may not be compensated for by improved employment prospects in the private sector due to the credibility, prestige and symbolic value of a public sector post in many countries.

The impact of an issue on stakeholders' interests will determine their position with respect to the proposed policy – whether they are supportive, neutral or opposed. As with identifying interests, positions may not be easily determined as they may be concealed or because publicly aired positions may be different than privately held ones (the latter often determining what a group may actually do). For example, a minister may publicly support a policy so as to win favour with voters or specific interest groups but may be actively working against the policy from within government. At times, actors may not be certain of their position as they are not sure how a policy might affect their interests. This may happen if the policy content is vague or if there are a number of policy options being discussed, each with different repercussions on the actor.

Activity 10.4

Identify the public and private positions of the five stakeholders you analysed in Activity 10.3.

Feedback

An example will illustrate the difference in public and private positions a stakeholder might hold. Doctors in a publicly-funded system might complain publicly about a lack of resources and patients having to wait for treatment. However, in private they might resist any attempt by policy makers to appoint extra doctors as this would jeopardize the size of their private practice and income.

In addition to assessing interests and positions, it is necessary to assess the importance of the issue to each stakeholder in terms of other priorities they hold. What you want to find out is the intensity of actors' commitments to the policy and how much of their political resources they are likely to devote to pursuing their interests through the policy. While a powerful actor may be opposed to a particular policy, the issue may be of marginal importance and the stakeholder may do little to block policy adoption or implementation. One can gauge the level of commitment of an actor by asking them, or from assessing how critical the issue is to the organization's mandate, or from the time that senior organizational figures devote to it, and so on.

It is important to attempt to determine each stakeholder's real interests, position and level of commitment for a proposed policy. This knowledge will play an important part in designing political strategies to affect change.

Activity 10.5

For each of the stakeholders analysed in Activity 10.4, list the interests they hold (what they gain or lose from policy change), their position (opposed, support, neutral), and their level of commitment to the policy issue (high, medium, low). Construct a table with the data including position and power (from Activity 10.1) for each of the actors – this is commonly referred to as a position map. As for the Activity 10.4, you may need to undertake some research.

Feedback

Each position map will look different depending on the policy content, actors and context. A position map of players in relation to health sector reform in the Dominican Republic is presented in Table 10.1. This provides a good starting point for thinking about who might form a coalition in favour of reform and which groups might undermine a reform.

High Opposition	*Medium Opposition*	*Low Opposition*	*Neutral*	*Low Support*	*Medium Support*	*High Support*
Dominican Medical Association	Private clinicians	Dominican Institute of Social Security	Church	President		Office of Technical Cooperation
	Employees in the organized sector	NGOs	Press	Partido de Liberación Domincana		International Development Banks
			National Health Commission	Dominican Institute of Social Security Director		
			Universities	Minister of Health		
			Beneficiaries	Ministry of Health bureaucracy		

High power   Medium power   Low power

Table 10.1 Position map for health sector reform in Dominican Republic in 1995

Source: Glassman et al. (1999)

The next step in a more sophisticated stakeholder analysis would aim to model how each actor's commitment and position would shift with a modification to the content of the policy. This issue will be returned to in the section on designing strategies for political reform. Before doing so it is useful to think about some of the limitations inherent in stakeholder analysis. On the one hand, it is perhaps too obvious to point out that any analysis is only as good as the analyst's attention, creativity, tenacity, and access to the information on the interests, positions, influence and commitment in relation to a particular policy. On the other hand, stakeholder analysis provides data only on actors and reveals little about the context and process of policy making which, you will appreciate, play equally important roles in policy change.

Developing political strategies for policy change

In Chapter 2 you learned that rational approaches are often used to identify the optimal policy for a particular actor and you can now appreciate how stakeholder analysis can be used to understand better the interests and positions of other actors in the policy arena. This is a good starting point but, to paraphrase Karl Marx, while philosophers have analysed the world in various ways, 'the point is to change it'. While your aims may be less radical than those of Marx, you will likely only be reading this if you are interested in policy change.

Roberts et al. (2004) suggest that the political feasibility of policy change is determined by position, power, players and perception. The viability of policy change can be improved by developing strategies to manage the position of relevant actors, the power or political resources at the disposal of key stakeholders, the number of players actively involved in the policy arena, and the perceptions held by stakeholders of the problem and solution. Based on their experience with health sector reform in numerous countries, Roberts and his colleagues provide useful guidance in terms of managing these variables.

Activity 10.6

While reading through the following summary of Roberts et al.'s work, make notes on which strategies you have used in your past efforts to effect change and others which you think might be useful within the policy context where you operate.

Position, power, players and perception

Position strategies

Roberts et al. begin by presenting four types of bargains that can be used to shift the position of actors with respect to a particular policy. Deals can be made with actors who are opposed or neutral so as to make them more supportive or less opposed by altering a particular component of the policy. For example, provider managers may drop their opposition to a proposal to introduce user fees if they are allowed to retain a percentage of the revenue to improve quality or provide perks for their staff. Second, deals can be struck through which support is sought for one issue in return for concessions on another. For example, a medical association may drop its opposition to a MOH proposal to train paramedical staff to assume additional medical functions, if the MOH agrees to drop its proposal to curb spending on teaching institutions. Third, promises can be made. If the medical association drops its opposition to the paramedic upgrading programme, the MOH can promise to consider the need to increase the number of specialists in particular areas. In contrast, threats can also be used to change the positions of actors. In Bangladesh, development agencies threatened to suspend aid if the MOH didn't proceed with agreed reforms while MOH staff threatened to strike if the reforms went ahead. A variety of deals can be struck and compromise made to change the position of actors without altering the balance of power in a given arena.

Power strategies

A range of strategies can be used to affect the distribution of political assets of the players involved to strengthen supportive groups and undermine opposition groups. These involve providing supportive actors with:

- funds, personnel and facilities
- information to increase expertise
- access to decision makers and the media; or
- public relations which highlights supportive actors' expertise, legitimacy, victim status or heroic nature

Roberts et al. suggest that actions can also be taken to limit the resources of opponents, for example by:

- challenging their legitimacy, expertise or motives
- characterizing them as self-interested and self-serving
- refusing to cooperate or share information with them
- reducing their access to decision makers

Player strategies

These strategies attempt to impact on the number of actors involved in an issue, in particular to mobilize those that are neutral and to demobilize those groups who are opposed. Recruiting un-mobilized actors can be achieved at times by simply informing a group that an item is on the agenda and what their stake in the issue is likely to be. For example, an association of private providers may not be aware that a particular policy is being discussed which may have consequences for its members. Player strategies can, however, be more difficult if new organizations need to be formed or if they involve demobilizing a group which has already taken a position. It may be possible to persuade the group that its stake or impact is different than it had previously calculated – but then efforts at face saving will also have to be made. Alternatively, it may be possible to undermine opponents by dividing them. For example, it may be possible to identify a sub-group within the larger group which might benefit from your proposal and whom you might win over to your side. Roberts et al. suggest that another player strategy involves changing the venue of decision making. This was a tactic employed by the donors in Bangladesh when confronted with opposition to reform in the Ministry of Health – they sought allies in the Ministry of Finance and the parliament who might support their cause. Player strategies aim to alter the balance of mobilized players by introducing sympathetic ones and sidelining opposing ones.

Perception strategies

Throughout this book the power of ideas and the role that the perceptions of a problem and solution have on the position and power of important stakeholders have been highlighted. A variety of techniques are used to alter perceptions. Data and arguments can, for example, be questioned as can the relative importance of a problem or the practicality of a policy solution. The appropriateness of public or private action can be attacked using economic theory or philosophy to shift perceptions on an issue. Associations can also be altered to give an issue a greater chance of political and social acceptability. Those seeking to eliminate congenital syphilis attempt to disassociate it from syphilis, which is often stigmatized and connotes licentious adults, and associate it with a condition inflicted upon innocent and needy infants. Invoking symbols can also change perceptions of issues. Thus, reforms can be linked to nationalist sentiments, imperatives or celebrities. Employing celebrities to endorse new reforms and initiatives is becoming common as is the branding of public health interventions. The latter places great emphasis on simple messages and the do-ability of a particular course of action so as to appeal to policy makers and the public.

Feedback

You have now reviewed the range of tools which Roberts et al. have identified as useful in influencing the position, power, players and perceptions associated with policy change. Some strategies are open to most players, for example, sharing or refusing to share information, changing the perception of an issue, or mobilizing groups. Some strategies may, however, only be available to certain groups. For example, the tactics to increase the political resources of supportive actors require that you have access to resources to distribute to them. Similarly many strategies which aim to change the position of actors require access to decision making over other issues that can be traded. Moreover, power is often necessary to deliver credible threats.

Data for policy analysis

It will come as no surprise to you that the quality of your policy analysis will depend on the accuracy, comprehensiveness and relevance of the information that you are able to collect. These, in turn, depend on the time and resources available to you, your official mandate, as well as your contacts in the relevant policy domain. Evidence for policy analysis usually emanates from documents and people.

Policy documents

Policy relevant documents might include academic books and journals (such as the *Journal of Health Politics, Policy and Law, Social Science and Medicine, Health Affairs, Health Policy, Journal of Health Services Research and Policy*, or *Health Policy and Planning*), reports and evaluations produced by interest groups, think tanks and consultants, government and inter-governmental (e.g. WHO) reports and documents, and the media. A literature search would likely start with a topic search on your health problem or policy using an indexing service such as the *Social Science Citation Index* or the US National Library of Medicine's MEDLINE (www.nlm.nih.gov). In the age of the Internet, there is likely to be a wealth of information about most policies and many policy contexts which may be searched with web-based search engines. Yet in contrast to journals, the information on the Internet is not necessarily subject to peer review nor is it always obvious which group or individual has published the material (which may have bearing on its credibility). Unpublished reports, email messages, minutes of meetings, memoranda and other 'internal' documents can be particularly useful in revealing the true interests of actors – but are generally difficult to access. Internal tobacco industry documents, made public as a result of litigation against companies in the USA in 1998, provided a rare and rich account of industry aims, interests and activities related to a number of health policies and organizations (e.g. undermining the Framework Convention of Tobacco Control and exerting influence over WHO). Figure 10.1 is a copy of one such internal document which reveals the manner in which Philip Morris sought to influence policy decisions in the USA.

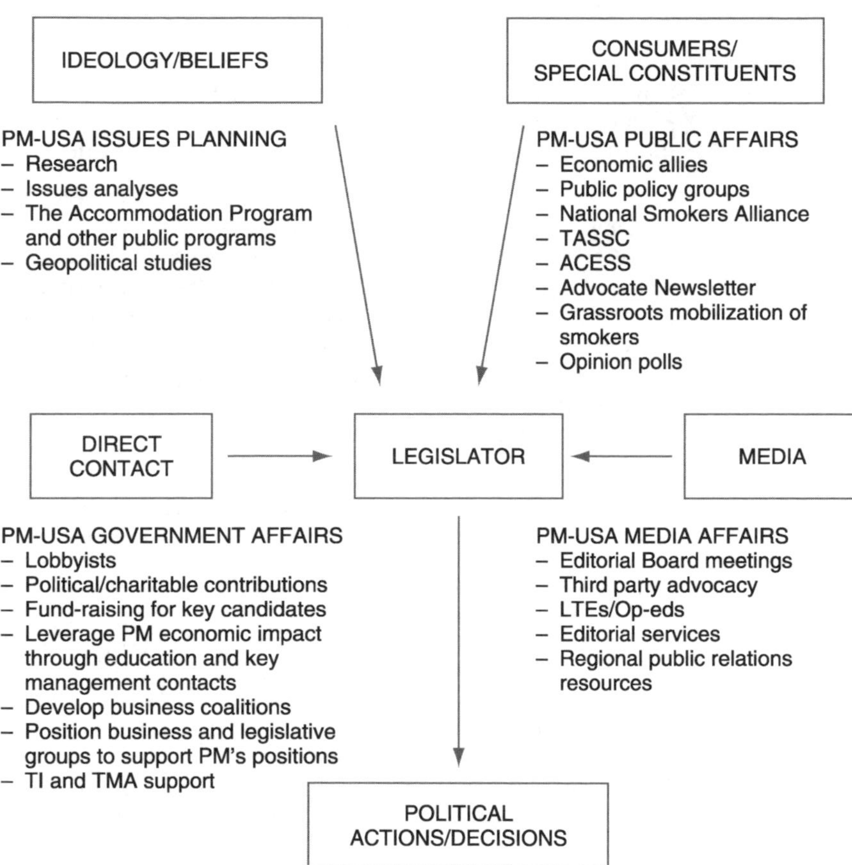

Figure 10.1 Tools to affect legislative decisions

Source: Philip Morris (PM) (no date)

Depending on the issue, you may also wish to consult statistical data sources, for example, to verify the magnitude of a problem so as to assist you in framing a problem or undermining an opponent's argument. International organizations, such as WHO and the World Bank, provide policy relevant data as do most governments and sub-national agencies of government (much of which is available on their websites).

The purpose of documentary analysis is to provide evidence that explains or predicts policy change. Therefore you are looking for evidence on relevant contextual variables (situational, structural, cultural and exogenous), actors (their power, interests, positions and commitment), content (policy aims), and process. Although there are a number of approaches to extracting data from documentary sources, most policy analysts will rely on content analysis, of which there are two types. First, quantitative content analysis is a systematic approach that seeks to quantify the content within documents according to pre-determined categories. A policy analyst might, for example, search through a sample of national newspapers to record the number of column inches devoted to different health policy issues, such as AIDS, over a particular time span so as to gauge media and public interest in a policy issue. Here the pre-determined category is AIDS. Alternatively, an analyst may go through a broader range of document types to reveal specific stakeholders' positions with respect to a particular policy over a period of time – in which case the actors and positions would be the pre-determined categories.

In contrast, qualitative content analysis aims to uncover underlying themes in documentary material. The policy analyst searching through newspapers for coverage of AIDS, for example, may examine the editorials to understand whether there is support for the government's policy on AIDS or to determine whether the press is spreading scientifically inaccurate messages in relation to the disease. Alternatively, an analyst might search documents for evidence of the philosophical argument used to support or frame a particular policy stance. The themes extracted using qualitative content analysis are often depicted using illustrative quotations from the document.

The utility of document analysis rests upon the quality of the documents upon which it is based. Bryman (2004) suggests that a number of questions should be posed to assess critically documentary sources, including:

- Who wrote and published the document?
- Why was the document produced?
- Was the author in a position to be authoritative about the subject?
- Is the material authentic?
- What interest did the author have?
- Is the document representative or atypical – and, if so, in what way?
- Is the meaning of the material clear?
- Can the contents be corroborated through other sources?
- Are competing interpretations of the document possible?

Gathering data from people

Talking to actors and undertaking surveys of key stakeholders can provide rich information for policy analysis. These methods may be the only way to gather valid information on the political interests and resources of relevant actors or to gather historical and contextual information. Surveys represent a quantitative method for collection of information predominantly by questionnaire or structured interview. Surveys, which can be administered in person or through the mail or email for self-completion, are occasionally used by policy analysts to generate basic information in relation to stakeholders' perceptions of a problem or their position in relation to a policy if this information cannot be obtained from documentary sources.

Semi-structured interviews are generally more useful than surveys in eliciting information of a more sensitive nature. The goal of the interview is to obtain useful and valid data on stakeholders' perceptions of a given policy issue. Typically, what is called a topic or interview guide will be used to prompt the analyst to cover a given set of issues with each respondent – as opposed to using a pre-determined set of questions. The idea is to allow flexibility and fluidity in the interview so that it resembles a conversation in which the respondent feels sufficiently comfortable to provide a detailed account and to tell their story. Hence, questions should be open (i.e. those which do not invite a 'yes' or 'no' response) and should be sequenced in such a way as to deal with more factual and less contentious issues before tackling more difficult areas and at deeper levels of understanding.

Health policy interviews tend to be undertaken with senior decision makers and representatives of powerful interest groups and are, therefore, of a special nature. These are sometime called elite interviews. Elite interviews pose special challenges. First, it is often difficult to recruit respondents into the study as they may be wary of how the results might be used, particularly if they are concerned that the analysis may undermine their own policy aims. Second, elites may not have sufficient time for an interview. Third, policy elites may simply provide official positions which may be more efficiently obtained through policy documents. Often it is more productive to interview such officials outside the office (or office hours) which may encourage them to provide 'off the record' comments which are more informative.

Relevant individuals to interview can be initially identified through the literature and document review which should reveal organizations and actors with an interest in the policy issue. These individuals will likely be able to identify further informants who may in turn identify others (called the 'snowball' technique). Interviewing retired staff from interested organizations can yield more forthright and analytical perspectives as these individuals will have had time to reflect and may not fear reprisals – and may also have more time available to allow them to participate in an interview. It has been suggested that it is best to approach first those individuals with rich sources of information, power, and who are supportive of the proposed policy, while those who may be hostile or may block access to other interviewees should be interviewed later in the process.

Interviews need not be conducted in person but can be undertaken over the telephone or through email correspondence. Thought needs to be given to introducing the purpose of the interview in such a way that is upfront and ethical and yet yields good data. Similarly, it will be necessary to inform the respondent how you will use the information and whether s/he wishes to keep his/her responses anonymous and out of the public domain. The pros and cons of using a tape recorder need to be weighed up but whatever decision is taken, the importance of transcribing the results immediately after the interview cannot be overemphasized.

The central limitation of interview data is that they concern what people say and how they say it, as opposed to what people actually do or think. This problem can be overcome by 'triangulating' the responses with responses from other informants, or with data gathered through other means, including observations of meetings or documentary sources.

In summary, both documents and people are equally important sources of evidence for policy analysis and both quantitative and qualitative approaches will be required to gather it. Multiple sources and methods increase understanding and the validity of the results. Once you engage in a real policy analysis, you will likely have additional questions on gathering data and would be well advised to consult a social research methods guide, such as that by Bryman (2004).

Data analysis: applying the policy triangle

Although the policy analysis triangle provides an extremely useful guide to make your exploration of health policy issues more systematic, it is more difficult to apply when you come to writing up your data because the different concepts, such as actors and processes, are so integrally intertwined. A few scholars have presented their policy analysis by talking separately about content, actors, processes and context.

Trostle et al. (1999) analysed policies on AIDS, cholera, family planning and immunization in Mexico to understand the extent to which researchers influence decision makers. They found a number of common factors enabling or impeding interactions between these two sets of actors and analysed their data by looking at the:

- content of each policy and the factors that promoted (e.g. good quality research) or constrained (e.g. academic vocabulary, unrealistic recommendations) the relationship
- actors involved in each policy and the factors that enabled (e.g. networks that agreed on priority issues) or impeded (e.g. lack of technical background among decision makers) the relationship
- processes, which included communication channels and events that intervened to promote or impede the use of research
- contextual factors that enabled (e.g. the stability of the state) or constrained research influencing policy (e.g. centralization of power and information)

This is just one way to organize your material. But on the whole it is usually easier to approach your analysis like a narrative: a story with a beginning, middle and end. For example, if you arrange your data and analysis chronologically, around the stages heuristic, you will start with agenda setting, go on to policy formulation and implementation, and end with an evaluation of what happened in this particular policy 'story'. This last part could be an overall discussion of how to understand what happened in this particular issue.

In gathering your data, you may well have produced a time-line: writing down the dates over a period of time of a series of events, meetings or conferences, results from research studies, media stories, or a change in government, which will have informed your analysis of how the issue got on to the policy agenda. You may start your narrative by describing the background to the issue you are looking at, referring to some or all of Leichter's four contextual factors of situational, structural, cultural or external you learned about in Chapter 1. Having done that, you will move on to the agenda-setting phase, saying how the issue got on to the agenda, whether there was a single focusing event or several, what role particular actors played in getting attention for the issue, whether the media were involved, and so on.

Having established how and why the issue reached the policy agenda, you can go on to describe who was involved in formulating the policy: was it largely prepared within a government department, how far did it involve others, such as the finance or social welfare ministries? You may refer to the extent to which non-government organizations or the private sector were consulted, or not; or how far they tried to influence the formulation of the policy and go on to describe its content (e.g. who was covered by it, or the cost implications).

The third stage is that of implementation, and you might here refer to what happened once the policy was formulated – how was it executed? Was there good communication between policy makers and those putting it into practice? Or was this a top-down instruction, which implementers were expected to carry out? Pitayarangsarit (2004) presents the results of her policy analysis of the introduction of the universal health insurance policy in Thailand in such a fashion.

Pitayarangsarit's early chapters provide the background to Thailand's radical policy reform. Chapter 3 is on the agenda-setting process – describing how universal coverage, having been discussed for years, was taken up by a newly formed political party, the Thai-Rak-Thai Party, which, when it gained power in 2001, put universal health care at the top of its political agenda. The next chapter focused on the policy formulation process after the election, and showed which actors (policy elites) and networks (tight policy communities) negotiated the design and shape of the policy, and who were excluded (consumers). The next chapters were about implementation of the policy, at the national, provincial and local level, and again, demonstrated the complexity of putting the policy into practice, and what strategies were used in implementation (e.g. allowing some flexibility at the local level).

In taking such an approach to your narrative, you will be looking very closely at both processes and actors – and having analysed your data from interviews and documents – you will be making a judgement about who exercised their power or influence at each stage of the process. Remember you need to demonstrate that you are presenting your analysis based on your data and not just making a judgement according to your own beliefs. You need to support your analysis by giving the source of your analysis: 'Fourteen (out of sixteen) interviewees suggested that the Prime Minister and her commitment to this policy was the single most important factor in getting it on to the policy agenda'.

Politics and ethics of policy analysis

In this book you have learned that policy change is political and in this chapter that analysis for policy typically serves political ends. Making policy alternatives and their consequences more explicit and improving the political feasibility of policy are neither value-neutral nor immune to politics. Policy analysis, therefore, will not invariably lead to better policy (e.g. policy which improves efficiency, equity or addresses problems of public health importance), or to better policy processes (e.g. fair decision making processes in which all stakeholders are provided opportunities to air their views and influence decisions). The substance and process of policy analysis are influenced by who finances, executes and interprets the analysis.

As you will appreciate from this chapter, ongoing, systematic analysis of a policy can be a resource intensive endeavour. Not all policy actors are equally endowed with resources. Everything else being equal, policy analysis may serve to reinforce the prevailing distribution of power and economic resources: those with political resources are more likely to be those who can finance analysis and influence who will use the analysis and how it will be used. Those groups with more political resources are in a better position to develop political strategies to manage the positions, players, power and perceptions surrounding a policy issue. In this way, policy analysis may reinforce the status quo.

Policy analysis is influenced not just by interests and power but also by interpretation. These issues raise questions about the role of the analyst, or of the organization for which the analyst works, in the analysis. If the analysis is for policy, it is almost inevitable that the analyst will have a preferred policy outcome. The policy goal may be at odds with 'good policy' as discussed above (e.g. many well-intentioned health professionals champion causes with poor cost-effectiveness). As no-one is value neutral, it is difficult to produce policy analysis which is unbiased. While there are ways to minimize bias, for example, by triangulating methods and sources of information and testing results with peers, it is probably necessary to accept the fact that the results of policy analysis will be biased.

Policy analysis raises other kinds of ethical issues. For example, is it ethical to allow any group to participate in the policy process so as to develop a more powerful coalition? Is it ethical to undermine the legitimacy of opponents or to withhold information from public discourse for tactical purposes? How far should one compromise on policy preferences so as to accommodate and win over a policy opponent? Your values will dictate how you answer these questions. In thinking about your response it may be useful to assume that other actors use these and other techniques to manipulate the substance and process of policy to their advantage. This may lead you to decide to join in the process of strategically managing the policy process to achieve your aims. Alternatively, you may feel uncomfortable with some of the strategies and decide that the ends do not justify the means. While these means may relate to values and ethics, they may also relate to the time, resources and emotional costs of pursuing, and at times failing to achieve, a particular policy change. There is nothing inherently wrong with abandoning or adopting a political strategy – particularly as it will now be based on a solid grasp of the fact that successful policy change requires a political approach.

Summary

In this chapter you have reviewed the retrospective and prospective uses of policy analysis. A stakeholder approach to policy analysis was presented. You used this approach to identify policy actors, assess their power, interests and position with respect to a policy issue of your choice and developed a position map on the basis of this analysis. A range of strategies to manage the position, power, players and perceptions associated with policy change were reviewed as were sources of information for policy analysis. With these tools in hand, you are now better equipped to pursue policy change. While the tools call for both evidence and creativity, they demand judgement and will be infused with values and ethical questions. While analysis may more often serve to reinforce the status quo, without the use of policy analysis tools groups without power will remain at a perpetual disadvantage.

References

Bryman A (2004). *Social Research Methods*. Oxford: Oxford University Press

Glassman A, Reich MR, Laserson K and Rojas F (1999). Political analysis of health reform in the Dominican Republic. *Health Policy and Planning* 14: 115–26

Kingdon JW (1995). *Agendas, Alternatives, and Public Policies*. 2nd edn. New York: HarperCollins

Philip Morris (no date) PM tools to affect legislative decisions. October 2003. Bates No. 204770711. http://legacy.library.ucsf.edu/tid/

Pitayarangsarit S (2004). The introduction of the universal coverage of health care policy in Thailand: policy responses. Unpublished doctoral thesis. London School of Hygiene & Tropical Medicine

Reich MR (1996). Applied political analysis for health policy reform. *Current Issues in Public Health* 2: 186–91

Reich MR and Cooper DM (1996). *Policy Maker: Computer-Assisted Political Analysis*. Software and Manual. Brookline, MA: PoliMap

Roberts MJ, Hsiao W, Berman P and Reich MR (2004). *Getting Health Reform Right. A Guide to Improving Performance and Equity*. Oxford: Oxford University Press

Trostle J, Bronfman M and Langer A (1999). How do researchers influence decision makers? Case studies of Mexican policies. *Health Policy and Planning* 14: 103–14

Varvasovszky Z and Brugha R (2000). How to do a stakeholder analysis. *Health Policy and Planning* 15(3): 338–45

Weimer DL and Vining AR (1999). *Policy Analysis: Concepts and Practices*. 3rd edn. Englewood Cliffs, NJ: Prentice Hall

Glossary

Actor Short-hand term used to denote individuals, organizations or even the state and their actions that affect policy.

Advocacy coalition Group within a policy sub-system distinguished by shared set of norms, beliefs and resources. Can include politicians, civil servants, members of interest groups, journalists and academics who share ideas about policy goals and to a lesser extent about solutions.

Agenda setting Process by which certain issues come onto the policy agenda from the much larger number of issues potentially worthy of attention by policy makers.

Analysis Separating a problem into its constituent parts so as to better understand its whole.

Audit Review of performance usually judged against criteria and standards.

Authority Whereas power concerns the ability to influence others, authority concerns the right to do so.

Bicameral/unicameral legislature In a unicameral legislature, there is only one 'house' or chamber, whereas in a bicameral legislature, there is a second or upper chamber, the role of which is to critique and check the quality of draft legislation promulgated by the lower house. Normally, only the lower house can determine whether draft legislation becomes law.

Bottom-up implementation Theory which recognizes the strong likelihood that those at subordinate levels will play an active part in the process of implementation, including having some discretion to reshape the dictates of higher levels in the system, thereby producing policy results which are different from those envisaged.

Bounded rationality Policy makers intend to be rational but make decisions that are satisfactory as opposed to optimum due to imperfect knowledge.

Bureaucracy A formal type of organization involving hierarchy, impersonality, continuity and expertise.

Cause group Interest or pressure group whose main goal is to promote a particular cause.

Civil society That part of society between the private sphere of the family or household and the sphere of government.

Civil society group Group or organization which is outside government and beyond the family/household. It may or may not be involved in public policy (e.g. sports clubs are civil society organizations, but not primarily pressure groups).

Company Generic term for a business which may be run as a sole proprietorship, partnership or corporation.

Content Substance of a particular policy which details its constituent parts.

Context Systemic factors – political, economic, social or cultural, both national and international – which may have an effect on health policy.

Corporation An association of stockholders which is regarded as a 'person' under most national laws. Ownership is marked by ease of transferability and the limited liability of stockholders.

Decentralization The transfer of authority and responsibilities from central government to local levels, which are thereby strengthened.

Discourse (epistemic) community Policy community marked by shared political values, and a shared understanding of a problem, its definition and its causes.

Dissemination Process by which research findings are made known to key audiences, including policy makers.

Elitism The theory that power is concentrated in a minority group in society.

Evaluation Research designed specifically to assess the operation and/or impact of a programme or policy in order to determine whether the programme or policy is worth pursuing further.

Evidence Any form of knowledge, including, but not confined to research, of sufficient quality to be used to inform decisions.

Evidence-based medicine Movement within medicine and related professions to base clinical practice on the most rigorous scientific basis, principally informed by the results of randomized controlled trials of effectiveness of interventions.

Evidence-based policy Movement within public policy to give evidence greater weight in shaping policy decisions.

Executive Leadership of a country (i.e. the president and/or prime minister and other ministers). The prime minister/president and senior ministers are often referred to as the cabinet.

Feasibility A characteristic of issues for which there is a practical solution.

Federal system The sub-national or provincial level of government is not subordinate to the national government but has substantial powers of its own which the national government cannot take away.

Formative evaluation Evaluation designed to assess how a programme or policy is being implemented with a view to modifying or developing the programme or policy in order to improve its implementation.

Global civil society Civil society groups which are global in their aims, communication or organization.

Global public goods Goods which are undersupplied by markets, inefficiently produced by individual states, and which have benefits which are strongly universal.

Globalization Complex set of processes which increase interconnectedness and inter-dependencies between countries and people.

Government The institutions and procedures for making and enforcing rules and other collective decisions. A narrower concept than the state which includes the judiciary, military and religious bodies.

Implementation Process of turning a policy into practice.

Implementation gap Difference between what the policy architect intended and the end result of a policy.

Incrementalism Theory that decisions are not made through a rational process but by small adjustments to the status quo in the light of political realities.

Industry Groups of firms closely related and in competition due to use of similar technology of production or high level of substitutability of products.

Insider group Interest groups who pursue a strategy designed to win themselves the status of legitimate participants in the policy process.

Interest (pressure) group Type of civil society group that attempts to influence the policy process to achieve specific goals.

Interest network Policy community based on some common material interest.

Iron triangle Small, stable and exclusive policy community usually involving executive agencies, legislative committees and interest groups (e.g. defence procurement).

Issue network Loose, unstable network comprising a large number of members and usually serving a consultative function.

Judiciary Comprises judges and courts which are responsible for ensuring that the government of the day (the executive) acts according to the laws passed by the legislature.

Knowledge transfer Strategy incorporating a variety of 'linkage' and 'exchange' activities designed to reduce the social, cultural and technical 'gap' between researchers and the policy community.

Legislature Body that enacts the laws that govern a country and oversees the executive. Normally democratically elected in order to represent the people of the country and commonly referred to as the parliament or assembly. Often there will be two chambers or 'houses' of parliament.

Legitimacy A characteristic of issues that policy makers see as appropriate for government to act on.

Monitoring Routine collection of data on an activity usually against a plan or contract.

Multinational corporation Firm which controls operations in more than one country, even if it does not own them but controls through a franchise.

New public management An approach to government involving the application of private sector management techniques.

Non-governmental organization (NGO) Originally, any not-for-profit organization outside government, but, increasingly, used to refer to structured organizations providing services.

Outsider group Interest groups who have either failed to attain insider status or deliberately chosen a path of confrontation with government.

Parliamentary system The executive are also members of the legislature and are chosen on the basis that the majority of members of the legislature support them.

Peak (apex) association Interest group composed of, and usually representative, of other interest groups.

Pluralism Theory that power is widely distributed in society.

Policy Broad statement of goals, objectives and means that create the framework for activity. Often take the form of explicit written documents but may also be implicit or unwritten.

Policy agenda List of issues to which an organization is giving serious attention at any one time with a view to taking some sort of action.

Policy community (sub-system) Relatively stable network of organizations and individuals involved in a recognizable part of wider public policy such as health policy. Within each of these fields, there will be identifiable sub-systems, such as for mental health policy, with their own policy community.

Policy elites Specific group of policy makers who hold high positions in an organization, and often privileged access to other top members of the same and other organizations.

Policy instrument One of the range of options at the disposal of the policy maker in order to give effect to a policy goal (e.g. privatization, regulation, etc.).

Policy makers Those who make policies in organizations such as central or local government, multinational companies or local businesses, schools or hospitals.

Policy Process The way in which policies are initiated, developed or formulated, negotiated, communicated, implemented and evaluated.

Policy stream The set of possible policy solutions or alternatives developed by experts, politicians, bureaucrats and interest groups, together with the activities of those interested in these options (e.g. debates between researchers).

Policy windows Points in time when the opportunity arises for an issue to come onto the policy agenda and be taken seriously with a view to action.

Political system The processes through which governments transform 'inputs' from citizens into 'outputs' in the form of policies.

Politics stream Political events such as shifts in the national mood or public opinion, elections and changes in government, social uprisings, demonstrations and campaigns by interest groups.

Power The ability to influence, and in particular to control, resources.

Presidential system The president or head of state is directly elected in a separate process from the election of members of the legislature.

Principal–agent theory The relationship between principals (purchasers) and agents (providers), together with the contracts or agreements that enable the purchaser to specify what is to be provided and check that this has been accomplished.

Private sector That part of the economy which is not under direct government control.

Privatization Sale of publicly owned property to the private sector.

Problem stream Indicators of the scale and significance of an issue which give it visibility.

Proportional representation Voting system which is designed to ensure as far as possible that the proportion of votes received by each political party equates to their share of the seats in the legislature.

Rationalism Theory that decisions are made through a rational process by considering all the options and their consequences and then choosing the best among alternatives.

Regulation Government intervention enforcing rules and standards.

Research Systematic activity designed to generate rigorous new knowledge and relate it to existing knowledge in order to improve understanding of the physical or social world.

Sectional group Interest group whose main goal is to protect and enhance the interests of its members and/or the section of society it represents.

Social movement Loose grouping of individuals sharing certain views and attempting to influence others but without a formal organizational structure.

Sovereignty Entails rule or control that is supreme, comprehensive, unqualified and exclusive.

Stakeholder An individual or group with a substantive interest in an issue (i.e. interest group), including those with some role in making a decision or its execution.

State A set of institutions that enjoy legal sovereignty over a fixed territorial area.

Street-level bureaucrats Front-line staff involved in delivering public services to members of the public who have some discretion in how they apply the objectives and principles of policies handed down to them from central government.

Summative evaluation Evaluation designed to produce an overall verdict on a policy or programme in terms of the balance of costs and benefits.

Support A characteristic of issues that the public and other key political interests want to see responded to.

Top-down implementation Theory which envisages clear division between policy formulation and implementation, and a largely linear, rational process of implementation in which subordinate levels of a policy system put into practice the intentions of higher levels based on the setting of objectives.

Transaction cost economics Theory that efficient production of goods and services depends on lowering the costs of transactions between buyers and sellers by removing as much uncertainty as possible on both sides and maximizing the ability of the buyer to monitor and control transactions.

Transnational corporation. Firm which owns branch companies in more than one country.

Unitary system The lower levels of government are constitutionally subordinate to the national government. Lower levels of government receive their authority from central government.

Acronyms

AIDS	Acquired Immune Deficiency Syndrome
ANC	Antenatal Care
ART	Antiretroviral Therapy
CHSRF	Canadian Health Services Research Foundation
CSO	Civil Society Organisation
DOTS	Directly Observed Therapy, Short-course
FAO	Food and Agriculture Organization (UN)
FCTC	Framework Convention on Tobacco Control
GFATM	Global Fund for AIDS, TB and Malaria
GK	Gonoshasthaya Kendra
HIV	Human Immunodeficiency Virus
ICC	International Chamber of Commerce
IFPMA	International Federation of Pharmaceutical Manufacturers Associations
IHR	International Health Regulations
IPC	Intellectual Property Committee
IPR	Intellectual Property Rights
IUATLD	International Union Against TB and Lung Disease
MMR	Mumps, Measles and Rubella
MSF	Medicins san Frontiers
NGO	Non-governmental organization
NHS	National Health Service
NPM	New Public Management
PPP	Public-private Partnership
SARS	Severe Acute Respiratory Syndrome
SIDA	Swedish International Development Agency
STI	Sexually Transmitted Infection
SWAP	Sector-Wide Approach
TNC	Transnational Corporation
TRIPS	Agreement on Trade Related Intellectual Property Rights
UNAIDS	United Nations Joint Programme on AIDS
UNICEF	United Nations Children's Fund
USAID	United States Agency for International Development
WHA	World Health Assembly
WTO	World Trade Organization

Index